THE TYRANNY
OF MAGICAL
THINKING

GEORGE SERBAN, M.D.

THE TYRANNY OF MAGICAL THINKING

The Child's World of Belief and Adult Neurosis

E. P. DUTTON, INC.   NEW YORK

The case studies presented in this book do not refer to any specific individual. While the psychodynamic of each case is real, the persons with whom it is associated are fictional.

Published in the United States by E. P. Dutton, Inc.,
2 Park Avenue, New York, N.Y. 10016

Library of Congress Cataloging in Publication Data

Serban, George

The tyranny of magical thinking.

Includes bibliographical references.
1. Neuroses—Etiology. 2. Child psychology. I. Title.
RC530.S4   616.85'2071   82-2472
AACR2

ISBN: 0-525-24140-X

Published simultaneously in Canada by Clarke, Irwin & Company Limited, Toronto and Vancouver

10 9 8 7 6 5 4 3 2 1

First Edition

TO MY PATIENTS,

whose revealing thoughts, fantasies, and emotions
gave me new perspectives
on human inner turmoil
and inspiration for better ways
to alleviate or remedy man's mental suffering.

CONTENTS

I wish to express my grateful appreciation to my editor,

Jerret Engle, for her painstaking editorial assistance

in the publication of this book.

THE TYRANNY
OF MAGICAL
THINKING

Introduction

THE EVOLUTION OF BELIEF TOWARD LOGICAL THINKING

One of the main functions of reason is to rationalize man's irrational behavior.

In his quest for harmony with the surrounding world man has constantly modified, even changed, his concept of himself to better respond to the social and historical forces acting upon him. The evolution of human reason, reflected in man's fluid mythologies and philosophies, clearly demonstrates man's shifting perception of the world and his place in it.

Primitive man viewed his world as one of objects and things endowed with feelings and volitions similar to his own. Later he replaced this universal animism with the concept of particular gods and demigods. He began to fancy himself as the divine creation of these supernatural beings, who in turn controlled his destiny. Then, when he was confronted with the unknown or the uncontrollable, man's surrounding world became less terrifying to him because he was able to appeal and to pray to the gods, who could mitigate his fate. In time, man generally came to believe in the existence of one universal God, creator of all things and controller of life and death.

This notion of God has undergone successive changes paralleling the evolution of reason. As man's ability to reason abstractly became increasingly sophisticated, his concept of God developed from that of an all-powerful living being to an intellectual abstraction. When man began to use deductive logic to explain phenomena, he also developed comfortingly "logical" rationalizations for a divine design of creation, and the reassuring concept of the immortality of the soul. But even though man progressively accumulated tremendous knowledge about himself and the world, he was always unable to accept his own transient existence. While reason helped him to establish a causal relationship among the various phenomena in nature and, in fact, to affect those phenomena, this same reason was unable to explain to him satisfactorily why he should not also be able to control his fate. Man could not accept his own death as a mere phenomenon but felt the need instead to link it to a divine purpose. After declaring the soul immortal, man finally felt a bit more comfortable about "God's plan."

It was René Descartes who first used the foundations of the logical method actually to prove the existence of God. Descartes attempted to expound a rational basis for religion's truths. The rational in these terms became relational—limited to relating beliefs to demonstrable truths, and as such it gave a new foundation to religion. Later philosophers equated God with Reason. Some became convinced that Reason might have the power to decide and control fate. At this point, the fracture between science and religion that had threatened for centuries began to widen.

Nineteenth-century philosophers and social scientists celebrated Reason and continued to downgrade theological "truths" as a system of mere mythical assumptions. Many considered Hegel's dialectical method of reasoning to be the classic example of the correct fundamental approach to the interpretation of history and to man's understanding of his own existence. The new scientific approach to man, Darwin's evolutionary theory, shockingly demonstrated man's humble (not mythical) origins and further stripped him of any divine mystique. But it also helped scientists to understand better the primitive, unstructured emotions that still generated tension between man's spiritual aspirations and the world he was coming to know. From Darwin's *Descent of Man*, with its principles of human drives, aggression, competition, and survival, came the basic framework for the scientific study of human nature and motivation.

This new "science of man," separated from both philosophy and theology, questioned the inner mechanisms of human behavior. Previously, biological and social programming was seen as dictated by God's wisdom, and any irrational desire or maladaptive behavior was denounced as the work of sinful evil spirits or demonic possession. But with the advent of the psychological sciences such myths were discarded as naïve. Even before psychology became a science in itself, philosophers had long been intrigued by the "irrational processes" of the mind that were not explainable on a conscious basis, and they had ascribed them to a particular aspect of the mind called "un-conscious." Philosophers such as Herder, Platner, Schopenhauer, Fichte, and others used the term *unconscious* in speaking of human behavior they considered to be outside the scope of self-awareness. Gradually the unconscious came to replace religious theories as the explanation for irrational behavior. With the retreat of religious thought, philosophers, psychologists, and social theorists suddenly found in the concept of the unconscious an open field in which to advance various theories about human behavior. But at this point a new battle emerged among philosophers and psychologists, and it centered on the seemingly old issue of objective and subjective truth in understanding human nature.

The supporters of the subjective truths or human individuality, while accepting the general characteristics of human behavior, refused to reduce the individual to any systematic application of those characteristics. Instead many attempted to dramatically emphasize human uniqueness—to the point of making man his own God. Friedrich Nietzsche was the most eloquent advocate of this in his conception of the world as the creation of man himself. Nietzsche saw man as being in control, responsible for the creation of all the world's values and devoid of any supernatural power, fate, or meaning, except the meaning accorded to his values and behavior by his own mind and his will to power. For Nietzsche, human drives were reducible to the will to power. He felt that the "irrational" need should be overcome by the process of sublimation.

The partisans of the objective truth tried to develop a more objective science, a mathematical equation of human behavior. Those psychologists oriented toward the objective truth in science were trying to decipher certain laws of human behavior by studying the mechanisms of human functioning. One was Franz Brentano, a professor of philosophy and psychology at the University of Vienna and a contemporary of Nietzsche. Brentano felt that philosophy and psychology could both become sciences if they could present truths of universal validity. The method for both, he thought, should be similar to the natural sciences; that is, phenomena should be studied scientifically through data based on observation and experience. He based his approach on this understanding and through it reassessed some of the basic tenets of both disciplines. Through an observational approach he reached the conclusion that the human being not only perceives an aspect of reality but is fully aware that he himself is the perceiver. In other words, things do not just come into consciousness but are the result of perceived or projected experience. The process of this experience is now known as *cognition*. In this context, Brentano came to realize an important characteristic of psychic phenomena: "intentionality" of consciousness, a fundamental act of cognition directed toward something in which the personal object is internalized in relation to the person's past experience about that object. This ultimately determines the character of the act and gives a meaning to it. This method became the basis for the study of modern phenomenology and is extensively used in psychology today.

The importance of Brentano to psychology and philosophy becomes further evident, however, if we consider that one of his students was Sigmund Freud. In the spirit of his time, Freud, too, attempted to conceive a well-integrated mechanism of human behavior based on provable facts. But though his observational bases were clinical data obtained by free association, Freud's conclusions were hardly based on those data. In fact, he developed a sophisticated process of interpretation that really disregarded the scientific process so revered by his teacher, Brentano. Rather than attempting to understand mental phenomena as a conscious perception, he looked for answers amid the mysterious vagaries of the "unconscious." As moving and intriguing as Freud's theories proved to many, they almost immediately raised grave doubts in the scientific community about their validity as a scientific approach.

At best, scientifically speaking, Freud put together in a fluid theory many of the existing psychological concepts. His sublimation theory, for example, was based on the idea of conscious determinism described by Nietzsche, although Nietzsche had spoken of it in the context of overcoming oneself in reaching for the will to power. With profound insight (but no scientific method) Nietzsche had analyzed various aspects of human adaptation to reality and used such psychological concepts as repression, negative association, sublimation, and spiritualization. To some extent Freud's presentation of various mechanisms of psychological defense only filled out in detail the teachings of Nietzsche, Hartman, Breuer, Charcot, Bernheim, and others. Even repression itself, for that matter, had previously been described by Schopenhauer.

What Freud seems to have been creating is a new mythology, while searching for a predictable method to explain the psychic defenses used by man to overcome his instinctual drives.

Freud saw religion, fantasy, creativity, love, and the will to power as only tempering forces that could not ultimately help man escape the inevitable manifestation of his aggressive instinct, which tried to close the cycle of life with self-destruction. He felt that man's survival depended instead on his *superego* (socially developed moral conscience), which would check man's natural hostility and aggression, basically by means of guilt. The voice of guilt was understood as a fear of loss of love. Finally Freud explained neurotic symptoms as a substitute for an unfulfilled sexual wish in which an element of guilt was present as a self-punitive reinforcement mechanism. In other words, the old religious model for the explanation of abnormal behavior was only updated by Freud, in keeping with current biological and psychological knowledge. The neurotic was simply a sinner (real or imaginary) bothered by his uncompromising conscience. Freud himself said in an article titled "A Neurosis of Demoniacal Possession in the Seventeenth Century" that what in those days were thought to be evil spirits were in fact evil wishes derived from rejected and repressed impulses. Moreover, Freud assumed that the superego torments the sinful ego with feelings of anxiety and is on the watch for opportunities to have it punished by the external world.

It is fair in this context to question Freud's whole "revolutionary" concept of neurosis and man's nature. What was it, after all, but a new pseudoscientific terminology for an old description of human suffering? The major difference seems to be that, according to religious dogma, the sinner (Freud's neurotic) suffers unless he expiates his sins and is absolved by God's grace, and, according to Freud's psychoanalytic theory, he suffers regardless of the reality of his crime because of unfulfilled wishful (but sinful) thinking. If in religious terms the punishment is the loss of God's love, in Freudian terms it is the fear of the loss of parental love.

Interestingly enough, Freud himself mentioned in his autobiography that by the turn of the century the numbers of neurotics seemed further multiplied by the manner in which they hurried their unresolved troubles from one physician to another. Religion had gradually disclaimed any ability to help the neurotic. It was particularly hard for the Protestants because of their dogma denying the possibility of immediate divine grace and expiation of sins, which left their followers alone to struggle with their suffering. Psychoanalysis, however, offered them a chance to alleviate their torments. Freud himself felt that religion might help the individual, but he questioned the price one had to pay. According to him, in "sparing many people from individual neurosis, religion forcibly fixes them in a state of psychical infantilism and drives them into mass delusion."

Freud therefore ministered to the sinner-neurotic by a more "scientific" method appropriate to the scientific beliefs of the early twentieth century. His was a new form of confession by free association, which was called in scientific terminology "emotional abreaction." In order to encourage confession, the atmosphere was supposed to be dignified, ritualistic, symbolic, and mystical. The analyst, in accordance with the new dogma, interpreted sins not in terms of demoniacal possession but as originating in the abyssal miasma of the unconscious. If the guilt in religion was removed by penitence, in therapy it was eliminated by the simple act of declaring the individual irresponsible for his actions to the extent that responsibility was relegated to the unconscious.

The difference, then, between religious healing and psychoanalysis was really only a question of changing moral evaluation. The sinner-sufferer was seen as responsible for his evil thoughts or acts. The neurotic only suffered, powerless and basically unaware of the smoldering emotional conflict that surfaced from time to time from the depths of the unconscious. To the neurotic it was a very appealing doctrine, for it removed the burden of guilt and responsibility for his behavior.

Yet psychoanalysis has proved of little value in correcting human behavior. Why? Because the answers implied in Freud's understanding of irrational behavior did not succeed in explaining the behavior itself. Psychoanalysis mistook meaningful connections among various psychic processes for the actual causes of maladjustment. A superstructure of assumptions, built on inference and hypothetical constructs, led the Freudians to the elaboration of sophisticated theories of psychic symbolism explained by unconscious mechanisms. The theory claimed to deduce consequences of behavior prior to any verification from empirical data and on the basis merely of preconceived theoretical assumptions applied to a particular case.

All of these theoretical and therapeutic explanations were supposed to be accepted by the profession and patient as articles of faith. The correlation of various unconscious material with their symbolic conscious representation depended on the analyst's interpretation and could not be proved or disproved by the patient. Any lack of acceptance by the patient was considered an act of resistance—hence rebellion, undermining the therapeutic process. If the patient was not an obedient subject, he was responsible for the therapeutic failure. The therapist was virtually infallible; the fault rested with the patient and his lack of belief in the therapeutic process.

This element of belief, the transcendental, magic connotation of mental processes (the backbone of the psychoanalytic theory), brought about the success of psychoanalysis and its failure. Like religion, it appealed to man's fantasies and need for myth, and, like religion, it proved to be ineffectual in curing mental suffering. It was inevitable that Freud's controversial and unscientific theories about the human mind would be attacked even from within his circle. Many of his pupils rejected the narrowness of his theory. They rebelled from reducing the conflict only to the repression of the infantile sexual drive, and they shifted the emphasis to the interpersonal relationship. Yet Freud's own theories about man's psychic dynamics and the therapeutic method he developed remain unchanged.

Independent of Freudian theory, other psychologists were looking elsewhere, specifically to the growing field of neurophysiology, to find answers to the psychological questions of mental functioning. Using as a model Pavlov's research into animal physiology, psychologists attempted to develop a rigorously objective theory of human behavior. J. B. Watson, for example, was convinced that objective physiological methods could be applied to the understanding of human behavior. For him, as a behaviorist, psychology was a purely objective brand of experimental natural science. Man was "an assembled organic machine ready to run." In this context man could now objectively strive for perfection because he was malleable and manipulable. Behaviorism, according to C. L. Hull, another behaviorist theoretician, "should attempt to free psychology from the past contamination of humanism." Hull regarded human behavior as an automatic operation, with identifiable cycles determined by the rise of a need and terminated by its satisfaction. For scientific purposes, he felt that man should be regarded as a "completely self-maintaining robot" and his behavior formulated in terms that would enhance its predictability.

The strict implementation of these principles was pushed to the extreme by B. F. Skinner, who was driven to create an applied science of human behavior with its main purpose to manipulate and control. What is interesting about behaviorism is that, in order to be able to predict human behavior, behaviorists had to cancel out the major characteristic of that behavior: free choice. Further, implicit in behaviorism's denial of motivations is the assumption that, outside of the experimental situation, unlearned human behavior is in fact uncontrollable (which is why it had baffled man in the first place).

These theoretical shortcomings have been reflected in the limited therapeutic value of the behavioral approach in actual situations. This is largely because the elimination of a particular symptom does not change the neurotic's thinking about related conflicting conditions, which will continue to produce anxiety (and neurosis). The behavioral treatment relies on the principle of outside reinforcement and punishment as the main learning influences that determine behavior, and pays little attention to the complexity of the thinking processes that determine a behavioral response.

When, not too long ago, neobehaviorists had to reintroduce the cognitive process as a mediator of behavior, they tacitly admitted the failure of behaviorism's single-minded approach. The recognition of the influence of cognition (that is, the process of perception, fantasy, ideation, and judgment) in the organization of behavior brought us back to the acceptance of behavior as determined multidimensionally by external and by internal psychic factors. In other words, behavior could be influenced by personal perception and beliefs that might be at odds with the generally accepted view of the objective reality. Exactly like psychoanalytic theory, behaviorism had failed to pinpoint properly the origins of man's "irrationality" and hence had not been able to deal adequately with it. Essential questions were unanswered. The question is not whether the behavior is maintained by learning but *why* that behavior is learned. More important, why does some maladaptive behavior, once learned, persist, even contrary to the best interests of the individual?

In order to find the cause for this persistent irrationality, a different look at the whole concept of human conflict is required. The phenomenological method developed by another of Brentano's students, Edmund Husserl, offered a new approach not fully recognized in his time, which began to fulfill the criteria of scientific objectivity. Rejecting as naïve oversimplification the identification of man only with his behavior, Husserl attempted to understand man in terms of his totality of being.

The phenomenologist in the tradition of Husserl Maurice Merleau-Ponty and Martin Heidegger believes that any human behavior should start with the analysis of the act of consciousness. To analyze it means to relate that act of consciousness to the individual's specific interpretation of his own experience of life and his understanding of his environment. Since the factors affecting an individual's reactions are based on the patterns of thinking he has formulated in the course of his life, the therapist has to try to identify from his life history exactly which patterns determine his present and future behavior. His life history will show the way in which he has approached reality in the past, and, especially, his ability to grasp his own choices. The maladapted person has a different way of seeing and relating to reality. A phenomenologist's analysis of the neurotic's structure of thinking indicates that it is impregnated with a pervasive element of belief, of personal faith, which subverts the reality and which can be traced to the organization of thinking in childhood.

This mixture of childlike belief and adult logic controls the neurotic's relationship to reality. Like a child, he appears to retain insignificant areas of experience as elements of magical thinking. Like a child, he may often view an action or thing as imbued with a powerful and even mystical tone, thereby distorting the logic of all further thought on the subject. In many cases this resembles the thinking of primitive man. For instance, the neurotic often interprets significant experiences of his life, particularly those to which he attached a highly emotional meaning, in magical terms expressed as symbols and signs, which become, in turn, a way of relating to his entire environment.

But, in fact, magical expectations creep into the logical processes of most normal individuals whenever they cannot understand, explain, or control reality. The wider the gap between one's needs and reality, the more one will try to equalize the situation by the sheer power of fantasy. Modern life, which on the surface appears directed by strict logical judgment, is in reality still permeated by magic. One proof of this is the persistent appeal of superstition and the widespread acceptance of occult science, astrology, and palmistry.

Religion, then, attributed irrational thinking to evil spirits, while psychoanalysis relegated it to mysterious forces of the unconscious and behaviorism refused to acknowledge it as anything but maladaptive learning. But none of these approaches understood its true origin in the relationship between behavior and logical thought.

It has been hard for man to accept the idea that he is not always the logical being he wants to be. He has always confounded his rationalization of the irrational with "objective," "logical" thought. He has always treated his beliefs and myths with the same importance he accords scientific truth, until such time as they are replaced by confirmable scientific knowledge. But if magical thought is indeed an integral part of man's thinking, and consistently has been since primitive times, then it is important to understand its roots and its functions in the development of the individual. In the past the main difficulty in identifying the formation of magical-irrational thought has been that it was considered to represent an alien dimension in man's mind.

Another basic error in the understanding of neurotic thinking was the belief that both children and adults employed basically the same principles of logic, except that children did not have enough accumulated knowledge to draw logical conclusions. As a result, the examination of the child's thought was reduced to an interpretation of the child's world by adult standards of thinking, which infer adult perceptions quite beyond the child's understanding of reality.

Not until Jean Piaget did a scientist study and scientifically document the fact that children think differently from adults. What is significant for psychology and psychiatry is that the stages of the child's intellectual development, like man's throughout the course of history, parallel his changing concept of reality.

Two aspects of a young child's thinking determine his approach to reality: one, the inability to separate consciousness of himself from outside reality; two, the use of magical thinking to explain the surrounding world. The young child is convinced that he can influence events and modify reality or any relationship between things by the simple power of his thoughts and wishes.

External interference with the process of maturation will affect the perceptual development of the child, making him insecure, reluctant to try new responses, and likely to carry over into adulthood childhood convictions or a magical style of coping with reality. These isolated areas of infantile, pseudological thinking can remain latent until a time of crisis or remain consistently active in adulthood, creating conflict and disturbing an individual's normal mental functioning. In this book I hope to show that neurotic thinking is a distorted process of thought maturation, a deviation in the complicated process of adaptation, a mixture of logic and pseudologic formulated for the most part in terms of the magical thinking and egocentricity of childhood.

I

NORMAL
ADAPTATION TO LIFE

> The neurotic is striving unsuccessfully to reduce or to
> control the inconsistencies induced by his environment or
> by himself; but as Propertius said, he is like "one rowing
> with one oar sweeping the water, the other the sands."

HOW WE ADAPT

Some people succeed in adjusting to the variety of events occurring in their
lives, while others fail. Why? What mental processes are responsible for
adjustment? Psychologically speaking, adaptation or adjustment means a
mechanism for dealing with events that finds both socially acceptable ways to
meet inner needs and personally satisfying responses to the demands imposed by the environment. What is commonly known as coping with life, an
individual's ability to control that dynamic between inner needs and the
environment, depends on his capacity to recognize a problem correctly and
then discover and employ the best available strategies to solve it.

The crucial factor in this basic relationship is the act of appraisal, the
ability to evaluate both the problem and one's resources for solving it. When
an event is routine, requiring little attention and reasoning, the solution is
usually based on a preexisting repertoire of responses developed in the course
of previous experiences. However, sometimes an individual is faced with
completely new and hardly known conditions that appear either to threaten
his self-esteem or to run counter to one of his basic biological or social needs.
Then the answer cannot be based only on previous experiences, because
there are no such experiences. Instead, the situation necessitates a careful and
pragmatic evaluation of personally untested means for counteracting the
new, antagonizing situation.

Let us say that a person is criticized by his employer for the quality of his work. He has several possible ways of reacting: he can reject the criticism and continue to turn out the same type of work; he can quit after accusing his employer of unfairness; or he can accept the criticism as positive and attempt to change. His approach and degree of objectivity will be determined by various factors in his personality: his degree of self-control, flexibility, intelligence, motivation—in short, his level of psychological maturity.

In order to be able to cope well with new demands, an individual has to correctly recognize the gap between the difficulty posed by the problem and his own resources. This implies an attempt to objectify the event, to detach himself in order to reach a sense of neutrality about the facts; only then is he able to anticipate the various responses possible. He must take into account his personal capacities, his knowledge and experience, and then consider whether or not they give him a sense of mastery over the situation. Finally, he may have to consider the significance of the situation in terms of the total organization of his life and thereby increase or decrease his concern for finding the best available solution at all. All the components of his psychological makeup: his aggressive or dependent personality, his social values, his sense of self-esteem, even his mood and feeling of confidence with his final decision will intervene in the course of this evaluation and contribute to his response.

But how does an individual reach a detached, rational decision when strong emotions are attached to the event? Correct syllogistic judgment, meaning the ability to apply logical, objective thinking to any situation, regardless of its emotional implications, is an ideal response, but any extremely subjective factor may distort that logic. Emotional subjectivity can distort the individual's ability to construct a syllogism accurately in terms of his own real abilities to deal with the problem at the moment. Acquiring objectivity in such a situation demands an extremely realistic and open-minded evaluation of one's skills and defenses. These skills and defenses actually represent a combination of complex factors: attitudes, traits, characteristics, and disposition of personality (confidence, for example). Only if all these factors have been accurately measured and tested in the past through various experiences and events, can an individual gain a correspondingly accurate appraisal of his abilities in a new situation.

For example, the reaction of the worker mentioned earlier to the criticism he received from his employer will be based on his previous recognition of his own ability to perform the job and on the personality factors that affect his coping skills. Whether he is the explosive type or shy and dependent, his level of confidence about the quality of his work and even his evaluation of his ability to get a new job will all influence his response.

The worker's judgment will be correct when all of these factors, at least insofar as they are known to him from his previous experiences, are considered in deciding what response will meet his needs at the time. An unrealistic evaluation of his working skill or an inadequate understanding of his own personality will obviously lead to a poor adaptive response. Leaving his job in a poor job market if he is unequipped to deal with insecurity would obviously constitute a poor response. An appropriate appraisal of the situation will produce a certain degree of emotional detachment, a separation of his frustration with his job from his other economic and personal needs. This will permit him to gain the prespective necessary to find the right solution and to live with it.

But the more confused and frustrated an individual is about his own concept of life and about his expectations for himself and his work, the more he is unable to direct his thinking effectively. If our criticized worker feels that he is entitled to deliver poor-quality work because he thinks that he is underpaid, mistreated, or unappreciated by his employer, it will be difficult for him to judge his employer's criticism. If he has a correct image of his working skills but because of a shy, inhibited personality is afraid to discuss the matter of a raise with his employer, believing instead that by reducing his efforts he will force his employer to give him a raise and appreciate him, he will also be using poor judgment. Avoidance of a direct confrontation to demand his rights might result in further frustration and the ultimate failure to achieve his objectives.

There is no set of rules that defines the right approach to the solution of a conflict situation. In the final analysis, if the adjustment mechanism an individual utilizes helps him to promote his goals, meet future demands, and enhance his social standing without any damaging effect on his mental or physical state, then his coping strategies are effective.

Although the strategies used by each individual for approaching a problem may vary from one event to the next, a few general approaches emerge as characteristic of successful adjustment. One of the first rules for a correct approach to a problem is usually to attempt to identify the cause exactly without using inferred assumptions or marginal explanations. Many people attempt to avoid directly addressing the cause by using self-construed rationalization. This only compounds the problem and the tensions.

Consider a woman who complains of being unable to find a suitable partner. While she wonders why she cannot maintain a relationship with a man, she tends to justify her situation by accusing the men she meets of being immature or uninterested in an emotional commitment. She may be overlooking the fact that she places unrealistic demands on a man too early in the relationship, is critical of his personality, or that she simply relates to the wrong man to start with.

Some situations are not so well focused as to permit any direct attack on the problem. Usually, some of the contributing factors are unknown or at least unclear. When any direct approach is impossible, the next logical approach is a step-by-step exploration of the known options. This approach enables one to predict and appraise the potential demands of a conflict and to move cautiously toward determining what limited means are available for controlling or overcoming it. If, even then, the evaluation of the options does not lead to any conclusive course of action, then the only way to deal with the situation is by trial and error. The exploration of trial-and-error possibilities is at least a useful form of experience for future reference, and more satisfactory than either making an arbitrary but final decision without adequate evidence or postponing the decision, hoping that something miraculous will happen favoring the desired outcome.

A typical example of exploration by trial-and-error behavior is the process of finding a marital partner. Most young people pursue a few emotional and sexual encounters with the opposite sex before getting married, realizing, through these experiences, what characteristics and personality traits in the opposite sex most appeal to them. An individual's unwillingness or inability to follow this course, because of rigid moral attitudes or personality inadequacies, can easily lead to future frustration and unhappiness when he or she finally does marry. By the same token, if the chosen partner changes or reveals different personality traits during the courtship that make the continuation of the relationship undesirable or increasingly difficult, an adjusted person will reevaluate the exisiting situation and admit the error of judgment made in the past, while attempting to reorganize his or her life accordingly.

Sometimes neither direct confrontation nor the exploration of options by trial and error are possible because of very real adverse conditions that make any control over the frustrating events impossible. In such cases, the only possibililty remaining is deliberately to reduce the amount of pressure caused by the frustrating situation.

Let us say that the same individual, after repeated explorations, is still unable to find a desirable marital partner and becomes extremely frustrated. In this case it might be necessary for that person to accept involvement in a more casual relationship, while still attempting to look for a marital partner. This approach reduces frustration and permits pursuit of the desired goal. However, additional factors are often required for the further reduction of tension such as extreme self-control and the inhibition of secondary needs that might interfere with the pursuit of a main goal. In point of fact, most human activity requires that a flexible set of priorities be given to the most immediate and decisive interest. Each individual has to establish a dynamic of priorities and keep less important matters in perspective.

In some situations, the most realistic method of adjustment is actually to substitute one goal for another. But sometimes, when a person realizes that his initial goal or ideal solution cannot be reached, because of uncontrollable circumstances, the disappointment may simply cause him to continue to pursue that goal irrationaly, only to become progressively more frustrated. At the other extreme, the individual may renounce the goal, or the possibility of any solution or reconciliation, and fall into a state of despair and helplessness because of the loss of confidence and self-esteem he feels as a result of his failure. However, if he thinks more realistically, he may see another

option: that of changing the direction of his pursuit toward an equally meaningful but different activity that he has better opportunities to realize. A
well-adjusted person accepts losses in a situation and is able to learn from
mistakes, thereby moving ahead toward new opportunities. Such a person
can eventually find a substitute for a lost partner or an unrewarding career.
But for this adjustment mechanism to operate the individual must learn to
think in flexible, relative terms, shifting priorities according to available
opportunities. To cope successfully with unpleasant events an individual
must approach conflict situations with an open mind, regardless of how
painful they may be; otherwise, regardless of how goal-oriented his approach
may be or how much he would like to solve the problem, he is bound to fail.
By unrealistically pressuring himself he has merely compounded his crisis
with the further (though in some respects inevitable) problem of stress.

The amount of stress that an individual is able to handle varies not only
according to exposure to it in the past but also according to his biological
constitution. Clearly, there are vast differences in individual abilities to tolerate stress. Though some scientists emphasize the role of social learning in
stress control, often an individual's constitutional qualities or defects make a
significant difference. Furthermore, environmental factors—family, education, and society—may play a major role in the formation of an individual's
personality and thereby of his ability to cope successfully with stressful
situations.

The most powerful environmental influence on an individual is the
family. The child's relationship with his parents, particularly with his
mother, is very significant to his development of good coping skills. The
sense of inner security and belonging is developed within the family, and
parental influence is extremely significant in the formation of his identity.
Parental rejection can lead to aggressiveness or submissiveness. While harsh,
brutal parental discipline can lead to hostility, insecurity, withdrawal, and
loss of self-esteem, overprotection and overindulgence can reduce an individual's tolerance for frustration. All these family-related factors can cause a
child to grow up unprepared to cope with the demands of society or to
withstand the pressures of daily life. These negative personality traits can
lead to a further three-way conflict between the individual's view of himself,
other people's view of him, and the way he would *like* to be seen by others.
This clearly exacerbates the clash between his increasingly unrealistic expectations of himself and his true possibilities.

PERSONALITY: A SINGULAR VIEW OF REALITY

The totality of the individual's adaptive and coping mechanisms, however
they evolve over the years of his maturation, are ideally integrated into his
unique interpretation of reality, his own style of thinking. A few patterns of
thinking are obvious examples of ways in which individuals sometimes fail to

develop a truly socially adaptive style of their own. One pattern is a tendency toward intolerance of ambiguity. An individual may develop a propensity to perceive and evaluate things only as falling into definite categories, and be unable to distinguish nuances or intermediate grades. This type of categorization is often associated with children raised in authoritarian homes in which discipline demanded that the child follow strictly prescribed patterns of behavior evaluated only in terms of absolutes. This style of thinking can be conformist, prejudicial, and inflexible, and can lead to an inability to adapt or make decisions in situations in which absolute values conflict.

Another polarized thinking style is to perceive a situation as either too simple or too complex. Some people oversimplify situations, not considering any but the most basic variables. Others see too many significant variables. Other common styles of thinking are to respond to group pressure and social expectations to be other-directed, or—the opposite extreme—to be inner-directed and act for personal satisfaction alone.

These cognitive styles only begin to broadly categorize a few of the faulty means individuals may develop for interpreting and thereby dealing with reality. While each cognitive style generally suggests a dominance of either parental influences (such as intolerance of ambiguity) or societal learning (as in responding to group pressure), it would seem incorrect, as the Freudians have suggested, to conclude that only the familial and social learning of the very first years of childhood contribute to the fixed patterns of personality that remain with the individual throughout his lifetime. Certainly, to the extent to which the process of learning goes on throughout life, various experiences in later years add their influence, modifing the attitudes of the individual toward himself and others.

Still, it is based on whatever thinking patterns an individual has developed that he will appraise events and will formulate his personality and then his coping responses. Often the *coping style* acquired during various periods of childhood (in order initially to overcome what *a child* perceives to be stressful or anxiety-producing events) will persist in a modified form in adulthood as a learned method of avoidance of similarly unpleasant situations. These defenses, when carried into adulthood, can become the source of an adult's maladjustment. At other times in the course of an individual's conflict with society he may exhaust his usually adequate coping resources and fall back on the same primitive defenses he used in childhood. This can happen when a previously well-adjusted individual discovers that his current means of perceiving and coping with the world has run afoul of society's sometimes contradictory norms, or shifting values, and he begins to doubt his ability to understand, evaluate, and deal with them as usual. The resulting confusion is extremely frustrating and in fact may induce a serious psychological maladjustment in a previously "normal" individual.

Ideally, a mature individual should have learned to adjust to high stress and to the demands of change and conflict in his life regardless of the circumstances. In real life, such a high tolerance for frustration and high level of flexibility may be required that an individual is simply unable to find within himself the means and understanding that he needs. But he can only continue to try to come to terms with the new situation based on his capacities or past learned responses, in other words, his personality and related coping style. Anyway, his childhood coping patterns will affect his ability to tolerate crisis and to develop further ways of understanding his experiences and coping with new stress and frustration.

THE FREUDIAN-BEHAVIORIST DEBATE

This, however, touches on the biggest controversy in psychiatry. Does an adult's maladjusted behavior stem from symbolic defenses used in childhood against repressed infantile drives, or does it stem from simple learned responses that are developed to avoid specific unpleasant experiences. Because these contradictory theoretical explanations have led to opposite concepts of therapy (which unjustifiably claim unique and indisputable success), they have in fact reduced the possibility of understanding and helping the neurotic, instead of offering further options. Though the historical dynamics of this debate has already been discussed in the Introduction, it is useful to look more closely at the respective therapies and to compare them to newer forms of therapy that attempt to answer the questions of perception and coping we have just raised.

Until recently, the prevailing view in psychiatry was based on the Freudian theory that the neurotic conflict is due to unconscious infantile sexual drives that interfere with the individual's normal processes of adaptation to the social environment. For Freud, the development of a child's personality depended on the resolution of the conflict induced by the child's repressed infantile sexuality. Any emotional conflict that the child might have developed at any stage of his sexual development (defined by Freud in terms of oral, anal, and genital stages) was seen as affecting his later years of emotional growth. Broadly speaking, all of the child's experience up to the age of five (the age of the resolution of the Oedipus complex, when the boy renounces the desire to sleep with the mother and to eliminate the father) became the bedrock for understanding the adult neurotic maladjustment pattern.

Freud assumed a few basic premises in reducing human maladjustment to the repressions of infantile sexuality. First, he posited the existence of an unconscious psychic activity that controlled the expression of the undesirable infantile sexual drives. Second, he asserted that the once-conscious infantile sexual drive of the child had been "pushed" or repressed into the unconscious because it was irreconcilable with the child's love for his parents and with his sense of morality. Third, he assumed that the difference between child and adult thinking consisted in the amount of knowledge accumulated through experience. Freud shared the current belief of his time that children and adults employed basically the same logic. He also believed that the individual developed various defenses against his infantile sexuality in order to integrate himself into the social mainstream. Finally, he maintained that society itself was neurotic because of the repression of infantile sexuality.

The premises used by Freud, far from being original, represented a compilation of the existing views of his time. As stated in the Introduction, the concept of the unconscious, for example, was widely held by philosophers and psychologists in the late nineteenth century. In fact, it was a philosopher, E. V. von Hartman, who wrote the most comprehensive book on the subject, *The Philosophy of the Unconscious,* in 1868. In Hartman's book all the unexplainable phenomena of the mind were documented by the existence of this special function of the brain. Hartman's *unconscious* was the counterpart of another concept of physics of the time, that of the *aether,* which attempted to explain unknown mechanisms of physical phenomena. The unconscious was responsible for the inexplicable "irrational" behavior of man. The idea was a more sophisticated attempt than religion to explain human behavior, which failed to conform to the widely held concept of man as a rational being, and Freud eagerly embraced this rationale. If in the past irrational behavior had been attributed by religion to evil spirits, now, with the advent of nineteenth-century scientific inquiry, a new concept was found: that of evil wishes unsuccessfully repressed by the individual.

The successful treatment of hysteria by Jean Charcot and Ambroise Liebeault and the empirical studies of Josef Breuer convinced Freud that repressed sexual trauma resided in the unconscious and was indeed the cause of irrational human behavior. Freud replaced their use of hypnosis with talk therapy—free association—in order, he said, to bring back into consciousness the long-forgotten memories buried in the unconscious. He became convinced that the infantile sexual drive, though in conflict with ethical or personal values, was still contained in the unconscious by a process of repression. *Repression* he conceived of as an active process, preventing these impulses from reaching consciousness. In other words, Freud thought that there were a set of mental processes with a life of their own of which the consciousness was not aware. Independent of consciousness, these mental processes containing conflicting instinctual needs were able to influence the conscious act by crossing the barrier (or censorship) of consciousness under particular circumstances.

Freud hypothesized that the repressed, the instinctive, material went in and out of the unconscious according to the dynamics of the principle of reality that governed an individual life as controlled by that person's superego, the socially evolved moral censor. But in exchange, he maintained the superego itself developed from the internalized aggressiveness and guilt created as a result of the individual's repressed instinctual drives due to parental prohibitions. In this way the cause became the effect and the effect the cause. The explanation for the mind's dynamics was circular. For Freud, the unconscious became the product of repressed human behavior and at the same time the controlling and directing force of the same behavior. The individual was trapped, his motivational organization of life determined by the inescapable childhood sexuality of his past. Furthermore, according to this libidinal theory (of the pursuit of sexual pleasure as part of the instinctual drive), individual response was channeled into certain patterns of expression, according to the person's infantile sexual conflict, which without treatment remained fixed and immutable for life.

These theoretical assumptions led Freud to the conclusion that civilization itself was the result of the renunciation of the sexual instinct; that human history was the history of attempted mutations of the sexual instinct in favor of civilization—an outgrowth of the repressed collective ego, so vulnerable to reality-testing. Indirectly, he saw all of civilization as an outgrowth of human psychopathology in which the individual was a pawn of unconscious forces that, though masked by "decency," could become violent, like monsters from the depths, to try to overpower the weak conscience. In this context all of us are neurotics.

Recently, with the progress of science and the increase in our knowledge of psychology, the tenets of Freud's theory have started to disintegrate. In the past his theoretical assumptions, while attacked emotionally, could not be fully refuted scientifically because they were untestable. But scientific methodology has now made possible the accumulation of a wealth of data that have totally changed our concept of the aspect of the mind's dynamics that is responsible for human maladaptation.

The first documented attack on Freudian theories came from the conditioned reflex theory, which developed an entirely different concept of maladjusted behavior. The behaviorist learning theories that evolved from the work of I. Pavlov, J. B. Watson, C. L. Hull, and B. F. Skinner postulated that human conflict is determined by maladaptive learned behavior. The behaviorists disregarded the role of any specific psychic conflict related to infantile sexuality in the development of adult neurosis. Later, these learning theories, combining genetic and environmental factors in the formation of mental symptoms, conceived neurosis as the result of a pattern of abnormally learned behavior in a constitutionally predisposed individual.

For instance, according to Hans Jürgen Eysenck, an English research behaviorist, the individual's susceptibility to a neurotic condition is determined first by the reactivity of his autonomic nervous system, which Eysenck called the "degree of neuroticism." This, he maintains, accounts for the great variability in individual responses to the same noxious environmental factors. In general, behaviorists agreed with Freudians that anxiety played a central role in the development of neurotic symptoms but disagreed about its formation mechanisms. Learning theories perceived neurotic anxiety as a conditioned emotional response that could be established experimentally or clinically by any classical conditioning. Thus, the conditioned anxiety acquires the properties of a drive to avoid the noxious stimuli.

On the basis of knowledge gathered from classical and instrumental conditioning, a few psychiatric conditions could be explained and treated behaviorally. Symptoms of phobic reaction, obsessive-compulsive neurosis, psychosomatic conditions, and sexually maladaptive behavior could be partially or totally explained or treated within this theoretical framework. But, although conditioning was able to explain direct behavior, it was unable to explain or to influence the mental processes that often made this behavior suddenly reappear in a crisis situation. The symptoms could be treated by behaviorists, but the personality dynamic and pattern of thinking that led an individual to respond to a situation in a particular manner remained beyond the immediate boundaries of learning theories. Also, theorists were becoming dissatisfied with the experimental analysis of behavior offered by behaviorists based on the principles and procedures of operant conditioning. They were particularly unhappy about the minor role assigned in the course of the scientific investigation to the subjective element in events. Cognitive processes and personal perceptions were rejected by behaviorists as superimposed, on the assumption that they did not exert any real causal effect on behavior.

A partial liberalization of this approach was attempted by neobehaviorists, who contended that the mind's symbolic representations of any anxiety-producing event were part of an individual's conditioning to that event. In this context the emotionally colored image of the stimulus object became the primary focus of the treatment of systematic desensitization (de-conditioning). Yet any cognitive formulation in these behavioral techniques was reduced to background material, part of the historical data about the individual's maladaptive behavior. Coping was still viewed as a question of conditioned response.

At the same time the social learning theorists extended their approach to the understanding of human behavior, maintaining that the regulation of behavior, while controlled by external factors, was significantly determined by an individual's cognitive processes. It was their hypothesis that cognitive activity is responsible for the maintenance and activation of a learned behavior and can reorient or modify the organization of that behavior. Therapeutically, this reciprocal determinism of behavior permitted a kind of manipulative self-control. In other words, the individual was given back a certain amount of responsibiity for his actions, but he was still viewed primarily as a product of his environment. A diversity of other therapeutic approaches have been developed within the cognitive theoretical framework, therapies that have expanded or changed the focus of the cognitive relearning.

Although shifting the focus from the restrictive sphere of classical and operant conditioning to the cognitive processes has broadened the base of behavioral therapy, it has not solved the fundamental issue of just how much the organization of thinking patterns is also responsible for maladaptive behavior. The irrationalities of the patient's logic are at best still categorized by neobehaviorists as superimposed misconceptions in an otherwise logical individual. In the behavioral context the therapist becomes a simple teacher who, after assessing the maladaptive learning problems of the patient, attempts to correct them by a simple educational experience. This learning is reinforced by the constant feedback of the therapist. Yet the learning experience in itself has proven in most cases to be ineffective in the long term, even with the support of the therapist in guiding the behavioral changes. It may be that learning and physical exposure to the anxiety-producing situation are not ·sufficient to assure extinction of an anxiety. What appears to be important is the patient's change of attitude toward his problem and sense of his ability to overcome it, which transcends any particular type of specific behavioral therapy. Instead of correction, he must come to perceive the problem differently. In this context, cognitive behavior therapy has not demonstrated any clear superiority over strictly behavioral therapy, and both of them have proved to have limited applicability.

CHILDHOOD THOUGHT: THE MISSING LINK

While all types of therapy, Freudian or behavioristic, attempted to deal with the irrational behavior of the neurotic individual, they failed either to place it within the right context or to solve it. For one reason or another what they missed was to trace correctly the origins of irrational thought.

For instance, although Freud attempted to relate neurotic conflict to the development of the child, he formulated this relationship in terms of adult reasoning, terms purely inferential as to the child's real understanding of reality. Freud assumed that children and adults used the same type of logic, the only difference being, as said before, the degree of knowledge obtained through experience. This was his fatal error. Freud's lack of knowledge about the development of thought in children (and this was where he placed the greatest weight in his theories) led him to construct a pseudoscientific theory of human behavior. He was never able to trace accurately the origins of "the irrational" thought that existed in an adult.

Furthermore, Freud built his theory on the then-prevailing assumption that man is a logical, rational creature who thinks irrationally only when disturbed by a neurotic conflict. But scientific and empirical evidence indicates that, on the contrary, irrational elements such as belief, superstition, and fantasies are integrated into the logic of all humans and act as motivating drives of behavior. These irrational elements in fact represent the internal reality of an individual, part of his conscious process; they influence perceptions and behavior.

Meanwhile, the behaviorists had discarded all aspects of consciousness and childhood influence, and focused on the behavior itself, because according to them this was the only observable reality. Therefore, for different reasons, both the Freudians and the behaviorists ignored the conceptual perspective of the individual, the inner, personal meaning of an act as developed according to his particular way of perceiving reality and based on his pattern of thinking. Most important, no one looked at the development of these thinking patterns in the context of childhood, since before the studies of Jean Piaget it was assumed that the child thought like a little adult.

In order to explore the structure of personal meanings and constructs with which an adult builds his phenomenal experiential world, we have to go back to the child's concept of reality. We have to follow an individual's stages of intellectual maturation until he reaches the adult's logical level of reasoning. This will help us to find the origin of any maladaptive pattern in adult thinking that has been maintained since childhood.

In simple terms, what is called irrational thinking in adults, as expressed by neurotic behavior, is based on the child's mode of thinking, which has infiltrated adult logic. The most important point to be demonstrated in this book is that any disturbance in the process of the child's adaptation to reality at any stage of his intellectual development, induced either by adult influences and behavior or by his own confused interpretation of an unfavorable situation, can lead to the formation of neurotic responses, and these responses are often carried into adulthood. Such isolated instances of pseudologic can be either latent or active in adulthood, often creating conflict and disturbing the individual's mental equilibrium.

2

THE CHILDHOOD
ROOTS OF
NEUROTIC THINKING

The logic develops as a child's thought becomes socialized.

—JEAN PIAGET, *The Child's Conception of the World*

The development of personality is essentially a long, difficult struggle toward the adaptation of an individual to his environment. It is a gradual process starting with the infant's dependency on his mother and his immediate environment, from which he slowly frees himself in order to be capable in adulthood of negotiating and creating his own independent social milieu.

One of the best formulations of the psychological theory of adaptation is based on the work of Jean Piaget, the Swiss psychologist. Piaget revolutionized the psychology of the child by demonstrating that the child's intellectual development goes through two basic processes—assimilation and accommodation. Piaget viewed adaptation as the balance between the assimilative and accommodative processes. In *assimilation*, he asserted, the child reacts to a situation with a behavioral response that incorporates the environmental stimuli into a preestablished pattern of behavior. In *accommodation*, the child modifies his response according to the new situation, thereby developing a new behavior.

These two processes can be followed through all stages of a child's intellectual maturation. The child's mental development, according to Piaget, starts with very simple reflexes that are modified through learning in order to reach a new combination of responses of higher complexity. Progressively, the organization of behavior changes qualitatively for the first time at

24

around the age of eighteen months to two years. At that time language emerges, as does the child's first primitive organized thought. The comprehension of signs and symbols gives a child the ability to evoke absent objects and extend his world beyond the momentary perceptions of things and immediate events. The surrounding environment then becomes stable, better organized, and more meaningful to him.

With the appearance of symbolic processes, the function of imitation does become more sophisticated; however, the child's imitation of adult behavior is not necessarily a photographic repetition of that behavior. It is modified and interpreted by the child according to his own understanding of what he has observed. The child integrates the adult symbols and signs and selects them on the basis of his own mental capacity to understand them. The result is the formulation of his own unique concept of things. This concept of reality is different from the adult's because the child's thinking structure is different from adult thought.

These new findings, documented by the extensive research of Piaget and others, represent a giant step toward understanding the mental laws governing the child's evaluation of reality. They can also explain the origin and causes of maladjusted patterns of behavior. The evolution of a child's intellectual development is a progressive socialization and with it an adaptation of his own thought to the adult's world and to the laws of logical reasoning. Therefore, the interaction between adult influences and the child's own mental responses is weighted according to the child's stage of thinking development at the time of each experience.

Piaget followed the child's intellectual development month by month, year by year, pointing out the child's own originality in conceptualizing the world and the progressive maturation of his thought toward the acceptance of mostly preconceived adult beliefs and convictions. Piaget found that the child's thinking undergoes a continuous change from an initial self-centered position in which there is no consciousness of the "self" to an objective, realistic concept of the world. As the child grows and his thinking changes, he is gradually able to understand adult reasoning better and to identify with the adult's concept of reality. The various stages in the emotional and intellectual development of the child offer a clue to the formulation of various problems of adaptation, or rather maladaptation.

A CHILD'S STAGES OF LEARNING

Despite some psychological theories that would lead one to believe that soon after birth the child is able to understand his environment, the overwhelming evidence indicates that the child's "self" is *not* conscious of itself. All of the infant's reactions are centered on his own body and his own actions, without any conscious emotional or mental interpretation. Conscious emotional reactions, or *affective responses* (emotional responses affected by outside factors), and the beginning of any organization of thinking processes gradually appear as the self becomes more firmly differentiated from external reality. As the child grows, the development of the ability to locate and recognize an object by its shape and form, and its place in space and time, will parallel any emotional meaning that the object might take on. These emotionally toned perceptual abilities develop in the second year of life and soon become firmly established elements of the child's thinking patterns. Yet it will be years before the child's organization of thinking will follow the adult's rules of logic.

By the age of seven, the mental development of the child reaches a third level, that of *concrete operations*. At this time the child becomes capable of organizing his thought based on mental manipulation of objects. In addition, his gradual progress in the logic of classification makes him able to relate objects in a logic of simple mathematical calculations. For instance, the child might make the association that when it is about to rain or it rains people protect themselves with umbrellas; thus he comes to believe that if he carries or opens an umbrella he can cause rain if he has had similar experiences in the past. The child's thought, however, is not yet a logic based on the projection of conclusions or causality. Piaget calls this type of logic *transductive;* that is, logic that puts together separate facts unrelated to each other yet linked in the child's mind and identified as having a similarity or reciprocal causality. This stage of thinking gradually disappears by the age of eleven or twelve years, when another major qualitative change takes place.

Only at this age does the preadolescent start to use *operational abstract thinking.* This new level of thinking brings him close to adult reasoning. Now he is able to consider hypotheses that may or may not be true and attempt to follow them to their final logical conclusion. He is able to master the hypothetical deductive reasoning of science and to theorize about the concept of relationships. This last stage in the development of thinking in the child is called the stage of *formal thinking*.

THE CHILD'S WORLD AND REALITY

Because these stages in the child's intellectual development are important in understanding the formation of maladjusted or neurotic behavior, it is necessary to consider how they interact with the child's socialization process. There is a close relationship between the processes of the child's socialization and the normal development of his ability to reason. Both factors determine the level of the child's comprehension of reality. The reality to which he has to adapt is that of the adult world. This process of adaptation is based on the influence of adult behavior and on the adult imposition of norms of behavior. When the child's concept of the world or his relationship to it is undermined, disrupted, or negated by untimely adult imposition of beliefs, actions, or demands beyond the child's capacities, then an adaptational conflict erupts.

This conflict, the product of the clash between the reality a child perceives and his ability to cope with that reality, arises because the child lacks the necessary perspective to integrate these demands properly into his system of thinking so that he can either respond to or dismiss them. These are, in fact, the roots of maladaptive behavior. The most salient aspects of the child's thinking, the aspects that shape his view of reality, are those of egocentricity and magical interpretation. These are also the two aspects of a child's world that directly conflict with the adult approach to reality.

During childhood, thinking is permeated by the child's egocentric orientation—he sees himself as the center of his own small universe. He learns to distinguish between his internal nature and external reality, but it takes him years of mental development to become conscious of his own thought. For instance, up to the age of six the child may believe that he thinks with his mouth, which emits words, not with his brains. By the age of eight he comes to the conclusion that he thinks as a result of a voice in his head. Up to this age, the child is unable to trace the chain of reasoning that led him to arrive at a particular conclusion.

This lack of introspective observation of his own mental operations limits the child's ability to reason logically, to find justification for his judgment, or to evaluate the judgment of others. He is neither able to define objects correctly nor to explain the causes of actions or events. Piaget called this thinking level *precausal* because the child can explain a relationship between objects and their actions only in circumstantial terms. He has not yet developed the mental capacity to see the relationship between cause and effect correctly, between his actions and the effect produced by them (this has significant implications for the development of maladaptive behavior, as we shall see in the next chapter). In fact, the child attributes his own intentions, motives, and failings for the most part to objects. He confuses his "self" with surrounding things. At the same time, he does not have the need to verify the truth of his beliefs. This attitude gives him a self-assurance unshaken by the contradictions between various statements that he makes at the same time. Furthermore, in his thinking there is a genuine acceptance of opposites. For instance, if the child is corrected by an adult for inexactly presenting a particular event, the child is able to reverse his position totally, accepting the position of the adult and denying the one he previously held. He changes his opinion without any realization of the switch. In fact, he assimilates the new explanation given by someone else and considers it his own.

Most of the time the child does not see the contradictions in his statements because he uses only partial definitions in describing objects or actions, and his perceptions of those things are limited by those definitions. A child may think "the moon is alive" because it moves, while an airplace is not alive even though he admits that it moves too. He may think that a teddy bear is a toy because he plays with it and at the same time believe that it is alive because "it is an animal." A child may operate with numerous inter-changeable beliefs according to the situation with which he is faced. If for the adult reality is coherently organized and governed by the same general prin-ciples, for the child it can exist on different planes, depending on the type of activity in which he is involved. The child lives in a world of contradictions that he is unable to recognize as such because his whole concept of reality is fragmented in an unstable equilibrium, changeable from day to day and from situation to situation. In this world, definitions of objects and things undergo reevaluation and modification under the pressure of adult influence. By imi-tation and assimilation the child attempts to identify the external world, yet the knowledge accumulated about it is not understood by him in terms of logical relationships or causality—it is fragmented, unsystematized, and dis-connected. The unifying point of reference is his egocentrism, which pro-jects him into the external reality he perceives. The result is that of confusing the functioning of self with the actions of surrounding objects, which is natural to a child, because his thinking is subjective, animistic, and magically oriented. His thought is inseparable from its object because he does not yet see a distinction between the psychical and the physical world: thoughts, images, words, and things all are somehow indistinguishable.

This state of undifferentiated consciousness that projects itself onto his surrounding world causes the child to interpret the relationship between himself and other things or beings as one of influence on each other through what is called *participation*. This mental process by which he appraises reality can create serious difficulties later in his acceptance of adult reality. The concept of *participation*, the reciprocal influence between an individual's be-ing and external objects or other beings, was introduced by Lucien Levy-Bruhl to describe primitive thought. Piaget applied it, in a more restrictive context, to the child's thinking. Piaget demonstrated that the child believes he has the magical power to influence things in his own way, while other beings or things are endowed with similar powers. When the child moves, the moon moves—when he stands still, the moon stands still. He believes that the moon follows him, watches him, listens to what he has to say. This is one of the most dominant aspects of a child's organization of thought, and it plays an extremely powerful role in influencing his interaction with others. The longer a child maintains this magical thinking as a part of his way of understanding and relating to the world, the more maladapted he will be later on in dealing with the reality of adult life.

The importance of the magic quality of the child's thinking escaped Freud, and he related it to the child's belief in the omnipotence of his own thought, part of his narcissism. *Narcissism*, as identified by Freud, was a stage of personality development in which the child, in love with himself, is preoc-cupied with the satisfaction of his own needs and desires. But this theory presupposes that the child differentiates clearly between himself and others—which is not the case. Further, the child's "sense of omnipotence" is actually a consequence of his inability to separate his "self" from the external world. The child appears to be a narcissist to the extent to which he lacks consciousness of himself. He is egocentric to the extent to which he sees himself as the center of the world, and he relates to the world as he relates to himself, because he sees no clear distinction at this stage. His inability to understand his internal process of thinking makes him attribute similar "thinking" qualities to surrounding objects. This confusion between thought and external objects, together with other aspects of precausal thinking, becomes the basis of the child's magical interpretation of reality.

One of the most common forms of the child's magical thinking is the belief that the performance of a particular action or thought will have the power to determine the course of an event important to him. For instance, the child may believe that he will be successful in his examinations in school if by the time he reaches a set distance from school he counts an odd or even number of some type of car. A variant of magical participation by action is the use of symbolic words or thoughts to master a situation. Words or specifically developed formulas, children often believe, can decide the direction of their activities or even the activities of others merely by being spoken. Whatever the means, the more a child desires or fears something, the more he will attempt to control the situation by "making believe" that it will happen as he would like it to happen. The performance of the right act or utterance of the right word is somehow linked with the desired outcome, assuring the child that his wish will be met.

This practice of what we adults call magic is for the child a natural approach to daily living in dealing with uncontrollable, anxiety-producing events, whose control he believes depends on his power of thinking. This magical thinking is present in all areas of his activity. If he is afraid of the dark or sleeping alone in a room, the child may associate a specific act or movement with the power to ward off any potential danger. If this association is established between a thought or act and a projected activity, then it is repeated in the same manner in similar situations in order to achieve the same results, but the act must be executed in a specific way, in a definite order, and at a given time in order to succeed.

For example, a child may relate bad dreams to disorder in his room and feel he must go through a ritual: put his clothes on the chair in an orderly way, pull the shades down, check in all corners of the room, tuck himself under the blanket well (the blanket may or may not cover his head). If the performance is not executed in a predetermined manner, then the danger is not fended off, and he has to repeat the same ritual in the right order. Obviously, for him, the ritual has the power to make things happen or not happen. Using the same line of reasoning, some objects are entrusted by children with the power to control and decide events of which actually they are totally independent. The connection is made purely accidentally or whimsically by the child in the first place, but as a result, he is assured that the object used will control the outcome of later, similar events. A boy goes to school and takes his marbles with him. In class he holds his marbles in his hand while he is solving a problem. If he solves it successfully, he believes that the marbles brought him luck. From then on, he will repeat the same activity in similar circumstances. Remnants of this type of magical thinking are found in gamblers who believe that a particular chair, a pack of cards, or a day of the week will ensure their success. Broadly speaking, there is little difference between the magic words or specific numbers used by the child for securing the grace of his parents and superiors and the prayers of the adult for help or absolution from God. From this magical approach to reality seems to stem obsessive-compulsive behavior in adulthood.

MAINTENANCE OF CHILDHOOD THINKING IN THE ADULT

If the child's thinking is so strongly permeated by a magical dimension, then how does the adult replace this with logical thought? Unlike adult logic, the thinking of the child on the preoperational level is not based on a logical relationship between objects; the child thinks not by syllogisms but by assumptions and inferences from one particular proposition to another. He does not apply any general law of logic but, at best, moves from separate explanations to other separate explanations in his thinking about an event. He juxtaposes them, combines them, and reaches a conclusion. In his animistic formulation, clouds that move are alive because he himself moves and is alive. It is no wonder, then, that his explanations are purely subjective and haphazard, because the relationships found between things is for the most part imaginary.

The child's egocentrism reinforces the magical quality of his world even more. The experiences of his infancy have caused him to believe that there is a direct link between his ability to request attention on demand—by crying or screaming angrily until his needs are fulfilled—and the care extended to him by his parents. This belief is sometimes integrated into his later life in a magical construction of thought and extended to other situations that he would like to be able to control; animate and inanimate things are endowed with the same ability to submit to his needs. The magic satisfies the need to find an explanation, providing a pseudocausal relationship between things or actions and rendering the surrounding world nonthreatening. Practically, it softens the impact of responsibilities imposed on him by his parents or school that contradict his need for immediate gratification. It constitutes the connecting catalyst between his emotional life of dreams and fantasies, in which things happen his way, and the painful reality of living and experiencing life, doing things that he dislikes or that seem unbeneficial.

If this magical coping with reality is maintained throughout the developmental stages of childhood instead of being gradually discarded in favor of logical thought, it becomes integrated into adult thinking. An adult whose childlike need for attention and immediate gratification was never properly dealt with will, particularly in moments of crisis, be tempted to take refuge in magic.

AFFECTIVE EXPERIENCE: EMOTIONALLY CHARGED PERCEPTIONS

Another important aspect in the child's development, one with profound implications for his later adult functioning, is the integration (through socialization) of his emotional reactions into the thinking process. In the first stage of development, a child's emotional responses are related purely to his physical state. Initially, his behavior is directed toward the dominant stimuli from his environment, that is only strictly reflexive, directly related to his comfort and survival. The growth of his ability to deal with his environment goes hand in hand with the development of his cognition. Affective and perceptual development cannot be separated from each other, even in an infant, so normally, when the meaning of the act is changed, the child's initial emotional response changes according to his new level of understanding a particular situation. The exception to this is offered by the *innate releasing mechanisms* (biologically programmed responses to a specific set of external signs that represent stimuli). These signs and stimuli, when introduced into a child's affective-perceptual reality, can create bonds that are so intrinsic to his needs and ego functioning that the resulting behavior often becomes very resistant to reversal. The process of learning cannot always modify these innate patterns.

A first example of this is a child's love bond to its mother or mother figure. It appears that in the first stage of adaptation to his surroundings, a disturbance of the love bond affects the child's expression of his most basic biological needs, such as protection and security. It can be particularly destructive. The absence of the mother when she is needed releases a reflexive anxiety, expressed by crying spells that can gradually lead to a child's withdrawal from his surroundings. The reflexive connections between his biological needs and the means of their gratification have become disorganized. This in turn inhibits his proper emotional and intellectual development by reducing his security and thus his interest in exploratory orientation toward the environment, because his more basic needs have yet to be met.

There are other situations in which if a specific innate biological drive (sexual identity) is associated early in life with a meaningful perception, a particular type of behavior results, for instance, if a young boy experiences identification with a girl through cross-dressing. This when repeated and reinforced by the reward of love establishes an enduring pattern of comportment. This new *affective perceptual relationship*, when firmly established, is very hard to change. This partly explains sexual disturbances in the child's later development of patterns of sexual behavior.

Another area of emotionally charged perceptions resistant to changes is that of traumatic experiences. For instance fears of the dark, being lost, being attacked by an animal, or of various other traumatic situations are all maintained and amplified by the child's fixation on patterns of avoidance behavior based on experiences that he has interpreted as frightening. The prelogical child does not attempt to test the reality or evaluate the conditions of the actual event that originally produced the fear. For him, cause and effect are established independent of the factual reality. What decides the direction of a particular subsequent activity is really the *memory* of an emotional reaction. In this context it makes a difference to the child's perception of a situation whether his past similar experience has been motivated by reward, sense of obligation, or repeated fear.

As the child grows, the organization of his perceptual field gradually becomes freer from the once nearly total control of the affective element; however, it is never totally free of that element. The child's thought is always most immediately colored by his needs, which he completely integrates into his thought processes, whereas for the adult both perception and its integration are more subject, or at least are supposed to be, to the process of objective evaluation and logical thought.

But even in adults the perception of the gratification of a drive is influenced by the hierarchy of available responses that will reduce the tension that induced the particular drive in the first place. Obviously the responses change according to the drive. For instance, if an individual has a high sexual drive, his perceptual readiness will be particularly directed toward signals that are sexually meaningful. However, if conditions do not permit the satisfaction of this drive, he will turn his attention toward some other pressing demand of another drive. This is not true for the adult whose rational evaluation of his alternatives remains patterned on the childhood level of immediate gratification; then the discrepancy between an emotionally colored perception of reality and reality itself underlies and interferes with almost all of his activities. This is because the affective response has remained a controlling factor in the growth of his personality. In this case he is unable to distinguish between his subjective emotional experience and the objective laws governing his reasoning about reality.

In order to trace this inadequate integration of affect with cognition, it is important to examine the role played by emotions in the process of a child's socialization. His social interaction begins with symbolic play and the learning of language. At the beginning children play by themselves even when involved in play with other children. By the age of seven they are able to play by rules—the beginning of social ethics—and relate meaningfully to others in their games. The progressive awareness of the self as part of the child's growth increases the value of interaction with others and their responses to him. This socialization carries with it either an emotional reward such as acceptance, praise, or expression of love (first from his mother and later from a significant other) or emotional punishment and nonacceptance. The result is a child learns to negotiate his needs versus those of others, otherwise he does not have friends. The same applies to verbal communication. Language, with its powers of evocation and representation, elicits powerful negative and positive emotions from others, hindering or helping the child's mental development. In addition language, as communication, can also strengthen and maintain various beliefs according to the parental and cultural climate of the child's rearing, affecting his social interaction with others. In fact, the persistence of magical thought in adulthood is often partly due to the fact that it is collectively and socially reinforced. This explains why the whole gamut of superstitions, myths, and taboos have remained with mankind throughout history despite the growth of scientific knowledge. The cognitive and affective components of mental activities are intertwined in the social development of the child; any difficulty in either one of these mental mechanisms brings changes in the other.

THE ROLE OF MEMORY IN ADAPTATION

As already mentioned, integrated experiences of affect and cognition are stored in the memory. A child's memory is also the storehouse of experiential adaptive patterns and social values that influence his moral judgment. Memory is extremely important to the dynamics of the child's adaptation. Both the cognitive and affective components of memory have been the subject of intense controversy regarding their role in maladjustment.

The ability to remember and recognize objects develops in early infancy, as attested to by the infant's recognition of the nipple during nursing shortly after birth. At this early stage children cannot have stable, integrated memory because they lack the ability to *represent* (project) and reconstruct their activities and primitive perceptions in their minds. With the separation of self from the environment and the appearance of symbolic thought, the process of representation in the formation of images takes place, leading to the development of more complex behavior patterns that can then be evoked as image memories. But these image memories are not exact copies of real objects; they represent *the way those objects have been perceived by the child*.

Interesting experiments with memorization of different combinations of objects have shown that they are recalled not in their presented configuration but modified by the child's ability to conceptualize them. This indicates that the child stores the memories of significant events in his life according to his ability to understand them at that time, at his own level of thinking.

For instance, experiments have shown that children coming from poor families have a tendency to overestimate the sizes of coins as compared to rich children. This difference is obviously due to different past experiences related to the value of money. The thought processes transform these visual perceptions into concepts by means of a tendency of the brain to maintain a state of equilibrium through integration of visual perceptions into previous experience. What is important to realize is that concepts presuppose a higher level of abstract operations that makes them reversible and changeable. Visual data are incorporated into specific concepts according to the thought level of the individual. For instance, the child visually perceives the moon in the same basic way as an adult, but he integrates it on a different level of conceptual meaning because of his prelogical thought patterns and his limited experience.

Until recently, it was assumed by most psychologists that the child stores significant events from his past in the unconscious. It was believed by Freudians that when the unconscious becomes a source of motivation for conscious activities, the behavior that emerges is largely unrelated to the conscious logical meaning of the activity. It was assumed also that bringing repressed memories of childhood out from the unconscious would correct maladaptive behavior induced by the memories' interference with conscious reality.

A complex hypothetical construct of memory about its storage and recall raises questions about memory's function (evocative memory) in the preoperational stage of childhood thinking. What kinds of memories are stored by a small child (up to the age of five)? If these memories are "stylized" events, distorted in their meaning through the prelogical thought process, they can have little significance when the child recalls them later in association with seemingly similar events. At best, the stylized memories would be reconstructed to fit the new events in new interpretations that are stored again as new stylized events. It is only later, after the age of six or seven, that the child can begin to store events better in their factual form, with fewer distorted layers of emotional or magical overtones.

However, memories are not only reconstructed according to the child's level of thinking development at the time when they were perceived but they also undergo changes in recollection. A potent affective factor complicates the storage of memory according to the child's emotional state not only at the time of the original event but also at the time of the recollection, as a result of the child's change in understanding or perception of that reality. The unreliability of younger children in recalling events and their tendency to modify, exaggerate, or diminish the intensity of initial emotional impact are well known. If memory records events as experienced through the child's level of thinking, to be reconstructed at the time of recall, then we are talking about a dynamic memory, not a factual one. Up to the age of about five or six, children's significant memories are reconstructed in large part through repetitive reminders of events by their parents or other adults in the way that these people saw the events. This means that the child often gets information about significant past events of his life, and in turn develops beliefs and attitudes, mainly from his parents. From the reliable and unreliable memories of the past stored by the child, and the adult versions of the same events, a new set of memories emerges that becomes the basis of his life story.

However, the child gradually retains events more or less in their original form. The controversial issue of specific storage of memories from the first five years of life, the basic tenet of psychoanalytic theory, is highly questionable in terms of what we know now about the reconstruction of affective memory. The old concept of repression, which attempted to deal with the mechanism that controls the storage of memories in early childhood, becomes irrelevant if not meaningless, because in early childhood the child is able to categorize the environmental conditions and objects he perceives as pleasant and unpleasant only according to the amount of gratification derived from them. The repetition of similar experiences reinforces his associations with a specific emotional state, and these associations are recorded as memories. Yet they are not integrated into a conceptual or causal framework.

Let us say, for instance, that a girl of three sees her father in bed with the housekeeper. As the act has no meaning for her, her ability to interpret the event could vary from surprise at the new situation to the belief that she is seeing her father "taking a nap." At best, the memory is retained because of its novelty, and only later, when she is older, does she understand the meaning of the act, after additional information is supplied by someone else, reconstructing it on the basis of the stored memory. Only then might she become upset and angry at her father.

As we have mentioned, emotional factors exercise some influence on the memory, in the sense that the intensity of the stored events and facts depends on what feelings they aroused at the time or continue to arouse; thus, pleasant experiences would seem to be retained and recalled more vividly than unpleasant ones. Yet other researchers asked children to recall their earliest childhood experiences and found that most memories were unpleasant, running contrary to the psychoanalytic concept that children tend to forget (repress) the disagreeable, which then remains stored in the unconscious. The retained memories as presented by the person have been considered by Freudians to be *screen memory* for other memory that runs deeper and is hidden in the unconscious, but we really do not have evidence of this, apart from the belief of the Freudians.

In this context, the most documented attacks on the repression theory came from behaviorists like E. L. Thorndike, a research psychologist, who worked out what he called the *law of effect* that dispensed with the need for acknowledging repression in discussing the remembering or forgetting of unpleasant experiences. The law of effect simply assumes that a child tends to perform acts he knows are pleasant and to avoid those he knows to be unpleasant. The unpleasant acts are avoided because the child remembers that they make him feel uncomfortable.

However, this is not the whole truth; for instance, in small children an emotional response, fear, for example, may be induced reflexively without any clear understanding of the nature of the danger on the part of the child. The fear response of the infant is a purely reflexive reaction not based on any understanding of the feared object, because the infant functions on a sensory instinctual level. Yet if this state of fear persists long enough, the child, and later on the adult, will remain afraid of the object or of other, closely related objects, without remembering how the fear started. He cannot remember because his initial perceptual representation was not structured in any image memory that would allow him to evoke the event. His memory retains the emotional response associated with the feared object to which he has now been conditioned. The persistence of such a response after the early stage of childhood is a sign that the individual's evaluation of reality is seriously disturbed. This means that when experiences of the past that were aroused reflexively have come to be reinforced cognitively, the child will continue in adulthood to be unable to evaluate objectively a new, related experience.

In fact, both pleasant and unpleasant memories are retained according to their intensities and are recalled either because of the pleasant association that they evoked or because the child wants to avoid repeating them. In any case, most memories are distorted by the child's slanted view of reality. In fact, Freud himself realized later in his career that the experiences furnished by his hysterical patients presenting recollections of having been sexually traumatized by adults were purely fabricated stories.

If most memories of early childhood cannot be truly recalled in their factual content, then what remains valid about information that the individual in therapy offers about that period? What appears to be presented in therapy is only information about general events and patterns of behavioral interactions with others, interspersed with specific events combining factual and reconstructed material as recollected over the years. In these terms there is no need for the introduction of any unconscious mechanism to explain them. However, these memories lead to the formation of attitudes, patterns of reaction, and approaches to reality that become guiding principles for the organization of the child's (and later the adult's) behavior. In other words, memories are learning experiences themselves, stored for future reference as tools to be utilized in approaching and dealing with new, closely related experiences.

The adult also will retain significant experiences he appraises as either neutral, dangerous, or gratifying, and appeal to these past experiences for an estimate of his resources for coping with similar events in the future. These experiences are obviously not stored in the unconscious, but emotion does play a role in the process of recollection. It sensitizes the individual to the importance of an experience in terms of his adaptive survival, warning him of the nature of the confronting situation by the initial emotional reaction it produces in his body. This "gut reaction" not only gives qualitative meaning to an act but indicates its value to the individual's adaptation to the environment. In this sense there is a continuous interaction between his mental activity and the central and autonomic nervous system responsible for his emotional responses. Although some human behavioral reactions are strictly a result of the activity of the autonomic nervous system and its brain center, most behavior is the result of learning experiences from the environment that lead secondarily to emotional arousal and subsequent responses. When the individual is faced with a new situation or when his action is blocked, the central and autonomic nervous system is automatically aroused, alerting him to the difficulty that he may face in reaching his goal. This warning is part of the primitive, instinctual anticipatory coping system present in animals as well as in human beings. But in human beings there is a secondary cognitive or logical coping process that will more carefully reevaluate the situation in most cases before action is taken, possibly canceling the initial intended response.

These reactions take place because man is fundamentally organized to maintain a comfortable equilibrium between internal needs and external environment. The instinctual alert is directed only toward the reinstatement of comfort or a state of satisfaction. However, the child has not fully developed this equilibrium. Without a developed logic that will make the necessary secondary associations, a young child is unable to discriminate fully between beneficial and nonbeneficial events except for those bringing on immediate emotional and instinctual reactions such as pain, discomfort, or pleasure. This is, in fact, a natural state, since in evolutionarily lower species emotions are responsible for adaptation to the environment, instead of any logical testing. Primitive emotional responses constitute the most basic level of the child's ability to adapt to basic needs before the introduction of the organization of symbolic thought and language. This is why the separation from the mother in infancy causes acute anxiety or depression that the child cannot rationally understand or express. The attachment to the mother is a result of imprinting based on the child's biological functions for protection and survival, and the disturbance of this instinctual process can have a serious negative effect on the development of personality. It is this reflexive reaction to the absence of the familiar and instinctually recognized comfort of the mother figure that triggers the highly negative self-protective responses in the child discussed earlier.

The quest for satisfaction versus dissatisfaction becomes more complicated for the growing child to handle when he begins to see things in terms of an outside reality to which he has to adapt. Reality, in this case long-term survival in the environment, surpasses the immediate need for satisfaction and replaces it with this long-term goal. In the process of growing up, the child has to learn to forgo immediate for long-term gratification. He has to become future-oriented, which is difficult until about the age of six or seven, because until then he is unable to see any cause-and-effect relationship between his present activities and their future consequences. But even later the child might have difficulty freeing himself from the need for immediate gratification and thereby he forgoes the pursuit of long-term goals.

THE DEVELOPMENT OF PERSONAL JUDGMENT

Another area of the socialization of the child is his moral development, a major source of maladaptive behavior. It is well known that children have difficulty relating to and applying the adult code of moral values. In general, the child develops his first sense of morality as a result of constraints imposed by adults or by older children at play. This morality of constraints is external to the child's mind and must be obeyed as such, but because it has no justification in his mind, no moral statement can be interpreted or evaluated in terms of its intentions or motives. For this reason, all children go through a stage of difficulty in establishing a firm relationship between their moral conscience and its practice.

In general, for adults, the moral act is conceived as derived from a moral code, a reflection of one's conscience into valuation of the event. For the child, practical action is decided by his needs, viewed through the egocentric prism of self. He sees the moral act as an act of denial, as a limitation of his gratification, as preventing him from doing things he wants to do.

The difficulty in dealing with moral judgment can be observed in the child's attitude toward lying. The child's tendency to lie is a natural one built into his system of thinking, based more on beliefs than on facts. Later on, the ten-year-old child's judgment about lying is determined more by the material consequences produced by his act than by its intentional meaning. He is usually little interested in whether the act of lying may be an intentional act or an involuntary error (though he is able to distinguish between them). His interest is to avoid the punishment he might receive because of his act. This reaction is due to parental upbringing that has reinforced consequences. For example, a child who lies because he is afraid of being accused of doing something wrong that was purely accidental lies because he believes that if he does not he will be punished by the adult. The child, in fact, attempts to avoid punishment by *not* facing the imposed rules of constraint set up by his parents. The rules themselves he considers non-negotiable, categorical obligations.

The child's dilemma in lying, as Piaget rightly observed, is that his egocentrism directs him to protect himself from any punishment, ridicule, or wrongdoing, while the moral obligations forced on him by his parents, the supreme authority for the child, tell him to obey their rule of facing the truth. But he cannot see any point in it.

However, before the age of seven or eight, children have difficulty in clearly distinguishing what is factual from what are wishes and dreams, and for this reason they appear to be unable to tell the truth. Yet at this period they are not lying; they are confounding the external reality of facts with their own needs and feelings. The child functioning on this level naturally modifies the truth in accordance with his wishes, but the denial of the truth is not intentional. The truth is just disregarded in order to fit the scheme of things meaningful to his gratification. The child develops a sense of truthfulness only through social cooperation, as in play; the need for social acceptance by his peers; and the fear of punishment by adults. Later on, when the child develops a conscious realization of his acts, he understands that a lie is wrong in itself, independent of any potential punishment. He sees the value of truth in interpersonal relationships as a reinforcement of mutual trust; yet he will probably continue to lie selectively according to the danger to himself he sees in the situation.

But since the child's consciousness of lying first comes from the adult's moral constraints, any discrepancy between the parents' preaching and their observed actions could create serious confusion for the child. The same situation could result from a social milieu provided by other adults or friends in which the child feels that there is a flexible gap between moral thought and actions that can be manipulated by people according to their needs. In fact, this might lead the child to form a very dubious moral code derived from an isolated and egocentric position that becomes the point of departure for psychopathic behavior, manifested by cheating to win a game, stealing to get something he wants, or lying to manipulate others to his own advantage or to avoid responsibility. All of these types of antisocial behavior are aspects of a poorly socialized and developed moral consciousness resulting in a lack of feeling of cooperation with others and a lack of tolerance to frustration in facing adverse conditions.

THE ROLE OF SEXUALITY IN THE CHILD'S PERSONALITY DEVELOPMENT

One of the issues considered to be most important in the development of the personality of the child, that of sexuality, has a controversial significance for psychology. Given the general outline of the psychosocial development presented so far in this chapter, it would appear that sexuality does not constitute the main source of conflict in the child's personality formation. Obviously, sexuality (in terms of sexual gender-identity or the formation of sexual role), when disturbed in its normal course of expression by either adults' interference or genetic constitutional factors, affects the whole personality orientation of the individual. However, the claim made by the psychoanalytic school that sexuality decides the stages of development of personality is scientifically unfounded and misleading in understanding the true factors responsible for general maladaptive behavior in a child. To assume that the infant's perception of reality is colored by his alleged sexual preoccupations and aims is to identify infantile satisfactions with adult sexual ones.

To assume that infantile sexuality and its repression by society are the sources of all neurotic behavior is to restrict the complexity of human interaction to one important but not exclusive dimension. It is like hypothesizing that the initial gratification of the child's most basic instinctual needs—hunger, thirst, and so on—is purely erotically oriented. Then development of the personality, according to this concept, is a pure genital striving toward adult sexuality. The gamut of these conflicts is worth a Shakespearean drama, all taking place in the mind of the child of five years of age. Intrigue, jealousy, anxiety, guilt, sexual excitement in an atmosphere of high suspense are supposedly felt and thought by a child who happens to be in the precausal, prelogical, magical stage of thinking. A child who does not understand the meaning of adult genital sex, who has developed a longstanding attachment to his mother and affectionate interaction with his father, finds himself the protagonist of a conspiracy to murder one parent for incestuous purposes. Meanwhile, control of these feelings hypothetically causes castration anxiety in boys, and fear of loss of love in girls.

How was it possible to arrive at these conclusions, which appear so incongruous with our present knowledge about the intellectual and emotional development of the child? It was precisely this lack of knowledge about the maturational processes of a child's thinking that led to these errors. The best example in support of this situation is Freud's analysis of "A Phobia in a Five-Year-Old Boy," which for Freud represented a clear validation of his theory of the Oedipus complex. This case, in summary, is the story of Hans, a five-year-old boy who, after witnessing a horse falling on the street, became frightened of horses to the point of being afraid to go out on the street by himself. From Freud's point of view, the phobic reaction of the child was the result of his sexual need for his mother hindered in its expression by the father. The rivalry toward the father caused the boy to develop a death wish toward the father, a thought that at the same time frightened the boy. According to Freud, the conflict between the fear of wishing the father to die and his love for his father led the boy to the displacement of his emotions to horses, which resulted in a phobia. Freud's explanations of the child's conflicting psychological and sexual development were based on unfounded theoretical assumptions, notably his mistaken notion that the child's thinking differs from the adult's only in its quantitative level of knowledge. He believed that in reaching any conclusion about a human interaction a child would not follow a different pattern of thinking from an adult.

The neurotic conflict of the child was interpreted in terms of adult sexuality. In describing the boy's masculinity, Freud ascribed to it adult behavior, such as the ability to flirt, to pursue a girl in a manipulative and seductive manner; furthermore, he concluded that the same masculine drive caused the boy to desire to go to bed with his mother and to get rid of his father. Yet Hans was unable to find, by himself, any causal relationship between his fear of horses biting him and his desire to get rid of his father. This assumption was suggested to him by his father. Furthermore, Freud himself admitted that "Hans had to be told many things that he could not say himself"; that "he had to be presented with thoughts which he had so far shown no signs of possessing"; and that "his attention had to be turned in the direction from which his father was expecting something to come."

Freud and Hans's father had justified to the child the motives behind his fears, but Hans himself was unable to retrace the process and the meaning of his thoughts. This is further proven by the fact that he lacked any understanding of the sexual meaning attributed to his masturbatory activity. When his mother admonished him for fondling his penis he answered, "Why don't you put your finger there?"

Mother: "Because that would be piggish."

Hans: "Why is that piggish? Why?"

Mother: "Because it is not proper."

This discussion could not have taken place if Hans had had even a rudimentary concept of adult sexuality, as Freud had hypothesized he did.

These assumptions, and others even more questionable, became the basis of Freud's understanding of the child's normal and abnormal development. Though his concepts were often questioned, modifications resulting from the different interpretations introduced either by Freudian disciples or, later, by neo-Freudians reflected the same premise that the neurosis is rooted in the development of infant sexual conflict. Their explanations of the neurotic conflict remained based on the concept of repression. Two interrelated questions are posed by these assumptions: the universality of the Oedipus complex and the extent to which repression lies at the heart of the neurotic conflict. If the Oedipus complex is a product of family influence, then it is harder to account for it when the child is brought up in an institution. In fact, various experiments have proved that monkeys or children deprived of maternal care in the early years of life develop serious difficulties of personality different from those of their contemporaries brought up at home. However, psychoanalysts argue that children brought up in institutions allegedly develop the Oedipus complex when they find out about the existence of their family from other people, by imagining a nonexistent experience of sexual conflict with nonexistent parents. As this suggests, at best, the Oedipus complex is basically a superimposed cultural phenomenon, a myth that has nothing to do with the child's actual intellectual and emotional development.

The second question, that of the role of repression in mental functioning, raises the even greater issue of the very existence of the unconscious as already discussed. Perhaps, in his time, Freud could not do without the unconscious because no alternative model for human behavior was available, but now we have scientifically documented and workable models from two different sources, both behaviorism and Piaget's work. These concepts, supplementing each other up to a point, give a perspective on human behavior and the origin of maladaptation that was not available to Freud. Now we can look to childhood's perceptions and mode of thinking for sources of information of distortion of reality and need not rely solely on the catchall belief in the Oedipus complex. Following the breakthroughs of Piaget, developmental psychology has built a solid basis for the analysis of the development of mental processes, and it is now possible to examine closely the specific elements in adult thinking that maintain or contribute to the formation of abnormal behavior.

3

BELIEF

The Mythical Component
of Adult Thinking

But know that in the Soul
Are many lesser Faculties that serve
Reason as chief; among these Fancy next
Her office holds
—JOHN MILTON, *Paradise Lost*, Book V

LOGIC *VERSUS* BELIEF

It would be natural to assume that with the development of logical thinking in adolescense, the preoperational thinking of childhood would fade away, together with the world of fairy tales and make-believe. We tend to believe that the mature individual constructs his view of the world and of human interaction on those principles of causality and logical reasoning that are free from childhood beliefs and magical assumptions. Yet many adults do not achieve this. When confronted with a new situation, a mature adult should be able to use logical operations of thought to predict the outcome and to decide on an appropriate solution. Furthermore, such an individual should, after a careful evalution of the various facts involved in the situation, be able to project rationally a chain of possible subsequent events on which he will further base his decision. We would like to believe that we are totally logical yet, of course, no one is 100 percent consistent. But in some cases the adult's projections about the consequences of his acts are based not on logic at all but on an elaborate, inferential, subjective process, part of his representational thought. This type of thinking is derived from the mind's symbolic functions

43

and is composed in this case of a mixture of beliefs, imagination, and logic.

This ability of the mind to evoke, represent, modify, combine, or fragment reality according to the individual's wishes is one of the most significant functions of the human mind, a function not found in the primates. The organization of images into elaborate anticipatory systems of interrelationships of sequences of events is a unique quality of man. It is his claim to superiority over other animals, and it is also his source of mental conflict.

Man's successful adaptation to the environment depends on this ability to anticipate the course of immediate physical events and to see the sequence of their interaction. However, when he is unable to find a rational explanation for things based on his knowledge and rationality, he is driven to create an answer that can become part of his reality. Whenever he is faced with events or phenomena about which he lacks understanding or a causal explanation, he is inspired to use his imagination to integrate these events into his system of existing knowledge and beliefs. From the beginning of time, man has invented his own explanatory theories of things, which represent his operational reality. The concept of causality has thus always been maintained, but the basic premises are not necessarily subject to proof.

Auguste Comte associated the evolution of man with the evolution of human thought in terms of its development from the mythical to the scientific stage. The first stage he described as that of theological thinking. At this stage primitive man explained the existence of things surrounding him by analogy with the human being; in other words, he attributed to natural phenomena the feelings and the volitions that he himself had. The orientation of his thought was animistic and anthropomorphic. This was a world controlled by spirits; a world in which everything was personified and endowed with qualities similar to those of man; a world tailored to meet his needs, according to his own perception of reality, with no distinction between the justification of an act and the real cause of it. All natural or human phenomena that primitive man was not able to control directly were interpreted by him mythically, as a part of his existing reality. His explanations of things did not represent merely beliefs but the only reality that he knew. They gave him a convenient comprehension of the natural order, conceived as determined by the immutable laws of a hierarchy of Spirits or of a "Great Spirit." The myths and the magic were the result of a specific understanding of things and of the world.

For instance, to primitive man all objects had an emotional connotation: either good or bad, pleasant or unpleasant, friendly or inimical, protective or threatening. In fact, primitive man's reasoning seems to bear a close resemblance to the child's preoperational level of thinking. Yet they are not the same. We cannot say that the primitive adult behaved and reasoned like a child. Logical thought, the capacity empirically to link cause to effect, to conceptualize and to abstract, was present in an elementary form in primitive man, as demonstrated by the making of tools and utensils. From observing a log rolling to developing a wheel requires a process of projection and abstraction that indicates the potential of the primitive mind to transcend its animistic and simplistic boundaries. The philosopher-anthropologist Claude Lévi-Strauss believes that the magic of the primitive mind is a well-articulated system, a modality for acquiring knowledge, a method of collecting information, based on both perceptions of the concrete and imaginative explanations of things. But for primitive man, the world of belief, as expressed in myth and magic, became the guiding principle of his life. It described his relationship with nature, with his social group, and, most significantly, with himself.

The impact of mythical thinking of the life of primitive man cannot be better appreciated than by evaluating the amount of stress experienced by a man guilty of violating tribal taboos. Lévi-Strauss, quoting the American physiologist W. B. Cannon, gave a penetrating analysis of the psychophysiological mechanism of death resulting from the belief that one is hexed. The man who violated a taboo in Cannon's example felt doomed to die. The tribe believed the same and treated him as though he were already dead, excluding him from its daily activities. He became progressively more terror-stricken and succumbed to the unbearable stress. His death was probably due to an acute stress reaction that produced severe circulatory collapse, with fatal damage to the cardiovascular system. This physiological reaction would not have been possible unless the individual had believed in the power of magic, believed that he had been "marked," and unless his belief had been shared by the group. His exclusion from his tribal environment acted as an environmental reinforcement.

If belief can have such power over an individual, then perhaps we should analyze the nature of belief versus logic and reality. Belief belongs to the world of imagination disconnected from the empirical reality. While, in general, any particular sense impression is confirmed by experience, a belief is not. Belief has its roots in primitive man's explanations of things he could not explain empirically or control mechanically. For these things he invented explanations and then derived subjective, what we now call magical, ways to attempt to control them. This distinguishes belief from empirical knowledge. Whereas empirical knowledge is based on the observation and analysis of perceivable phenomena that can be classified, belief is based on assumptions about the unperceivable. By a process of analysis empirical thought breaks down the content of the event into its constituent elements in order to determine the cause-and-effect relationship between these elements. Empirical thinking leads to a basically objective view of the world; belief leads to a view of the world in which the distinction between the objective and the subjective is blurred and the nature of what is perceived is distorted by assumptions about what cannot be perceived. Thus cause is apt to be mistaken for effect, the wish confused with its fulfillment, the symbol with the thing. Empirical knowledge, the foundation of objective reality, passes the test of scientific validity; belief does not. The belief resides comfortably in a comparable form of mythical thinking we find routinely in the dream state.

THE REALITY OF BELIEF: DREAMS AND MYTH

Some students of mythical thinking find a striking parallel between the unstructured organization of the myth and the explanations of the dream experience. This observation, though not sufficient to explain the myth, does show more than a circumstantial link between myths and dreams as attempts by the mind to deal with unexplainable events. In fact, man has often treated dreams as part of reality and given them an extraordinary significance as potential experiences of the waking state. In an indirect way, modern man's mythical thinking and the interpretation of dreams represent two intertwined modalities for dealing with unexplainable realities, using the common underlying approach of belief. This is an important and significant similarity, even though the roles of myths and dreams have changed with the advent of modern scientific thought.

For primitive man, the organization of life and its activities was directed in great part by dream experiences; for modern man dreams represent only a particular state of consciousness. In the past dreams provided mythical interpretations of events and were often used to predict the future. Along with the astrologer, the dream interpreter played an important role in the life of noblemen and at the royal courts by claiming to predict the future. His predictions often influenced the course of historical events. Today the dream interpreter attempts to explain the hidden psychic conflicts in individuals. The most famous modern dream interpreters, Freud and Jung, attempted to give dreams a scientific status, as Paracelsus had with alchemy. Freud took seriously the popular belief that dreams have a hidden predictive significance and tried to develop a scientific method for their interpretation; it turned out to be as esoteric and mythical as dreams themselves.

Of course, Freud did not know about the REM* and non-REM stages of sleep, the amount of dreaming an individual does during one night, or the periods of recall and nonrecall during sleep. It is known now that dreams comprise about one-fifth of sleep time, averaging between one hour and half to two hours a night. Dreams occur cyclically about every ninety minutes, with durations of about ten minutes for the first dream to half an hour for the last. Everybody dreams, but not everybody is able to recall his dreams. In fact, nobody recalls an entire two hours of dreaming; only one or two dreams, at best, are remembered. They are not necessarily representative of the dreaming period and may be distorted when recalled. In fact, some experiments indicate that dreams reported when the sleeper is awakened are presented incompletely and are distorted, and later, in the therapeutic ses-

*Rapid-eye movement.

sion, they are not recalled. This would indicate that much dream material represents the waking fantasy of the patient. Apparently the combination of various lived events and experiences of the day reappear in a distorted version in dreams and are combined with the patient's waking fantasies. The therapist reinforces this mythical content with his own pseudoscientific explanations of its meaning. A final argument against the assumption of any deep psychological meaning related to the unconscious is the fact that dreaming periods exist in animals, and in people with cerebral trauma whose cerebral cortices do not function.

Had Freud known of these recent findings, he might not have considered dream interpretation "the most valuable of all the discoveries that it has been my good fortune to make." The eagerness with which his followers picked up the notion of dream interpretation proves the inability of the human mind to escape the need to create and believe in new myths. In his symbolic interpretation of dreams, Freud created a myth-making model that further supported the need of the patient for magical explanations.

It is not necessary, then, to go back to primitive man in order to reconstruct the formulation of mythical thought; we can trace its formulation to the reconstruction and interpretation of dreams. In dream recall, as in mythical thinking, no relationship is established between particular causes and effects, because things in dreams can happen independent of any sequence in time and space. The interpretation can be global, arbitrary, defying any logical deduction. The weak logical connections made between dreams and particular events in the dreamer's life are largely inferential and empirically unverifiable. Ultimately, the entire structure of the interpretation is based on belief.

Mythical thinking and dream interpretation have both been thought to hold the key to the individual's relationship to his world. Myths attempt to explain human existence and its interaction with the environment in terms of mysterious external forces that determine man's fate; dream interpretation attempts to explain human behavior as grounded in mysterious inner forces that reveal themselves in the symbolism of the dream. Both of these interpretative systems disregard any empirical evaluation of their contentions and both assume a hidden meaning behind phenomena. In both cases, the consciousness does not make a clear distinction between illusion and reality, between make-believe and truth. Thus, above and beyond concrete reality, another reality emerges—the reality of make-believe itself.

Where does this "reality beyond reality" come from, and where does it get the power it holds over man throughout his life? Why, for instance, are people still fascinated by dream interpretation, even in the light of recent scientific findings challenging its validity? Disregarding the modern neurophysiological explanations of dreams, which include no provision for their psychological interpretation, people continue to be fascinated with their esoteric meaning. Why? Or why, for that matter, do people continue to

patronize fortune-tellers and astrologers in this age of rationalism? The answer is simple: The dream interpreter (or the fortune-teller) offers a mystical
interpretation of reality that fits the need of humans to communicate with
forces or spirits who give the illusion of holding the key to the future, to the
dilemma of the unknown. Anything that gives the individual the feeling that
he knows something about the future, that makes him feel more confident in
facing the unknown, is valued.

At other times the adult has the need for magical escape from reality in
games or fantasy. This has a counterpart in the child's world of make-believe.
Symbolic play—that is, playing that involves make-believe—shares with daydreams the denial of reality and reinterpretation of reality on the level of
wishful thinking. In both, the distinction between the internal and external
worlds, and between object and symbol, is blurred. In symbolic play, a
mental representation of an object becomes fully integrated into the child's
view of reality (if on a provisional basis). Such play fits in perfectly with the
child's mode of thinking because he naturally sees empirical reality as undifferentiated from the world of fantasy and magic. And yet the child, while
seeming to believe in the symbols of the game, simultaneously knows that
there is another reality: adult reality. Thus the child who rocks a doll to sleep
and pretends that the doll is his playmate knows at the same time that the doll
is not alive. This double-leveled approach to reality reflects the fact that the
child lives simultaneously in the adult world, which bewilders him, and his
inner world, where he feels at home. Symbolic play is a part of the child's
world of beliefs; it is a part of his seeing and relating to his environment
according to his mental abilities. Yet this world of beliefs cannot be equated
with adult beliefs. The magic-oriented thinking of make-believe enables the
child to free himself from the uncontrollable variables of the adult world at
the same time that he is in fact imitating the actions of that world, safe within
his own fantasy. The child believes in his play world as an intimate reality
that he fashions to his own tastes and that he knows he controls.

The child's symbolic play as part of his marginal approach to reality and
the adult's dream interpretation or escape into fantasy or games represent
elements of a continuum in magical thinking and provide a link between
modern man's rational world view and the primitive world of magic and
rituals.

WISH FULFILLMENT AND FANTASY

The remnants of primitive mythical consciousness found in the modern adult
are maintained as part of his childhood developmental stage and are characterized by the failure to distinguish between a wish and its fulfillment. The
mythical consciousness does not see a causal sequence of events leading to
fulfillment but instead sees the wish as being implemented or frustrated by
the agency of benevolent or malevolent spirits. An important breakthrough

in man's view of the world was the change from attempting to control the world magically to trying to control it mechanically. Man learned how to differentiate the world of personal desire from that of impassive reality, yet he did not discard magic.

The fact is that causal, scientific thinking, while it enables modern man to understand and control much about his world and himself, can do little to assure him that his wishes will be fulfilled and cannot ultimately solve the fear of the unknown. Furthermore, logical theorizing has never been able to explain—and is not likely to resolve—the conflict between man's drives for instinctual gratification despite social norms and his need for social accept-ance; neither has it illuminated very well the many contradictory and unpre-dictable aspects of human behavior. Above all, man's rational, structured view of the world is of little help when he faces the uncertainty of the future and the inevitability of his own death. In fact, science makes matters worse in that it demonstrates his limitations and his transient place in nature. Science has taken away the mythical or religious concept of life and death but has failed to provide a comprehensive meaningful replacement for it. Thus man questions the meaning and value of his existence, and feels frustration and anxiety about his destiny. His thinking, though logical in organizing the details of his life, becomes magical in explaining or justifying life itself. What can be the meaning of any project in life, regardless of how sound and productive it may be, when it can be unpredictably and tragically terminated by death? Under these conditions, the individual's view of life tends toward rationalizations that assume the human need to give a magical-transcendental meaning to human existence.

This conflict between the supernatural meaning of life and the con-straints imposed by the objective reality of man's frail condition is irreconcil-able. The duality of a world unclearly divided into the mystical/mythical and the objective/logical becomes the source of man's basic conflict with himself. The individual's view of life and death tends toward rationalizations that seek to reconcile a rational point of view with his need for some kind of mystical meaning or supernatural endorsement of his existence. The schism between the yearnings of the mind and the needs and limitations of the body is bridged by fantasy and ritual.

The fantasy of adults is a sophisticated form of the symbolic play of childhood; it shares with symbolic play the attributes of magical thinking. In fantasy a person reconstructs reality in order to meet his unfulfilled needs; he performs this reconstruction in a realm beyond the scientifically controlled world of everyday life, in a realm where he has mastery over events and things. The link between the true and the fabricated reality is a loose one. Perception is replaced by mental representation and imagination.

The imagery of fantasy is organized into a kind of secondary world much like the child's world of make-believe. Although the individual knows that this world is unreal, the emotions experienced within it are completely real. This is because his feelings are indeed real and are part of a desire for a real absent object (for example, the absence of a lover or a desired event or situation). They are evoked by the image of that object, often with a nearly immediate intensity. Fantasy can reduce the tensions caused by frustrations in a person's everyday life. This is where the magical quality of fantasy lies: in its power to evoke real feelings and to provide a certain amount of real satisfaction, through the use of an unreal image or set of images representing a desired object.

Unfortunately, fantasy often results ultimately in even worse frustration in dealing with reality. The imagination acts to palliate the frustrated desire for a time, but the very vividness of the imagined experience reinforces the original desire, intensifying the need for its fulfillment in reality. Since he cannot achieve this real gratification, the individual is forced to resort again and again to fantasy, which further aggravates his inability to deal practically with his real prospects for gratification.

For some individuals, fantasy thus becomes a pattern of adaptation to the frustrations of life. They become unable to cope with frustrations in certain areas in which they encounter the most difficulties—or even in life as a whole. They not only fantasize about the fulfillment of their wishes but come to have a veiled belief that fantasies might become true.

Beneath most fantasy lies a desire magically to determine the real course of events according to a prescribed scenario. For the *believer* in fantasy, this magical impulse is so strong that he interpolates into his view of reality elements of make-believe, which become integral components of his logical system for appraising reality. Thus, his fantasy beliefs not only shape his attitude toward his life but affect his practical decisions, thereby changing the actual course of his life. Fantasy reinforces beliefs that otherwise might not find acceptable channels of expression and compensates for basic inadequacies of personality that conflict with an individual's aspirations, needs, and social demands.

Consider the example of a young man who fantasized frequently about achieving great things in life, believing that this was in fact his destiny. While fantasizing, he did poor work in college and flunked out after two years. Rationalizing that success in formal education was unimportant to him because his natural intelligence was certain to prevail in any event, he took an unrewarding job. Soon his arrogance made him unpopular among his co-workers. He became withdrawn and retreated further into fantasized successes. This world of fantasy, so at odds with reality, made him feel ever more estranged from his world. Instead of realistically evaluating his job opportunities and the sources of conflict in his social interactions, he told himself he was misunderstood, mistreated, and out of place. He became even more depressed and extremely insecure in his relationships with others. Finally he decided to get psychological help. With therapy he was able to stop the tendency toward fantasy that was indirectly responsible for his negative interaction with others.

Of course, an individual's fantasy world need not create such discord in relation to his real life; there are many people whose acts of imagination work as a kind of support and inspiration toward the achievement of goals that they actively pursue. Regardless of whether they are viewed as a visionary or maladapted, whether they win or lose in their attempts to change the world, without the inspiration of fantasy based on moral and political beliefs, social reformers and revolutionary activists would have no "dreams" for which to struggle. But in the case of the young man who fantasized about great success without working for it in practical ways, his fantasies became not a sourse of inspiration but a means of escape. Seeing reality as threatening and hostile, he created a new reality to suit what he felt were his needs. This separate reality became the more meaningful reality to him and hindered his success in the world.

THE PURE MAGIC OF SUPERSTITION AND RITUAL

One of the mind's most fundamental approaches in dealing with the unknown and the uncontrollable is the belief in pure magic. The use of magical ritual is another example of a characteristically childlike mode of thought that often persists as an underlying component of the adult's view of the world. Thus the modern, rational man, like the child and like the primitive human, sometimes still resorts to mythical thinking when he cannot explain particularly distressful phenomena, or when he is faced with events beyond his control; either way, events with which he cannot cope.

People like to believe that every event is produced by a specific cause either self-evident or beyond their knowledge—yet possibly discoverable. This approach represents a great relief for the mind and provides a sense of confidence in mastering situations. The more logical, rational, and scientific man's thought has become, the more need there is to explain the unexplainable. But because science is unable to penetrate the ultimate mystery of life and nature, people continue to rely on their own beliefs.

Two sets of magical beliefs are used in the attempt to adapt to reality: those that protect an individual against unknown dangers, and those that rescue him when he is overcome by danger.

Most magical beliefs are recognized as superstitions. Superstitions, as magical safeguards against the hazardous character of life, can become an integral part of a person's daily life. Examples abound in modern life: the use of ESP despite scientific studies disproving its validity; the use of astrological divination (in the United States alone, approximately 20 million people read the astrological columns daily, and 18.2 percent of the population between eighteen and sixty is influenced by astrology in making decisions about their lives according to a recent New York University study. Another study indicates that in England, one person in three has consulted a fortune-teller and one in ten believes in lucky days or numbers. The statistics are similar from studies done in Germany and Switzerland. This modern-day survival of primitive superstitions is commonly explained as being the result of the superstition's social transmission from generation to generation; but although this explains *how* superstitions survive culturally, it hardly explains *why* they are not more carefully scrutinized by modern adults versed in logical reasoning.

Psychologists have sought to explain the nature of superstitions in various ways. Freudian analysts, of course, used sexual-symbolic interpretation to reach their conclusions: they ascribed a symbolic meaning to a superstitious act or belief, thus linking it to some anxiety stemming from infantile sexual conflicts.

In this context let us examine one of the most common superstitious acts—knocking on wood to protect a favorable situation against unknown destructive forces. Psychoanalysts, following the suggestion of Robert Fliess, have attempted to explain it in pure symbolic sexual terms. Fliess, a close friend of Freud, identified wood with the mother, the finger with a penis, and "knocking three times" with the male genitalia. The knocking he interpreted as an act of intended destruction and impregnation, which symbolically controls anxiety against infantile sexual strivings. Others have explained this superstition as based on the need to express symbolic humility in order to hide the repressed hostility that the individual experienced toward his parents in childhood and that remained unresolved during the Oedipal phase. But the catch is that both explanations fail to clarify why the ritualistic act of knocking on wood succeeds in controlling fear or anxiety in adults. In fact, in both explanations the belief in knocking on wood is only replaced by another belief, the Oedipal belief.

Carl Jung assumed that superstition was part of the *collective unconscious*—a subliminal system of imagery that is an integrated part of a universal psychic heritage. He considered the symbolism of superstition to be a specific attribute of the human mind, which finds expression in primitive magical beliefs and in the shared religious and social beliefs of modern man. The main problem with these concepts is that they are impossible to prove or even to disprove scientifically, and as such do little to advance our methods for dealing with, or understanding, the irrational functioning of the mind. What can be surmised from the writings of Freud and Jung is the insight that superstitions are deeply rooted in the mind and can in fact be called to the surface by the process of association.

A seemingly more empirical understanding of superstition is suggested by behaviorists, who see it as a matter of accidentally conditioned behavior. According to B. F. Skinner, a superstition develops when a pair of stimuli occur together, so that an individual becomes conditioned to their association. In his imaginative experiments with pigeons Skinner describes the formation of "superstition in a pigeon"—in reality, a conditioning of pigeons to a peculiar behavior that was rewarded. But what Skinner calls superstition in a pigeon is not the same as what we call superstition in a human being, because for the human being the peculiar behavior arising from superstition is not necessarily rewarded. For instance, in the case of a gambler who uses a particular "lucky number" in roulette, the lucky number will retain significance for him even though he may be rewarded for its use only rarely or not at all. Still, he believes that the number will increase his chances of winning. Other people think of a specific day as a bad day or fear things such as spilling salt, to mention only a few superstitions.

What accounts for the modern survival of superstition, then, is both the cultural transmission of a given belief from generation to generation and the need of the individual for myth and magic to help him face the unknown. There is another type of superstitious belief, however, which derives not from the culture at large but from the private symbolism of an individual's childhood world of make-believe and prelogical thought. These individually developed childhood superstitions blend with the socially transmitted ones to form a network of magical beliefs that is woven into the seemingly logical fabric of an individual's everyday thinking processes. As he matures, a person must find some way to come to terms with the conflict between the magical thinking that gave him comfort during childhood, and the newly learned logical thinking that seems more realistic but perhaps less comforting. At this critical juncture the individual will adapt his style of thinking in ways that may have a far-reaching effect on his future dealings with reality.

THE TRANSITION TO CAUSAL LOGIC FROM CHILDHOOD THINKING

Consider the case of a seventeen-year-old boy, Jimmy, who was sent for psychiatric consultation after members of his family repeatedly observed him suddenly throwing one hand into the air, always making the same peculiar gesture. He refused to discuss the reasons for this behavior with his family or others. He was an A student in school, did very well socially, and had no evident emotional difficulties, but he admitted that he was troubled by his inability to get free of certain rituals that he had developed over the last six to seven years. He did not remember how they had started, but he realized that he believed, for instance, that in order to get a good mark in school he had to swallow three times before answering his teacher's questions. He felt that in general he was successful in his life and believed that he could bring himself good luck by his rituals. He never faced them logically and never discussed them with his friends or members of his family.

He continued practicing these rituals unnoticed until he went to college and had the opportunity to assist at a few criminal court trials. This world was totally foreign to him. The trials were of persons accused of various sexual or social crimes that surprised and appalled him. He felt like a good person when he compared himself to the criminals, yet he had such a limited understanding of the motivations for their crimes he was afraid he might somehow become one of them. If he swallowed three times, however, he felt that he could protect himself from the possibility of sharing their fate. Under the spell of the ritual he would be safe.

One day in court, assisting at one of the trials, he forgot to swallow three times before listening to the case. When he realized this, he feared that something might happen to him because he had not protected himself. In order to dispel this thought, he made a gesture with his hand as if to kill the thought. Indeed, the thought disappeared. This made him repeat the gesture whenever similar thoughts came to his mind. Sometimes he was successful, sometimes not; when he was not, he had to repeat the gesture three times in order to free himself from the thought. This last addition to his magical ritual complicated his existence because it betrayed to others his peculiar behavior; moreover, it secretly baffled him because he could not explain his conduct on any rational level. Yet still he felt compelled to perform the ritual.

Jimmy admitted to the therapist that this way of thinking was "crazy," but he was afraid to give up his rituals because he feared the power of criminal thoughts over his mind. Therapeutically, the only solution was to eliminate the whole illogical structure of his thought. He could do this only by first testing the results of his actions when he omitted his rituals related to good and bad "luck." When he realized that there was no relationship between the rituals and his "luck," he became convinced of the irrationality of his symbolic actions. Even then, however, he was not able to give up his ritual based on the fear of "criminal influence" until he was reassured by the therapist that nothing bad would happen to him as a result of abandoning the ritual. Ironically, his acceptance of this reassurance was based on his trust in the professional authority of the therapist, which in itself was a belief, if a more socially acceptable one.

The ritual performed to eliminate "bad thoughts" may be seen as an example of accidental conditioning due to the linking of two otherwise separate events (the gesture and the disappearance of an obsessive thought). Psychologically, the gesture disrupted Jimmy's thought process, cutting its repetitions. But this connection between two events would not have led to superstitious behavior unless Jimmy's thinking had already been oriented toward magical beliefs to explain intimidating events. Jimmy was vulnerable because he had not yet confidently made the necessary transition from mythical, prelogical thought to causal, logical thought.

Some people never succeed in making this transition, either because social reinforcement supports their mythical beliefs or because they are simply reluctant or unable to cope logically or realistically with particular areas of life for which they do not have explanations. Paradoxically, although scientific thought has sufficient flexibility to tolerate ignorance about the causality of an event, magical thought does not. The less scientifically oriented a person is, the more he will rely on a system of beliefs that offers security in dealing with the environment. Such a person, though adult, continues to disregard in certain stressful situations the logical laws of causality and to operate within a system of irrational beliefs. Sometimes this system of beliefs remains latent until it reappears in a time of emotional stress; in other cases the superstitions remain within the otherwise logical organization of the individual's thought and exercise an ongoing influence, though they may still be most apparent in particularly stressful areas of emotional activity, such as love relationships or coming to terms with death.

Such a duality existed in the case of a thirty-five-year-old, Bill, an engineer who required psychiatric attention because he felt bewitched by a fortune-teller. He had gone to the fortune-teller in order to regain the love of a woman. The fortune-teller told him about his difficulties with a woman before he had mentioned them, and he interpreted this as a clear sign of her supernatural talent. He proceeded to discuss with her the story of his unhappy love affair, during the course of which he spoke of his ethical and religious values concerning life and marriage, and of his despair. The fortune-teller then proposed to him a pseudoreligious magical scheme for regaining the love of his former girl friend. The scheme was simple. According to the fortune-teller, Bill's former girl friend was under the influence of the Devil, and in order to free her he and the fortune-teller must pray together to the Virgin Mary. At the same time, the fortune-teller would perform a special ritual that would counteract the Devil's influence. For the ritual to succeed, Bill would have to meet his former girl friend once more and put into her food or drink some ashes specially prepared by the fortune-teller. Meanwhile, he was supposed to sleep in a double T-shirt into which he was to sew a fifty dollar bill every day until the day he reached a state of "mental communion" with his former girl friend; to facilitate his reaching this state of communion the fortune-teller would periodically exorcise the T-shirt. One day, when he brought the T-shirt, the fortune-teller told him that it had fallen hopelessly under the control of the Devil, and she burned it. With it went his six hundred dollars. Even then, though the man believed that the fortune-teller had stolen his money, he was still convinced that the shirt had been bewitched. Consequently he developed episodes of dizziness, anxiety, and nightmares. He believed, in fact, that he had been bewitched by the fortune-feller and the Devil together.

Significantly, this did not interfere with his mathematical thinking applied at work. The worlds of scientific method and of magical belief were kept apart, each one within its sphere of influence in his life. He was unable to apply logical thought to the problems of his emotional life because the loss of the woman he loved was too painful to face realistically, and because logical thinking offered no means of modifying the situation. Bill's acceptance of magic, witchcraft, and ritual was based on the hope it gave him that he might win her back, whereas his logical assessment of the situation offered him no hope at all. As he rationalized it, he tried the ritual because he had nothing to lose if it did not work. However, he did not realize the power the magic had over him, which was in fact merely his own powerful desire for a solution to his dilemma. His deeply suppressed belief in magical thinking was brought to the surface by his emotional crisis.

Other types of stressful conditions can cause adults to resort to magic and magical thinking, particularly those involving great danger to life or well-being. During World War II, for instance, many American soldiers wore protective charms, amulets, or "lucky" articles of clothing. Often they admitted that this behavior was irrational, yet they felt that it was justified in war, in which they might meet with death at any moment. Like the engineer who went to the fortune-teller, many of them felt that even if these charms did not help, at least they could do no harm.

Similarly, when people confront the matter of health and illness, they tend to think in terms of superstitious beliefs and pseudoscientific procedures. Among less educated people, for example, spiritual healers are still of great importance. These healers make no clear distinction between mind and body in their concept of illness and its treatment. They include in their treatment of the body an incantation for the alleviation of the suffering of the mind; yet, by addressing themselves to the mind of the patient, they attempt to reinforce the patient's belief in the healer's magical powers. People who go to healers believe in them because they believe in magic; they believe in the magic of healers because it offers them some means, however illusory, of controlling or affecting the otherwise uncontrollable contingencies of sickness and death.

Together, the various aspects of mythical and magical thinking—dream thought and dream interpretation, fantasy, and the formulation of belief and superstition—make up the inner world of an individual. The degree to which this sort of thinking affects an individual's otherwise rational dealings with reality depends on the balance between the mythical elements of this inner world and the empirical perceptions gleaned from the world at large. The interrelation between these internally and externally stimulated mental activities is so complex that for the most part a person does not realize their impact on each other. Fantasies and magical beliefs can distort the individual's response to external events and thereby affect his interpretation of reality, as well as the motivational direction of his life. It is noteworthy that most fantasies are attempts to find solutions to unfinished situations and unresolved conflicts. Even though an individual knows that the solution is unrealistic, in order to relieve his anxiety and distress he may push his fantasy to the end, going so far as to introduce into it lively auditory and visual imagery, as in the childhood world of make-believe. But if on the other hand an individual can learn to distinguish the mythical thinking of childhood from the empirically oriented thinking of maturity, he may become capable of exploring his inner world of fantasy and belief and of achieving some control over its impact on his everyday life.

4

EXTERNAL AND INTERNAL SOURCES OF ANXIETY

No Grand Inquisitor has in readiness such terrible tortures as has anxiety.

—SÖREN KIERKEGAARD, *The Concept of Dread*

HISTORICAL PERSPECTIVE

Philosophers and writers consider our time "the age of anxiety." Researchers and clinicians have struggled for many years to understand the psychopathological causes and effects of anxiety. Despite the many theoretical controversies surrounding this issue, there is general agreement on one point: that anxiety is the prevailing emotional condition of Western civilization. Clinical researchers in mental health have found the malady to be widespread indeed. M. R. Salkind, using an anxiety inventory, found that in England, in 1973, 31 percent of the population suffered from some degree of anxiety. According to a recent national study done at New York University, 52 percent of the men studied and 60 percent of the women experience mild to severe stress reactions.

One of the first questions raised by these data is whether this large population suffering from anxiety should be considered normal or neurotic. Certainly much anxiety must be considered normal, because everyone experiences it at one time or another. Every individual from time to time experiences threats to his system of values or to his social, economic, or physical well-being, and to such threats he reacts with anxiety. In general, this anxiety is proportional to the objective magnitude of the threat and will not hinder the individual's attempts to deal with the threat according to his rational assessment of the situation. Neurotic anxiety, however, makes the

57

individual unable to proceed rationally; instead, he becomes preoccupied
with his fears about the situation.

The oldest and the most common anxiety-inducing conditions arise
from man's realization of his own limitations: his vulnerability to sickness,
death, and the forces of nature. The line of distinction between normal and
neurotic reactions to these contingencies of life is very thin. For instance,
normal anxiety about illness or eventual death may well involve transient
feelings of discomfort and self-pity but neurotic anxiety results in a continuous preoccupation with death that affects all aspects of an individual's life.
Furthermore, for a well-adjusted person the recognition of the inevitability of
death is a recognition of the necessity to give meaning to life through one's
own actions, spurring the individual toward self-actualization. Basically, the
well-adjusted individual tries to overcome his limitations by acting to anticipate and control his future in order to gain some measure of protection
against the eventuality of sickness and death. In this light a large segment of
human activity can be seen as directly motivated by the desire to reduce
anxiety.

But not all human anxieties are based on rationally perceived threats.
Because life itself is unpredictable and often seems directed more by chance
than by the laws of causality, people often do not approach it in a rational
way. In the seventeenth century Blaise Pascal observed that since rationality
is unable to offer any certitude to human existence, correspondingly uncertain and irrational apprehensions creep into the human world view. Pascal's
intention was not to question the validity of reason but to emphasize its
limitations as a guide for controlling the senses and emotions. He believed
that emotions have the power to override reason and that reason is often used
in the service of the emotions, as a rationalization for them. But the evolution
of theories about human thought has been influenced more by Descartes than
by Pascal. Ever since the enthronement of reason by Descartes, man has
become progressively more convinced that reason can free him from his
irrational fears and emotions. This conviction has been supported by the
outlook of science, which attempts to explain everything mathematically and
causally. But the fact is that the wider the discrepancy became between
technological advancement, which created only an illusory sense of security,
and the emotional needs of man for stability, certainty, and control of his life,
the more anxiety man has experienced. If in past centuries the individual
could explain and accept the vicissitudes of life as a result of an overpowering
destiny, the rational man of today has more and more difficulty operating
with this old framework of belief and myth. Thus modern man faces the
uncertainties of life stripped of the mythological beliefs that could offer him
the comfort of divine protection. This produces the anxiety that modern
writers have called *existential anxiety*—the anxiety of existence in the world.

Kierkegaard saw this existential anxiety as the result of man's need for
self-realization—the need to express his freedom and to give significance to

his life. Kierkegaard recognized that when an individual is aware of being "on his own" in life and of having the freedom to make his own choices and to act accordingly, he often develops anxiety about this freedom and responsibility. Because the structure of modern society tends to engulf the individual in the masses and promote a self-effacing attitude, the modern individual's drive for self-realization is likely to alienate him from the society around him (this theme has been elaborated by later existentialists such as Karl Jaspers and Martin Heidegger), and this too is an anxiety-producing conflict. All of this anxiety is inevitable and normal in the context of modern life. As such, it can become an energizing force that spurs the individual on to creative and productive action, or a negative force that causes him to retreat into irrational behavior in order to avoid the fears and doubts aroused when he confronts his condition in a clear-eyed manner.

The attempt to understand anxiety has not only involved the theoretical formulations of philosophers but also, more recently, has been taken up in the clinical studies of psychologists. Whereas philosophers attempted to understand the meaning of anxiety within the framework of the human condition, psychologists have undertaken a more precise exploration of its content and mechanism. One of these first attempts was made by Freud. According to the theory of anxiety that he developed in his later years, the condition resulted from an ego perception of a danger. This danger was associated with repressed sexual or aggressive impulses of early childhood, which were misdirected toward the parents. The expression of these impulses was repressed due to the fear of punishment and loss of parental love. Anxiety is caused by the poor resolution of this sexual conflict. In later life, Freud believed, the repressed anxiety comes back into the consciousness, associating itself with some symbolic object representing the early trauma. According to this theory, anxiety becomes associated with the maladaptive defenses of the individual. A classic example is the patient who is anxious whenever the door to his room is open. He has a compulsive need to close the door. Though the patient does not know the origin of his anxiety, analysis allegedly reveals that the traumatic childhood experience leading to it was being caught masturbating by his mother while the door of his room was open. The punishment that followed made him afraid of repeating the activity with the door open. The event was repressed, yet the anxiety remained with him, associated symbolically with the open door. In other words, the ego perceives the unconscious danger that, in neurotic anxiety, is a result of symbolic association between objective, external factors and unconscious fears. Symbolic symptoms and reactions are created by the individual to avoid the confrontation with the repressed instinctual danger lurking behind them.

A closer look at these assumptions immediately raises a few questions. If indeed the ego realizes the danger, why does it need another stimulus (that is, the appearance of the symbolic object) to inform it of danger that is already apprehended as danger? Why should the ego need to rely on repressed instinctual impulses that in a symbolic form are already allegedly arousing anxiety as a defensive signal, when the ego itself is supposed to be the organizer of the defenses? The intrusion of anxiety into the ego does not inform the ego about the nature of a danger unless the individual has already been apprised by somebody else—that is, the analyst—that the alleged danger should be translated in terms of certain repressed instinctual urges. And if there is this link with the past, why should the painful association necessarily be related only to infantile sexual memories and not to other developmental events in the individual's life? The introduction by Freud of another independent mechanism, that of unconscious repressed memories, in order to explain the appearance of anxiety, confused the issue all the more.

Freud's assumption was that emotions are controlled by the unconscious, which contains undesirable repressed events (in spite of itself) and as such rules the organized behavior of the individual. At first this approach seems enticing because it offers an explanation of irrational behavior. But although the behavior of a person who is afraid of crossing the street (or, for that matter, the behavior of any phobic person) may appear irrational, its explanation does not necessarily require the assumption of an unconscious mental agency. If the person facing a situation evaluates it as dangerous to himself, then he is conscious of the past similar events with which he associates it. This means that the mental processes responsible for his behavior belong to the area of consciousness, even if the judgment made about the situation is based on the reappraisal of forgotten events that have left only vague memories of discomfort. The event that triggered the discomfort may be forgotten, but the pattern of behavioral response induced by it, with its associated emotions, remains. Any new situation perceived as similar will bring out the same emotional and behavioral pattern. It could be said, then, that no emotion is aroused without a cognitive activity. Thus, the statement that "anxiety is signaling a danger" refers not to a danger of intrapsychic conflict brought about by repressed libidinal needs but rather to an immediate danger from the external world, or at least something perceived as such by the individual.

The individual's inner conflict then could be described in terms of conflicting judgments, those that assess a situation according to its objective characteristics and those based on the individual's subjective fears and beliefs about it. Whether one's judgment involves events affecting one's life, such as marriage, career, or relocation, or trivial acts such as crossing a street or riding in a car or elevator, making a decision requires a projection of oneself into an uncertain future condition, and as such involves an element of risk. The effectiveness of the individual's response will depend on his ability to appraise his possibilities in the situation, to predict his chances of overcoming it. Two processes are involved: evaluating the threat and coping with it.

Any evaluation of a situation first requires the collection of information.

The appraisal of a situation is a matter-of-fact affair if all the facts are known; but a complex and unpredictable situation can create anxiety for anyone. Also, the more emotional significance that is attached to a situation, the more anxiety-creating it becomes. Certainly this explains the normal anxiety of a student taking a major examination, of a woman giving birth to her first baby, or of a person working toward some important goal on which his future career depends.

Once an individual has evaluated the requirements of the situation, he must ponder the question of his competence to cope with it. He must ask himself whether the task requires physical, intellectual, or emotional skills beyond his capacities. His concept of himself, his past experiences, and his preoccupations will cause him to give more weight to some information from the environment than to other information. For instance, if someone is the "worrying type," then in a new situation he will tend to pay attention to environmental cues that suggest an element of uncertainty and cause the situation to appear threatening. Let us take, for example, a success-oriented person concerned about his social image, about his ability to convey a sense of his own importance. He will be very attentive to the reactions of others to his way of dressing and of speaking. He will continually search for signs of recognition and interest in him. His inability to elicit the desired responses may induce discomfort or anxiety. He will question the effectiveness of his social behavior and will attribute total or partial failure to his alleged difficulty in coping with the situation or inability to produce his projected results. He is likely to conclude that there is a defect in his ability to apply his previous social learning to this new situation. Although it may appear that his anxiety has caused him to evaluate his performance incorrectly in the situation, the fact is that the anxiety not only impairs his evaluative judgment but also hinders his performance, due to his sense of insecurity.

The key to understanding a particular emotional reaction, though, is in the individual's thinking patterns as developed over years of reacting to the environment. The arousal of anxiety is based on the individual's assessment of an entire situation, which leads us back to his distorted cognitive interpretation of events. These thinking patterns are the bases of his interpretation of and response to any situation or event. In a given situation, these thinking patterns bring in a set of associations derived from the individual's memories of past experiences, which alert him to difficulties he might encounter in the present situation. These emotionally slanted memories are fed into the information process he is using in dealing with the present event and integrated into his coping system. The individual is fully aware of both competing sets of cognitive information—that of the past (which is anxiety-related) and that which is directly associated with the present event—and both participate in the judgment that will result in his final response.

There are various types of anxiety-loaded memories and associations that can blur his appraisal of a situation confronting him. Perhaps the most anxiety-inducing are those associations related to the evaluation of his own competence. His perception of his competence is based on his experiences as he has assimilated and internalized them. This varies within the same individual according to the area of social activity, for instance, someone's sense of competence might be very high professionally but very low socially.

The experiences formulating an individual's concept of his own competence represent the long course of social learning that started during his period of prelogical thinking, in childhood. The child's sense of competence develops as he learns to master situations commensurate with his possibilities. But without the right adult support and guidance, the child's self-evaluation could go wrong. He could come to overestimate his ability to master tasks, which would lead later on to frustration. Overprotection or too frequent "put-downs" by significant adults might have made him feel incompetent or stupid. Under these conditions, the child's ability to develop a sense of competence is seriously affected if not irreparably damaged. His already persistent insecurity in dealing with others increases; he feels surrounded by uncontrollable and even hostile forces. And so he retreats into a world of fantasy and magic. He comes to believe that through various special manipulations of his surroundings he will be protected from threatening situations.

This is the beginning of feelings of inadequacy that the individual attempts to control with superstition and beliefs. They may remain throughout his life. As an adult he crosses over the threshold of his house in the morning with his right foot first in order to have a good day, or he believes that a black cat crossing his way is a sign of bad luck. He still may attempt to deal with an anxiety-arousing situation by a particular magical procedure used in childhood against potential negative encounters.

PHOBIA

Most children begin to develop fears related to particular events or objects that lead to obsessive avoidance of those things at around five or six. This avoidance response is called *phobic reaction*.

In general, the fear that gives rise to such a response can be produced in various ways, whether by the actual experiencing of traumatic events or the accidental association of some event or object with a painful thought. In the first type of case, the child becomes afraid of an animal or an uncomfortable physical environment (darkness, heights, closed spaces) because of a frightening experience. Most of these types of phobic reactions disappear in later years.

In the second type of case, the child (or even an adult) becomes conditioned to being fearful of a situation that otherwise would be neutral. This happens when the child or adult pairs a neutral experience, such as crossing a street, with an unrelated but strong physical sensation such as dizziness, fainting, or blacking-out that occurred on one occasion at the same time as the neutral event. The unpleasant physical sensation could have been induced by an unpleasant thought or an unrelated physical distress. The thought of repeating that situation produces anxiety because the individual infers a causal relationship between the two separated events.

The first type of case—the memory of a bad experience—is a typical example of Pavlovian conditioning, which happens often in children. However, the second type of case, the association of unrelated events, involves a more complex conditioning that requires an illogical mental operation to be maintained in adulthood and indicates a deficiency in logical thinking. An example might illustrate this condition.

A young woman in her twenties, Susan, was traveling by subway to visit her boyfriend for the weekend. Their relationship had been somewhat strained because of their frequent arguing about his lack of commitment. While riding, she wondered whether his reception of her would be a pleasant or a cool one. During the subway ride she was remembering scenes from their last few meetings when suddenly she felt dizzy and nauseous, and had the sensation that she was going to faint. A sense of panic set in. She waited, frightened, for the next stop. She wanted to get out of the subway, but she was afraid that she might not be able to make it. Finally, another passenger observed her pallor and sweaty face and offered her help. He escorted her off the train. Outside, however, she became more frightened about being left helpless in a desolate station, and panicked. Finally the other passenger called her boyfriend to come and pick her up. After that experience she was afraid to travel by subway alone, fearing that she would have another anxiety attack.

This could be considered a simple case of a conditioned emotional response to a traumatic experience, in which neutral external stimuli have been paired with unpleasant internal stimuli: riding on the subway was paired with feelings of dizziness evoked by thoughts and fears of separation from her boyfriend. But this would be an oversimplification. Susan eventually overcame her anxiety about her boyfriend but retained her fear of subways. On closer examination it appears that the internal stimulus—dizziness—was in itself anxiety-producing because of Susan's fear of her own helplessness. It is important to determine the underlying cause of Susan's fear of helplessness and of being unprotected when facing adverse life situations.

In fact, this was Susan's established pattern of relating to unfavorable events, a pattern begun in childhood and developed over the years. According to Susan, she had always been afraid that things might not work out well for her. This insecurity appears to have been triggered by frequent separation from her father, who had often left her mother and her. At these times family conditions became difficult financially and emotionally, and Susan felt the burden of these difficulties. She grew up with a distrust of men and as an

adult had only superficial relationships. Her first serious romantic involvement at the time of the subway incident coincides with the development of
her phobia. Yet the anxiety-arousing memories of her insecure childhood and
fear of rejection by her father, and of things her mother had said about men
in general, were still fresh in her mind. The same anxiety that had in the past
been caused by her father's departure was now activated by the thought of
her boyfriend's departure.

The pattern of Susan's thinking is clear: constant insecurity in her relationships with men, from whom she did not know what to expect. Her
present problem appeared to stem from her inability to separate two distinct
sets of experiences; that of childhood from those of adulthood. The unstable
relationship with her father, the only learning experience about men available to her as a child, had been reinterpreted and reinforced by her mother
until it became a basic belief about all men. Thus, her associative thought
process, leading from father to men to lover, reinforced Susan's feelings of
helplessness in relating to men.

It is clear that this case of subway phobia was induced and supported by
an underlying type of thinking that interfered with an objective interpretation of reality. This might explain why, later on, when she could reflect upon
her experiences in the subway, Susan persisted in her fears, though by this
time she could see that nothing was likely to happen to her as a result of
riding on a subway, yet the fear was stronger than any logic. The fear that
something still might happen to her on the subway was initiated by the fear
that something might happen to her if her boyfriend left her, which itself was
built on her anxiety experienced in the past with her father and therefore
could not be dissipated at once by simple logical persuasion. This associative
trend of thought, blown out of proportion by her fantasy, became fixated on
the subway because it was supported by the magical conviction, maintained
since childhood, that she was the center of all dramatic happenings and the
target of invisible forces.

In this respect there is little difference between the child's organization
of thought and that of the neurotic adult in interpreting the phobic object.
Yet, though it is easy to explain phobias in the child, it is not so easy to
explain them in the adult. In the child, phobias are based on an unrealistic,
subjective appraisal of reality resulting from lack of knowledge and lack of
ability to interpret events correctly. The child's magical thinking supports
this element of irrationality. But what of the adult? If the distorted perception that causes irrational fear in the adult, which he cannot justify rationally,
is like the distorted perception of the child, then behind the immediate fear
there must be a more general fear related to a belief carried over from childhood that *something* unfortunate is destined to happen.

In other words, some adults retain in certain areas of their thinking a
childish level of beliefs that affects the interpretation of reality. Adults with

this belief remain phobic, or at least sensitized to a state of generalized fear. From one area of experience, the fear could extend to another object in the same category: for instance, the fear of moving objects, from cars to airplanes to elevators; in the case of animals, from dogs to cats, mice to snakes; in the case of spatial situations, from closed to open spaces. In some adults a fear persists from childhood to adulthood by simple reinforcement of the avoidance of the situation or object feared. Others may have a generalized fear reaction—panphobic reaction—morbid fears that, in situations perceived as terrifying or uncontrollable, "things" could or would happen. In both cases the fear is experienced as real, but the belief does not have a real basis.

In those cases, the appraisal of reality is altered by the belief, unsupported by any evidence in the real situation. This kind of belief belongs to an infantile mode of human thinking. It is based on the idea of avoiding situations to which the individual has attributed a special meaning, a magical power of producing disaster. The "proof" of this magical power is the anticipatory anxiety that precludes the phobic activity itself. However, the anxiety has nothing to do with the real activity. It is instead mentally induced as the *symbolic representation* of the real activity viewed as a possibly terrifying experience. In this way a vicious circle is created: the fear of the event or object produces anxiety, which in turn maintains the avoidance of the feared object. But the true threat is never tested, and its avoidance is supported by a judgmental confusion between the imagined disaster and the true situation.

The next question to ask is why some people become phobic and others do not, since surely all people go through the same stages of mental development. Another factor contributing to the development of phobia and as a matter of fact of other neurotic reactions is the factor of genetic predisposition.

Modern researchers in psychology have come to the conclusion that neurosis—which is mainly induced by a state of anxiety—develops in individuals who have a genetic predisposition to it. Eysenck asserts that there are dimensions of "personality emotionability" (or "neuroticism") as opposed to stability, and of "personality extroversion" as opposed to "introversion." He believes these factors to be genetically predisposing toward neurotic behavior. According to his findings, both neurotics and psychopaths have high degrees of emotionability (neuroticism), which makes them react abnormally to events. (In addition, neurotics are high in introversion.) This means in part that neurotics have a tendency toward strong reactions of the autonomic nervous system, the part of the nervous system that alerts the person by automatic reactions to stress, inducing such symptoms as shortness of breath, increased heart rate, and so forth. This in turn leads to fast arousal and slow response under conditions of emotion-producing stimulation. This peculiar aspect of their physiological makeup has definite consequences for certain individuals' appraisal of life situations. For instance, these people are much more susceptible to conditioning and they very readily acquire maladaptive patterns of response. Some researchers and clinicians attempted to reduce the phobia in these individuals to merely this aspect of avoidance-conditioning to a specific traumatic experience.

Although evidence of this predisposition may help explain the differences in individual reactions to fear-producing situations, it fails to explain the persistence of phobias throughout adulthood, contrary to any logical rethinking of the situations. Unfortunately neurosis is not a simple case of biological control. Admittedly, an individual can become conditioned to respond phobically to a given situation, but his conditioning still permits an element of discriminative judgment about the rationality of his behavior. That most individuals do overcome fear-producing situations, while only a minority become phobic, suggests that another factor besides conditioning and susceptibility to conditioning is responsible for the development of phobic behavior. This determining factor, as already mentioned, is a part of the individual's judgment, which distorts his view of reality according to preconceived patterns of thinking. This aspect of judgment, though basically irrational, is blended with rationalization to give it the illusion of rationality.

The phobic individual, then, is a person conditioned to a belief that is reinforced on a reflexive level by the responses of the autonomic nervous system. Based on this belief he interprets events in the context of his private perceptions of himself and of the world. In the case of the phobic individual, this involves the perception of himself as unable to control specific anxiety-creating situations. Other people, although not strictly phobic, can suffer from a similar type of fear. Their fear, triggered by a more symbolic conceptualization of events but based on the same fear of the uncontrollable, takes the socially accepted form of superstition.

It is important to note the relationship between phobia and superstition and to see how both of these relate to magical thinking. Phobia and superstition are different aspects of a unitary belief system. In their approach to events they are based on the need to avoid projected but untested threatening situations. Both attribute to the situation or object of fear special power to produce disaster, without any demonstrable evidence of that power. Anxiety is induced by the anticipation of these uncontrollable catastrophes. In superstition, anxiety is produced by encountering a particular situation that allegedly will bring bad luck; in phobia, anxiety is produced by a specific situation associated with "unexplainable" fear.

The type of judgment used by a phobic individual in a situation in which he is afraid clearly shows a departure from the logic used by others. To demonstrate this point, let us again consider Susan, the young woman who was afraid of riding on the subway, to see what kind of judgment she used. When millions of people ride the subways daily, why should she be afraid of getting into one? Her fear was induced by the experience of feeling sick and forlorn in the subway. That she continues to be afraid to travel by subway suggests that she believes that the subway somehow has the power to make her sick, and this is exactly her reasoning. She anticipates a remote possibility, which for her becomes so real as to interfere with any attempt she might make to ride a subway. Though she is able to admit that people are traveling by subway without getting sick, she is unable to subject herself to the same laws because she sees her situation as special. She agrees with the general premises of any syllogistic reasoning that might be used, but she is unable to arrive at the same conclusion based on these premises.

A person who is not phobic about subways will reason as follows:

1. People do not get sick just because they ride in subways.
2. I am like other people
3. Therefore, I can ride the subway safely.

The phobic individual formulates it somewhat differently:

1. People do not get sick just because they ride in subways.
2. I am like other people, but from my past experience I have a feeling that something might happen to me in the subway. (I will get sick.)
3. Therefore, I cannot ride the subway safely.

Notice that the minor proposition of the syllogism is different for the phobic individual. Although she thinks that she is like everybody else, she includes a set of new possibilities that for her are real and make her special. She projects onto the execution of the activity an element of belief; that is, she predicts that something will happen to her that will not be under her control. The inferential belief in the main proposition has changed the conclusion. She is anxious because of her inability to transcend the impending danger, which, strangely enough, she does not see as self-induced. The belief triggered by her experience in the subway which produced the anxiety attack was reflexively repeated through its projection onto future similar possibilities. But the projection in itself only produces further anxiety in that it reinforces the belief, making it seem real. In reality, the denial of the act (the source of anxiety) appears to be logical as long as some danger is real. However, she goes one step further in denying the execution of the action by this new concern based on her projection of sickness and her sense of helplessness. In her appraisal of this particular event Susan introduces two beliefs—first, that she will be faced with an uncomfortable, unpleasant situation, and second, that she will be helpless and unable to get out of it safely. If she is asked why she believes in this particular sequence of events, she is unable to give a logical answer. She admits that the mere fact that it has happened once is no reason to believe that it will happen again. Yet she is unable to visualize herself comfortable in a subway. As long as her judgment rests on irrational beliefs it will reinforce her negative feelings any time she invokes the situation.

The reinforcement of irrational fears lies in the phobic's tendency to visualize the situation or event that is the object of his phobia before it occurs. Mere visualization is enough to cause anxiety. Behaviorists have recognized the importance of this visualization before the undertaking of an action and the anxiety-producing effect that such visualization can have (such as, for the woman afraid of subways, the anticipation of actually riding one). For this reason, some behavioristic techniques for the modification of phobic behavior involve the purposeful and graded visualization of the feared act or event under conditions of minimal anxiety to the patient. This can help recondition the phobic person toward a new, anxiety-free concept of the act or event. The opposite technique, that of "implosion," uses the visualization of the worst that could possibly happen in a feared situation, in order to exhaust the anxiety and free the individual from it. Both methods can free a person from a phobia, but he may later experience some new phobia or state of anxiety in a different area of his life. This can happen as long as he maintains the belief that disastrous things that he cannot control might happen to him.

PHOBIA: SIMPLE MALADAPTED LEARNING OR A FORM OF MAGICAL THINKING?

A specific phobic reaction might be the result of a learned fear, but it also reflects a type of personality that is prone to anxiety when confronted with uncertain situations. Therefore, the behavioristic assumption that phobic symptoms are simply learned patterns of behavior is only part of the truth. That learning procedures can modify existing phobic symptoms does not prove that the primary source of phobia is defective learning. It is important to keep in mind that this type of learning depends in the first place on the quality of an individual's appraisal of an event, the nature of the reinforcement he receives, the level of his symbolic thinking, and his beliefs. The integration of all these factors within the context of his developing thought can lead to the development of an anxious personality, which will react fearfully to isolated events and circumstances (as in phobia). Even certain behaviorists have recognized this, in observing, for instance, that phobic reactions in adulthood occur particularly often in unhappily married women who feel trapped in marriages from which they are afraid to disengage because of their basic insecurity and fear of loneliness, fears that may have an earlier source.

An example is Mrs. K, a forty-two-year-old housewife, unhappily married, who came for treatment because of a phobia. Her husband, a forty-four-year-old stockbroker for a Wall Street firm, did not care about her well-being, spending most of the time outside the home, in a bar or chasing other women. Mrs. K was afraid of being left by him with two relatively young children and was unsure whether she could manage by herself. Her husband accused her of being too dependent on him, inadequate, and socially awkward. She admitted having such personality problems as low self-esteem, dependence, and lack of assertiveness. In her childhood she had been over-protected by her parents. Recently she became afraid to go to the supermarket by herself, fearing that she would get an anxiety attack. She had the first one in the supermarket and another in a department store. She did not remember how it started, only that she suddenly became dizzy, felt discomfort in the pit of her stomach, and wanted to run out of the store. Yet she could not, and this made her more fearful. She recalled, however, that on both occasions, that morning she had an argument with her husband, who threatened to leave her. Since the attacks her house had become the only safe place, and any departure was visualized as a loss of her security base, which automatically led to an anxiety attack when she actually went out. She attempted to free herself from the phobia by undergoing behavioral modification, with no success. Her insecurity and sense of helplessness remained untouched; her basic pattern of thinking was not corrected, and she remained phobic.

Mrs. K's sense of insecurity, unrelated to the phobic reaction, was based on a distorted appraisal of her possibilities for self-assertion, which was in itself anxiety-producing. Yet her insecurity rested on her belief that she would not be able to control events in some areas of her life. This conviction had evolved gradually during her life. She learned to avoid situations that she believed she could not master; this in turn reinforced her sense of inadequacy.

It is obvious why behavioristic therapy failed in this case. Mrs. K's phobia goes beyond any avoidance response; it is part of her anxiety response to all circumstances perceived as unfavorable. Her anxiety is a psychobiological warning sign to pay attention to what she *believes* will be detrimental to her physical or emotional safety, regardless of evidence to the contrary. Her judgment is based on all-controlling beliefs. Thus, the solution to her phobia rests in her ability to change her basic beliefs about herself.

OBSESSIVE-COMPULSION REACTION

Another major type of anxiety neurosis is the obsessive-compulsive reaction. The individual experiences this either as the persistent recurrence of an unpleasant thought or as an uncontrollable urge to perform a particular ritualized act. The obsessive thought might be absurd, distressing, or meaningless, yet he is unable to dispel it; it comes and goes by itself. In the case of the compulsive act, its ritualistic repetition defies any logic or satisfactory explanation in terms of present theoretical models.

Freudians believed that the obsessive idea was merely a substitute for an unconscious impulse or tendency, such as hostility or guilt, which is unacceptable to the individual on a conscious level. The intolerable unconscious idea creates anxiety that the individual attempts to control by substituting a more acceptable idea, the obsessive one. This theory does not explain why the obsessive thought persists after being recognized by the individual as related to hostility, guilt, or some other unconscious impulse.

The compulsive act, according to psychoanalytic thinking, is the result of a forbidden drive, usually sex-related, which was repressed into the unconscious and replaced by a symbolic act that is less anxiety-creating. Because the conscious activity is only a cover-up for the unconscious need, the person's explanations for his behavior are irrational. His rituals appear meaningless to him, yet if he attempts to discard them he experiences great anxiety. The compulsive act, according to the Freudians, serves to alleviate anxiety aroused by the unconscious sexual-anal impulse. But this formulation does not explain why anxiety persists even after the symbolic compulsive act is performed, neither does it tell us the origin of the particular ritualistic behavior.

The psychoanalytic school recognized that the compulsive act contains a kind of ritual magic but related it to attempts to cancel the effect of an unconscious idea. But how did the individual reach the decision to resort to magic? Why does he believe that the magic ritual can dispel the assumed danger? Although psychoanalysts noticed the close association between these magical rituals and the ceremonies of primitive people, they offered no explanation of the organization of the adult's thoughts into magical patterns.

On the other hand, for the behaviorists the understanding of compulsive behavior is reduced to the act itself, independent of the thinking that directed that behavior. For them, compulsive behavior is a conditioned response to an anxiety-arousing thought that otherwise is poorly controlled. They admit that the complex conditioning of the obsessional thought makes treatment very difficult, particularly in this case. The suggestion that this kind of thought could be part of an obsessional personality prone to excessive orderliness only complicates the issue for behaviorists. Instead, the compulsive act when considered as a kind of conditioned approach-avoidance response to conflict situations in childhood has a more defined therapy.

Both psychoanalysts and behaviorists overlook the fact that obsessive-compulsive behavior represents a childlike level of thinking and response to an anxiety-creating situation with which the individual does not otherwise know how to deal.

Take the example of a child who cannot go to bed unless he goes through a particular ritual, such as arranging the pillow in a particular way, tucking the blanket under his feet, holding his teddy bear, and so on. All of these acts are somehow connected with the ability to sleep, yet all of them presuppose a particular type of thinking in which separate acts are linked together and control a particular unrelated activity. In this case, the child endows this series of acts with the magical significance of bringing a good sleep. This approach belongs typically to the pseudological thinking of the child.

The adult compulsive act is a continuation of the same type of activity, unquestioned by adult logic. It is unquestioned because the individual is afraid that discontinuing the behavior will bring back painful anxiety for which he does not have an explanation. Here is a clinical example.

Dorothy, a twenty-seven-year-old college graduate with a good job, came to therapy because of obsessional thoughts and compulsive acts that seriously interfered with her social life and her career. She described herself as having been extremely fearful of things that might happen for as long as she could remember. At the age of five or six she felt that her parents did not like her, because they traveled for long periods and left her at home with a relative. At that time she developed the fear that her parents might not come back or that her father might die on one of his business trips. She began to believe that if she did things in a particular way that she knew would please her father, he would get home safely. When her father came home, she believed that his return was the result of her actions. Then she began to believe that if she thought of good deeds, or prayed in the morning, or dressed in a particular manner, she would have the power to influence events positively or negatively. Gradually, particular rituals took on the power to control events in her life and in the lives of those close to her. Each act had to be performed meticulously, in a particular manner in order to ensure the success of the day or of the activity to which that act was related in her mind. The fear of not correctly executing the act made her repeat it until she was sure that it was right. Any failure she attributed to her having done something wrong in a different area of her life, which only made her extend her practices to those other areas.

In adulthood, her main anxiety was focused on her doubts about the inexact execution of a few ritualistic acts that were strongly associated in her mind with her ability to overcome apprehension related to other events and situations in her life. For instance, the fear of not correctly turning off the gas stove, or some electrical switch, was related to a possible tragedy in her family life. Her fear of intruders made her doubt that she had correctly locked the door of her home, with the result that she would go through a routine to ensure the exact performance of the act. Failure to carry out the routine made her anxious and unable to concentrate on her daily business. Another compulsion that this young woman had developed was related to checking the contents of her purse before any important business appointment to reassure herself that everything was there: her keys, money, checkbook, and so forth. Some of these acts were performed in a repetitive pattern, others in a particular ritualistic sequence that was supposed to secure the desired result. If she did not strictly follow the ritual, she had to repeat it until she did it correctly.

Dorothy was also preoccupied with her alleged power to influence the lives of others by performing her rituals. For instance, if one of her girl friends was competing for a position or seeking a raise, she believed that her undertaking would be helped by Dorothy's performance of a ritual for bringing success. If she did not perform the ritual, she would feel guilty and anxious because she had failed to help her girl friend. She was tormented on one side by her fears that she might perform her job poorly if she did not execute her rituals, and on the other by her distress about not being able to free herself of these compulsions. Though she questioned to what extent her ability to carry out her duties was dependent on the performance of her rituals, any attempt to stop them would throw her into a state of anxiety followed by a prolonged depression.

Behavioral modification therapy helped reduce her compulsive behavior, but she became depressed to the point of functioning poorly socially. Why did she feel depressed, if her condition was only a learned ritual to reduce anxiety in response to a behavioral maladjustment? If this were the case, she should be free of anxiety and depression when deconditioned. Yet she was not. In her case, the magical thinking typified by her belief that the performance of some ritual would bring her father safely home gradually became all-powerful in the decision-making process with regard to significant aspects of her life. A pattern of approaching critical situations was created in which she believed that the outcome of the situation would be influenced by her set of rituals. Without them she felt helpless and thus depressed. Any unfavorable possibilities in life, such as someone's death, or failure in business, could be confronted without excessive anxiety only because of the element of magic introduced into her perceptions.

In psychological terms, she conceived the world egocentrically; her relationship to it was magical; and she could protect herself against undesirable, fear-producing happenings by using specific formulas, self-developed and described as rituals. But is not this approach characteristic of the prelogical phase of childhood? If this is true, what remains to be explained is why Dorothy persisted in her childish, compulsive behavior in adulthood, when this approach contradicted any logical concept of reality. In order to answer this question, we have to see how it was possible for the magical thinking of the child to fit into her adult logic.

What was Dorothy's thinking in performing her obsessive-compulsive rituals? Not all of her compulsions were of the same intensity, yet her thinking was the same in all of them. For instance, one of her compulsions was to wash her hands for five to ten minutes after touching objects she considered contaminated. In this instance, her thinking ran as follows:

1. Properly washed hands are clean (free of germs).
2. My hands are not properly washed (unless they are washed ten times).
3. Then my hands are clean (free of germs).

Her difficulty started with the second, minor, proposition, in which "properly washed" is used in a highly personal, subjective context differing from its use in the first, major, premise. In a sense there is ambiguity and subjectivity in the middle term, which is inferred from the assumption that properly washed hands are hands washed for a period of ten minutes or washed ten times. Here we can see that for Dorothy the minor premise has a particular inferential meaning, and through it she attributes an arbitrary significance to the completion of an act. For her, washing her hands or checking the lock are unfinished activities unless she exhausts all possibilities of doubt related to their termination. She is uncertain about the completion of those acts unless that completion becomes controllable and definable by a set number of repetitions. Although she is conscious at every moment of the execution of the act, she denies that it is complete unless the magical ritual takes place.

Why is she unable to stop the repetition? Simply because she is unable to see the end of the act as final without magical reassurance that it was done in a particular manner. For her, the termination of the act is based not on factual reality but on a system of hidden meanings carried over from childhood. The minor premise is changed from a descriptive, factual one to a conditional one, uncertainly defined, and the conclusion of her syllogism is then sidetracked, carrying in it an element of belief treated as a categorical fact. The completeness of the compulsive act is decided arbitrarily by the number of its repetitions, which ensure success in the execution of the act and which give the act exactness and perfection. This means that the ritual has a double connotation for the compulsive person: on the one hand, its completeness is defined as the exhaustion of all possible variations in its performance; on the other hand, its completeness is defined arbitrarily by a set number of repetitions. This seems to be the basic dynamic of compulsive thinking.

It is important to emphasize that the compulsive individual is not compulsive about only a particular activity; in fact, all of his actions are to some extent dictated by a rigid conceptualization of the world and of human interaction. This orientation is basically a product of his childhood beliefs or the very mode of *perceiving* the interrelationships between things as based on his notions of perfection, exactness, and order. The compulsive is in a continuous search for a static mental equilibrium, which he forces upon his immediate surroundings.

Phobic or obsessive-compulsive behavior can be classified as situational anxiety reactions. The phobic individual simply attempts to avoid the anxiety-provoking situation, while the compulsive individual ritualizes the activity in order to eliminate the anxiety produced by its improper termination, a point to which he attaches a magical significance.

DESERTION ANXIETY

There is another type of condition, however, wherein anxiety is not merely a situational reaction but is generated in the very core of the individual's personality by his beliefs about himself and his skewed view of human interaction. This is anxiety about desertion induced by fear of disapproval or of rejection by others. These feelings may begin in early childhood in the form of anxiety about separation from the mother, or later in life, resulting from a difficult family or social life, leading to the formulation of a poor concept of self. The result is always the same: anxiety about feeling unaccepted and eventually rejected by others.

The insecurity induced by separation from the mother in the first years of life has been the subject of extensive research. Among the possible long-range psychological scars produced by this emotional deprivation, anxiety traits are predominant. The child becomes fearful due to the sense of loss of closeness to the mother and of the protection that he instinctively needs. This need for protection is part of the child's biological programming and arouses anxiety, as previously discussed, in the case of an absence of the mother image. But many individuals who develop fear of desertion resulting from childhood emotional deprivation did not necessarily experience actual separation from the mother; more often, the situation involved lack of interest or rejection by the mother or mother figure, or threats of abandonment or even of death invoked by the mother to enforce rules of good behavior. Unable to cope with the mother's threats or attitudes, the child develops anxiety, depression, feelings of worthlessness and guilt, or in extreme cases antisocial behavior patterns that can become permanent. As an adult he may suffer anxiety or depression in any situation suggesting separation from or rejection by significant people in his life.

While there is a clear and direct cause-and-effect relationship in the case of the fear of desertion produced by a poor mother-child interaction, a similar type of anxiety may be induced in a less direct way by the combination of factors contributing to the child's development of a positive or negative self-image. This is the result of his interaction with other members of his family and with his peers, as interpreted by him according to his tendency toward low or high degrees of emotionability, introversion or extroversion. This interaction between these constitutional factors and environmental ones is so complex that there can be no truly objective clinical separation of them. In this light it seems best to concentrate on the contribution of the social factors (which are the observable ones) to the development of a fear-of-rejection syndrome.

In the life of the child the importance of others besides the mother becomes more evident if we consider the obstacles that the child has to overcome in order to meet his ever-changing needs. He has to master his sense of weakness, inferiority, and inadequacy by emulating the adults close to him, who, in turn, must appreciate, encourage, and help him. The child who does not have a favorable interaction with his family or the people with whom he has close contact is likely to suffer from an intensified feeling of inferiority and dependency. This dependency makes him afraid of any separation from or rejection by those he feels close to, including peers and friends. The degree of their acceptance of him becomes the measure of his self-esteem. As a young adult, he transfers his dependency from the parent or parent figure to the lover, attempting to maintain the same model of interaction with the same symbolic connotation of protection. As a result, the loved person is not only admired but overvalued and invested with unreal or exaggerated qualities. This overestimation of the love object is paralleled indirectly by an underestimation of the self as compared to the lover.

In fact, the overestimation of the lover has its source in the insecure person's feelings of inferiority. It compensates for the lack of desirable traits that the insecure person feels in himself. The loved one appears self-confident, secure, able to handle any difficult situation—in short, able to protect the insecure person from any threatening situation. This entire psychological process is based on beliefs, untested assumptions, and irrational projection of needs; instead of developing adequate psychological mechanisms to cope with the stresses of life, the insecure individual functions at a prelogical level of affective dependency, hoping that the lover will accept him and take care of all his needs. When a person, in the name of love, seeks from another person compensatory protection for his own feeling of inadequacy or inferiority, that is neurotic.

It is neurotic because the insecure person tries to cope with his anxiety by attaching himself to someone else who will magically have the power to take care of all his needs, doubts, and worries. The belief that the love of one person can support an individual's sense of self and security throughout life is based on the belief in the power of magical protection through love. It is unreal because love is a volatile, undefined feeling of elation about someone that in itself is based on a magical transformation of reality. In the majority of cases, when this magical phase of love fades away lovers see each other more realistically and want a more meaningful level of interaction, not mere dependency.

The neurotic's hopes in love are highly unrealistic, and they become the source of great conflict in his life. "Love," said Miguel de Unamuno, "is the child of illusion and the father of disillusion." The relationship with the lover is plagued by the insecure partner's fear that he may displease and be rejected by the stronger partner. By continuously attempting to please the stronger partner, the insecure partner reinforces his sense of inferiority, which in turn reinforces his insecurity. The relationship, instead of bringing the longed-for peace of mind, gradually deteriorates because of the increasing inability of the insecure partner to achieve that peace of mind. He is always frustrated by the feeling that he is not worthy of the love of the stronger one, and at the same time he becomes accusatory toward the stronger one for making him feel inferior, and this behavior in turn reinforces his fear that he will be rejected.

In this way the vicious circle is closed: The striving for security brings about more insecurity, because the individual has used the unrealistic magical approaches of childhood in his attempts to gain inner security. His judgment has been muddled by fear, and instead of confronting these fears he seeks to alleviate his anxiety by a kind of infantile clinging for protection, which in adulthood is unrealistic and self-destructive. The established pattern will continue reinforcing his sense of inferiority; it will extend to his entire view of life and paralyze his attempts at self-realization.

Consider the example of Jane, a woman in her late thirties, attractive, twice divorced, financially very comfortable (through inheritance), yet extremely insecure. She became increasingly frightened that she would grow old without having someone in her life to take care of her. Though it was easy for her to relate to men and to secure a lover, her relationships with her lovers were strained by her inability to get them to accept her on her terms. Her terms were not easy ones. On the one hand, she wanted a successful, strong man whom she could look up to who would be in control; on the other hand, she needed to manipulate the emotional interaction in order to feel totally accepted by and the equal of him. In her relationships with men she oscillated between submission and arrogance, between self-denial and spurts of independence. Even these areas of conflict would have been possible to resolve if she had not been extremely selfish and immature, in addition to being insecure.

Finally she succeeded in developing and maintaining a long but turbulent relationship with a man who met her terms and was ready to accept her with some modifications of her erratic behavior; but her low self-esteem made her progressively more doubtful about her ability to sustain his interest. They were together for several years, and she continually pressed him to reconfirm his love and his lifetime commitment to her, but she was unable to free herself from the fear of his final rejection. When she received an offer of marriage from another man with whom she felt more secure, she abruptly terminated the earlier relationship. The new man, in his sixties, divorced, and at the end of a moderately successful career, married her for her youth and money, hoping to be able to handle her moods and insecurities.

In reality, this marriage was the admission of her failure to mature emotionally, to free herself from her need for magical protection. She wanted to be loved and accepted unconditionally by a man in order to reinforce her self-esteem. Her married life became a magical reenactment of her childhood, when she had felt secure and loved, but with a substitute father—the husband offering her protection, security, and admiration according to the financial and social rewards he received from her. But her anxiety and insecurity did not subside. She worried not about whether her husband would leave her for another woman, but about whether he paid more attention to his grown-up children and grandchildren than to her. She was still insecure about her future financial condition and about her dependence on a man who was relating to her in a "fatherly manner," but with dubious motives. Her insecurity was magnified by the realization that her married life would become unstable should her husband become chronically ill. At other times she worried that he would find out about her past emotional problems, which would make him question her credibility and hence free him from any commitment toward her. She felt that her husband was more and more critical of her shortcomings and that his family treated her too casually. Furthermore, she felt that her ability to attract the interest of men was on the wane. This reduced her social confidence, already undermined by her general insecurity. Her attempt to return to the magical childhood state of protection through marriage to a fatherly figure turned out to be a disappointment.

It is true that more women than men suffer from the fear of desertion. This is due for the most part to a built-in biological need for protection of offspring, and to cultural conditioning that encourages dependency. But although men often appear to suffer less from feelings of rejection when rebuffed by their lovers, this is not always the case. Sometimes men develop a feeling of total dependence toward women, fostered by the relationship with the mother. They develop acute anxiety and depression when the magical protection is threatened by separation from the partner. The impact of a skewed mother-child relationship on the development of this type of irrational male fear of desertion is illustrated by this example.

Bob, an intelligent, financially successful man in his early thirties, was experiencing acute anxiety and depression because his wife of ten years wanted to divorce him. He had married quite young, and soon after the marriage he and his wife had realized that their emotional needs and personalities were incompatible. They remained together because of her financial needs and his need for emotional security. Over the years she became more independent and assertive, less willing to play her motherly role toward him, which led to stormy arguments. As a result she left him a few times, only to return at his insistence because he could not stand the loneliness. Although she had been unfaithful to him, he continued to rely on her emotionally and to seek her company because it made him feel secure. He would call her constantly from work or while traveling on business to get magical reassurance from her that he would be all right. When she was not home, he would become anxious, imagining that terrible things had happened to her—disasters that would result in the loss of her emotional support. He felt relieved only when he could talk to her, receiving the ritual acceptance. Yet he was not sexually attracted to her, nor did he like the way she managed the household or share her major interests.

Eventually he developed a phobia about airplanes. Though he appeared to be afraid to fly, in reality he was afraid of being away from home and from his wife. Gradually he developed other fears. He was afraid that he might choke while eating or have a heart attack while away from home; this gave him further anxiety attacks. Finally his wife, totally dissatisfied, decided to move out and divorce him. He responded ambivalently, with relief at being freed from a poor relationship but with concern about his need for emotional support. He negotiated a new situation: the right to call her whenever he needed her emotional support, in exchange for which he would continue to support her financially. He started to look desperately for a woman to replace her but was unsuccessful. This increased his insecurity and anxiety even more.

Finally, an attractive young woman was attracted to him, but she found it progressively more difficult to relate to his constant need for reassurance and protection, which was not evident to her from the beginning of the relationship. She felt the nature of their relationship had changed. Then Bob's father, with whom he had always had a somewhat distant relationship, suddenly died. After the funeral, Bob felt that his world had collapsed. His wife had left him, his father was gone, his mother was self-absorbed, his girl friend was not supportive enough. He felt deserted. He realized that his need for protection was irrational, but he was unable to function without it. His anxiety became unbearable. Tranquilizers did not help, though he took large quantities. His despair reached a point at which he began thinking seriously of suicide.

Bob's life history illuminates the source of his fear of rejection and provides an example of magical coping. His mother, a businesswoman, had difficulty showing affection, although she was interested in the problems of her children. His father was uninvolved in family matters, somewhat authoritarian, and intolerant. Bob was the younger of two children four years apart, and the favorite of his mother. The relationship between the parents was quiet, businesslike, and punctuated by arguments about money or their way of life. Bob's earliest significant recollection dated from about the age of five, when both his parents had gone on a trip and left him at home with a maid. He had become extremely upset because he missed his mother. He remembered little about the circumstances except the fear he experienced. His actual behavior, related to him later by his mother, he described as a terrible tantrum, with crying spells and fear of being alone in a room. The parents interrupted their trip and returned home. His condition improved immediately.

The next serious attack of anxiety occurred when he started kindergarten: he had a fear of leaving his house and playing with other children. His condition improved gradually, and he was able to attend school. But when he had to change junior high schools, he had another acute anxiety episode. For a short time he saw a psychiatrist who considered his emotional reaction the result of stressful puberty. Bob felt somewhat better after treatment, but the worst was yet to come.

After graduating from high school, he decided to go into the army in order to increase his self-esteem and get away from home. After five weeks of basic training he started to develop anxiety attacks and telegraphed his mother to come and take him home. Meanwhile, he was confined to the hospital, unable to undergo training. He was discharged from the army and taken home by his mother, and his emotional condition improved. A few years later he decided to get married, and he transferred his dependency from his mother to his wife.

In analyzing Bob's dependency on his wife, we must ask just what he expected from her. He wanted her to protect him, but against what? In the case of any real disaster, how could she protect him? Her lack of real love for him meant that she could not even offer him support in loneliness. His dependence was not based on anything objective. It was irrational. His logic stopped at any attempt to explain her alleged power to protect him. He admitted that it had always been the same way, that this was his belief, and it was hard to shake. His need for protection, stemming from the separation anxiety of his childhood, never changed. He projected in any significant relationship with a woman the same childhood fear of desertion. He did not feel inferior or inadequate, yet in close interaction he changed the role of the woman-lover to that of a mother-substitute. The need to reestablish the threatened sense of security became the overriding need of his life.

Another way in which the need for protection sometimes continues in adulthood is in the form of its original biological expression between infant and mother—that of bodily contact. In this case, the insecure person attempts to secure a sense of well-being in a love relationship by maintaining a close physical body contact with the partner. Absence of this contact produces anxiety and depression.

Pam, a young woman, a college graduate, divorced her husband after a short marriage because of her inability to get emotional gratification from the relationship. Their sexual life was satisfactory physically but not emotionally. She had an overpowering need for physical contact—to be held, embraced, kissed—that was not being fulfilled in the marriage. After her divorce, she gradually drifted into a homosexual relationship, partly because of her close association with a militant feminist group, partly because she felt better understood by women. She responded very well to homosexual love, particularly in a relationship in which she could have a close contact of hugging and embracing. The physical closeness was more important to her than sexual intercourse. She could spend hours in close embrace with her lover. The sense of acceptance and closeness gave her emotional comfort and had the magical power to create a sensation of total peacefulness. When, after a few years, her first relationship broke off because of her lover's infidelity,

Pam became acutely depressed and developed intense attacks of anxiety. She not only felt rejected but became overpowered by the fear that something disastrous might happen to her without her lover's protection. At the same time, she missed the other woman's soothing touch, which had given her the feeling that she was accepted and protected.

She remembered that she always had the need to be held close in her mother's arms whenever she felt upset or insecure. Her craving for bodily contact had its roots in a lack of warmth on the part of her parents. Her mother had believed in a "spartan upbringing" without the expression of emotion; she had been supportive of the child intellectually but not emotionally. Her father had been friendly but busy and inconsistently affectionate. She had grown up feeling unwanted and rejected.

She remembered that as a child she had often become apprehensive without any evident reason. In her relationships with her peers she had felt insecure and inadequate. Sometimes she had felt like crying because she felt unloved. At around the age of fourteen she had seen a therapist because she was unhappy. At nineteen she underwent regular therapy because of frequent anxiety attacks, feelings of loneliness, and lack of interest in pursuing a career. With the advent of adulthood, her insecurity became masked by an air of defiance, arrogance, and contempt for conformity. At twenty-one she had gotten married only to leave home; she did not love or even attempt to please her husband, whom she considered immature and inferior to her.

After divorce she drifted from job to job, but always with a sense of insecurity beneath the mask of self-assurance. Her attacks of anxiety never left her; they were sometimes so severe that she could not leave the house. She did not know what she was afraid of, but she felt lost, aimless, and fearful of being squashed by the outside world. After the termination of her love affair with the other woman these anxiety attacks became frequent, almost daily. She looked desperately for someone to replace her lover, only to be increasingly disappointed in her search for the lost intimacy.

Finally, after two years of emotional drifting, she believed that she had found what she was looking for in a woman who was interested in sharing the same type of intimacy. Unfortunately, this woman refused to commit herself to the relationship. She wanted to continue to experiment with other women and with men before getting into any deep emotional involvement. When she was not available for a date, Pam would have an acute anxiety attack lasting for hours. It passed only when she felt secure in the arms of her lover. The fear of losing her lover was unbearable, triggering uncontrollable anxiety. Pam felt lost and inadequate without the affection of the other woman. In her attempt to obtain the elusive feeling of missed maternal affection, this insecure woman endowed her lover with magical powers to give meaning and value to her life. She was not even aware of the extent of her need for close bodily contact until her "true love" relationship with the second woman. The absence of close body contact, of holding and being held by another woman, was extremely disturbing to her. Her sense of rejection in the absence of closeness was irrational; it was an enactment of a fantasy that could neither survive in daily living nor duplicate the mother-daughter interaction. Her judgment was suspended by this magical transformation of reality in the hope of recapturing her unfulfilled needs of early childhood. As long as childish beliefs continued to direct the organization of her life, she would succeed only in reinforcing her insecurities.

The power of childhood beliefs takes no more primitive and direct form than in the development of hysteria, an emotional condition in which anxiety plays an essential role. In a few words, hysteria represents the ultimate expression of control by an idea of the body's functioning. Hysteria will be discussed extensively in chapter 7; at this point it will be mentioned only as a different modality of magical coping with anxiety. In this case anxiety is "converted" into peculiar physical symptoms of the somatomuscular or somatosensory apparatus, which represent an attempt to solve the individual's difficulties in coping with life.

However, there are other persons who approach life experiences with anxiety. This type expresses his anxiety neither focused in a phobic reaction, nor controlled by obsessive-compulsive activity, nor related to a fear of abandonment, nor converted into functional signs, but attached to physical symptoms related to a disturbance in the organs innervated by the autonomic nervous system. Such a person is extremely sensitive to the implications of any irregularity in his physical health, because ultimately he is *afraid of dying*.

In most cases, this abnormal concentration on his state of health can be traced back to childhood, when, perhaps because he was extremely ill or was told that he would become ill unless he obeyed his mother, he developed a disproportionate fear of illness or death. Later, under stressful life conditions related to the possibility of becoming ill, he imagines that he is in fact ill, although his doctors are unable to diagnose the problem. This element of suggestibility, which has remained with him since childhood, affects his mode of response to stressful situations. Under stress, he interprets his autonomic bodily responses as signs of illness or impending death.

There are three factors present in the psychosomatic neurosis: a persistent stressful event with which the individual has difficulty coping produces an anxiety response associated with a third factor, the physical disturbance of an organ innervated by the autonomic "vegetative" nervous system. Yet the dynamic linking these three factors is based on beliefs and magical expectations.

Consider the case of Mr. N, a forty-three-year-old married businessman, who, if alone for long periods of time, began to feel anxious and experienced shortness of breath, heart palpitations, dizziness, and faintness. These symptoms convinced him, without medical evidence, that he suffered from a heart condition and would die if left unattended. He had repeated physical examinations, all of which indicated that his heart was healthy. But his belief that he might suffer a heart attack was unshakeable. In stressful situations Mr. N experienced palpitations, a rise in blood pressure, and dizziness. Sometimes he felt chest pain. After any sustained effort he felt breathless and faint and had to rest, during which time he monitored his pulse and breathing. His belief about his heart condition was strengthened when his seventy-two-year-old father, who had appeared to be in good health, died of a heart attack. Since he had been very close to his father and had the same type of personality, he felt that he might well meet the same fate.

A close analysis of his life brought out a few significant facts. He had been the youngest of three children and very much attached to his parents. The consensus of his family was that he had been a timid, tense, sensitive child, lonely, dreamy, and artistically oriented. He had had difficulty in making friends and had been afraid to get involved in fights with other boys and, later, to pursue girls. His first attack of anxiety appeared while he was in the army; he felt inferior, awkward, and afraid of not being able to sustain the effort required by military life. After the daily drilling he became extremely fatigued and suddenly developed shortness of breath, palpitations— and the feeling that he was about to die. Mr. N also admitted that he was afraid of dying in combat. He was discharged from the army. In civilian life he felt more comfortable because he could control the pressures of business, since he was in business for himself.

The second serious episode of anxiety came after the death of his father. The death of his mother one year later made his condition even worse. At that time he felt that he had lost the most important support in his life. He again became depressed and preoccupied with his health, and his anxiety was increased by his difficulty in functioning sexually.

It was obvious that Mr. N had a deep sense of inadequacy and a poor male image; it was also clear that he had poor methods of coping with stressful events like military training, relating to women, organizing his social life, or accepting the death of his parents. The association between the anxiety he experienced in facing a threatening event and its accompanying physical reaction was based on suggestibility and irrational reasoning.

For him, heart palpitations and shortness of breath were signs of forthcoming death. This was taken by Mr. N to be a universal proposition, applicable in all similar cases, despite medical evidence to the contrary. His reasoning was:

1. Shortness of breath and palpitations of the heart are possible signs of heart attack.
2. I suffer from shortness of breath and palpitations of the heart.
3. Therefore, I will probably have a heart attack at any time.

Obviously, Mr. N's judgment is distorted. The major premise is ambiguous because it is partially true. The minor premise has a double meaning: while he suffers from shortness of breath and palpitations of the heart, he has misidentified them as signs of a possible heart attack, whereas in reality they are the result of his anxiety, therefore the conclusion is certainly false, no more true for Mr. N than for anyone else.

Psychosomatic disorders demonstrate the extent to which the individual's appraisal of reality affects his emotional response to stressful events, which in turn can affect his physical well-being in areas of high somatic vulnerability. The somatic response can even result in outright physical lesions such as gastric or duodenal ulcers, or in symptoms of the cardiovascular system manifested by tachycardia or hypertension. The somatic reaction depends on the interaction of such variables as the individual's physical and psychological constitution, the length of his exposure to the stressful event, the significance he attaches to it, and the effectiveness of his coping mechanisms. The interaction of all these factors determines his capacity to adapt to the environment.

An individual's capacity to adapt is always on trial because of the constant conflict inherent in our society. As a result of this conflict he experiences anxiety. The less equipped he feels to overcome situations as he perceives them, the more anxiety he will experience, but in fact anxiety is present in almost all forms of maladaptive responses to the environment.

5

DEPRESSION

The Sickness of Despair

The thought of suicide is a powerful comfort: it helps one
through many a dreadful night.
—FRIEDRICH NIETZSCHE, *Beyond Good and Evil*, IV, 157

THE PAIN OF LOSS

Depression, like anxiety, is a common condition in our modern world. It is estimated that 10 to 15 percent of the U.S. population suffers from serious depression at one time or another. Like anxiety, it can be a normal and even healthy response to events. In a recent study at New York University it was found that approximately 37.7 percent of the adult population in the United States between the ages of eighteen and sixty complained of a subclinical depressive state. It is normal to become temporarily depressed, such as after the loss of a loved one, or after a failure in some social or professional undertaking. Most individuals, however, learn to cope with their misfortunes, adjusting to changed circumstances and overcoming depression. A person who cannot cope with his misfortunes, who remains depressed regardless of the available options for change and adaptation, is unreasonably or neurotically depressed. Such a person remains depressed because of the conviction that a given goal or object that he values above all else has been lost irretrievably *and is utterly irreplaceable*. The neurotically depressed person gradually becomes unable to function socially. His feelings of sadness are accompanied by pessimistic, self-denigrating thoughts, behavioral agitation or apathy, and physical reactions such as loss of appetite and libido, or aches and pains.

Many attempts have been made to explain the mechanism of neurotic depression. The most basic question has been whether the symptoms of depression are triggered primarily by psychological (affective-cognitive) factors or by biochemical factors. Of course, it can be argued that the psychological factors exist only as a result of the biochemical functioning of the nervous system. But while it is true that there is a given biochemical balance underlying every human mood, it is still important to consider in any condition whether affective-cognitive operations have induced a specific biochemical change or whether the change was what altered the affective-cognitive operations. In most conditions the relationship between the biochemical and psychological systems are intertwined, affecting one another reciprocally in so complex a way that, given our present knowledge, it is not always possible to separate cause from effect. In fact, there is evidence that in some cases psychological factors are most important, whereas in others biochemical factors predominate.

But even among adherents of the psychological approach to depression there is controversy. Some theorists, particularly the psychoanalysts, believe that depression is the result of an emotional dysfunction, a disturbance of mood resulting from an unconscious conflict. More recent theorists have favored the concept that depression is triggered by an impairment of cognition that secondarily produces the emotional response.

The psychoanalysts consider depression to be the result of internalized anger, which should normally have been directed toward the lost object. They believe that the depressed patient suffers from guilt based on real or imagined wrongs done to the lost object. Thus, their approach is to try to identify the roots of anger and wrongs and to evaluate their meanings in the light of the overall Freudian theoretical outlook. They analyze the patient's feelings toward his parents, and the repressed sexual experiences of early childhood, where the guilt is thought to have had its origin. The assumptions underlying this psychoanalytic approach have been impossible to test by controlled study. Their therapeutic value has been supported largely by anecdotal cases, which are scientifically unreliable.

Although there is general agreement among all schools of thought that the depressed person characteristically suffers from a loss of self-esteem and a sense of guilt and helplessness, the reasons for this vary according to the theoretical concept of each school. Theorists of the cognitive approach to depression recognize that all of these characteristics represent aspects of the patient's perception of himself and his relationship toward the environment. This perception is based on his past experiences and on his evaluation of his failure to prevent the loss of a valued object or to succeed in an important project or activity. The problem is that the judgment of the depressed person is too categorical and final, utterly out of proportion to the situation. His distorted perception of reality leads the depressed person to evaluate himself and to conclude that he is inadequate, helpless, and unable to overcome his loss.

Research involving this state of helplessness offers an insight into the mechanism of neurotic depression: A similar state has been observed in infants abruptly separated from their mothers. After experiencing acute anxiety, these infants fall into a state of withdrawal and depression. Also, in experiments on monkeys it has been found that infants separated from their mothers react with an initial period of intensive searching, followed by a deep apathy and withdrawal from their surroundings. In the last phase, the baby monkey exhibits immobility, inertia, and noncommunication. This condition is reversible in monkeys, especially if the infant is surrounded by other monkeys, but it is less so in the humans, particularly after a long separation from the mother.

Experiments with adult animal subjects indicate that if the animal is exposed to a series of unavoidable noxious stimuli, he loses the ability to respond normally, and becomes passive and indifferent. Furthermore, he extends these passive responses to other uncomfortable situations: he has learned to be helpless. The striking similarity between the animal's learned helplessness and human depression suggests a similar physiological mechanism. This is why behaviorists view depression as induced by the individual's inability to derive gratification from his relationship to his environment, because of a dysfunction of the reinforcement mechanism.

In behaviorist theory, the *reinforcement mechanism* is the psychological function whereby a person or an animal learns to consider a given behavior in a given type of situation either desirable or undesirable, depending on the desirable or undesirable results (positive or negative reinforcement) associated with that behavior. In the case of depression, behaviorists believe that this reinforcement mechanism is damaged by repeated subjection to situations in which the significant behavior is not positively reinforced. The reinforcement mechanism is damaged to the point that the individual begins to see little possibility of positive reinforcement for any behavior meaningful to his life; he becomes chronically depressed.

Of course, these conclusions are based on experiments with animals, in which the adaptive mechanisms are shown to be impaired when they are repeatedly unable to provide relief from noxious stimuli. But this futility of adaptive behavior is a result of outside control exercised over the animal; in other words, the animals are made literally helpless. But it is seldom that a human being is truly cut off from all possible ways to alleviate an unpleasant condition. (Perhaps prisoners are in a position analogous to that of helpless laboratory animals, but even under these conditions they do not always become depressed.)

Learned helplessness becomes part of the human response to the environment only when the individual believes that he indeed has no ability to protect himself against unfavorable events, or no means of striving for his self-defined goals in life. The distinction becomes clear: the learned helplessness of laboratory animals is objective, imposed from outside, while human helplessness is self-taught, self-imposed, according to the individual's own perception of his interaction with the environment.

This perception is greatly influenced by the individual's previous experiences and motivational orientation. The significance assigned to a particular situation depends largely on the set of assumptions and beliefs that he brings to that situation. When a person experiences a significant loss, he may perceive himself and his relationship with others differently if he feels that his equilibrium with the outside world has been upset. The world around him has to be redefined, which in turn requires that he redefine himself. Learned helplessness requires a personality prone to overreact to significant loss with a sense of failure that interferes with the realistic evaluation of subsequent events. The depressive person's personality and style of thinking bring him back to childhood and to the world of belief and magical expectations out of which these functions develop.

Consider the example of Ms. M, who as a child was told by her parents that she would become a movie star some day. She grew up building dreams about her wonderful career; she believed that she was beautiful and deserved the admiration of men. As a teen-ager she sensed that the great beauty she had expected for herself was not materializing, or at least that it was not fully recognized by others. Nevertheless, she went to college hopeful of being discovered and launched on a movie career. No such thing occurred, however, and she became progressively depressed and withdrawn, suffering feelings of rejection and inadequacy. She felt that her last hope lay in her ability to attract the interest of a successful man who could support her while she built a career. She met many men but could find none interested in marrying her. Each new adverse situation shook her confidence and further lowered her self-esteem.

After graduating from college, she moved to New York and looked for work as an actress. She found only minor roles. She worked as a secretary, and hated it, while studying acting assiduously. Her career did not develop, but she did achieve temporary happiness by marrying an actor who understood and accepted her. They were able to support one another's hopes and dreams, but not to find regular work, and the marriage ended after two years.

Ms. M's struggle to become a successful actress continued, but with no means of support she started to feel increasingly demoralized. She gave up acting and married a college professor from out of town, then divorced him, apparently because of his drinking, and returned to New York to try once again to succeed as an actress. By now she was thirty-four, but her childhood dreams still haunted her. She continued to fail as an actress and remained depressed. Eventually she joined an Oriental meditation group. There she gradually became detached from friends and reality, entering a world of dreams and shadows, brooding about reincarnation and the meaninglessness of life. But her meditation and her work with the group did not alleviate her chronic depression. At thirty-five she felt old, unattractive, and directionless. She felt beaten down by society and thought of herself as a loser.

Ms. M's pursuit of her acting career was an article of faith, rooted in the experiences of her childhood years and reinforced by a childlike perception of her adult expectations. Had she evaluated the causes of her failures more objectively—had she paid closer attention to her poor performances at auditions, or to the lukewarm responses of audiences—she might have realized the limitations of her talent. But her hopes of success were grounded in a fundamental *belief*, and her depression was the result of her repeated inability to fulfill those hopes. When all avenues of success as an actress led nowhere, her sense of the futility of life became part of her daily thinking. She began to feel helpless: that there was nothing she could do that could bring her satisfaction. Sadness and apathy became permanent features of her existence.

If Ms. M had been able to accept the limitations of her acting talent and to consider other possible directions for her life, she might have had some hope of escaping her chronic depression. Through the positive experience of some new activity—as, say, an acting teacher or casting director, or in some other pursuit related to her knowledge and experience—she might have found satisfaction, and with it, relief from her feelings of apathy and inadequacy. But this would have required a change in her way of thinking; as long as she persisted in her self-destructive belief that acting was the only possible source of fulfillment in her life, then she continued to be depressed.

Ms. M's depression is an example of a condition that developed over many years as a result of a general response to the experiences of life. Other forms of depression appear to develop suddenly, after some "precipitating event" such as the death or loss of a loved one, or a financial or social setback. This is perhaps the most common form of depression. The precipitating event is experienced by the individual as a traumatic, irreparable loss. The significance of the event is defined by the extent to which the person or object lost was endowed by the individual with unique powers to satisfy his own desires and needs. This reaction to the loss is normal at first; the grief, the mourning are natural responses to a real deprivation. But at a certain point the individual must begin to make a new evaluation of his possibilities in order to fill the void created by his loss with new choices and new opportunities.

The person who remains depressed after the initial period of mourning for a loss is unable to find a meaningful replacement for the lost object. For him, the loss is absolute. He sees himself as inadequately equipped to cope with the new situation, which takes on catastrophic proportions in his mind. He attributes his difficulty either to an overwhelming destiny of which he is the victim or to his own irreparable faults that brought the disaster upon him. In either case, he sees himself as helpless, without exit. These are his true feelings and thoughts, as triggered by the painful event, but how real and logical are they?

Consider the example of a man, Ed, who married a woman and lived happily with her for twelve years, until she fell in love with his best friend.

After a period of arguments and reconciliation, she decided to divorce him. His life remained almost unchanged: he lived in the same house, with the children, and continued the routine of his daily life. Nevertheless, after her departure he felt that his life was aimless and meaningless. Even after he became intensely involved with a young woman, he continued to seek the company of his former wife only to be rebuffed again and again. He became more and more depressed and, finding it difficult to work, he contemplated suicide.

Ed could not free himself from the need to maintain contact with his former wife. She became his obsession. He hoped to get her back, to make her understand his great love for her, to convince her of her mistake in leaving him. No other woman could replace her. He felt inadequate, unattractive, unsuccessful with women—in short, unable to reorganize his emotional life. He felt dead inside.

After a year of intensive psychoanalytic therapy he dropped out because in spite of the therapy he continued to feel depressed, if not suicidal. The explanations offered him in the course of therapy (about his masochism and his internalized hostility) neither helped him to understand himself nor alleviated his suffering. He felt that he was at the end of his rope. By most standards he had much to be happy about: he was professionally successful, was loved by his two children, and had a new woman in his life. However, the whole network of support from his family, his friends, and his lover was meaningless. A closer look into his life story may provide insight into why this was so.

In his early childhood he had been his mother's favorite son, and she had showered him with affection and attention. His father, on the other hand, had been distant, nonsupportive, and highly critical of his behavior. By his father's description he was socially awkward. In fact, he remembered his shyness, awkwardness, and feelings of inadequacy as the major aspects of his childhood and adolescence. He had felt mediocre, ugly, unable to live up to the expectations of his father. He had done well in school but had felt that this was because the program was too easy. In his late teens he had started to fantasize about girls, but he had been too shy to attempt to ask for a date. He had been afraid of ridicule.

In college Ed had dated occasionally. After he became a successful professional he started to date more frequently, but he always believed that women wanted him for his money. He was dating women toward whom he felt superior socially and financially. He thought of himself as a mediocre lover. Finally, at the age of forty, while traveling in Europe, he met a twenty-three-year-old woman who became interested in him. He married her six weeks after their first date.

This beautiful young woman's acceptance made him feel wonderful; it gave him confidence and a sense of recognition as a man. Because of her he also felt better accepted and appreciated socially. His image of himself changed for the better. When she left him, this image, built on his relationship with her, collapsed. The change he had felt in himself proved illusory; the old feelings of insecurity and inadequacy came back, aggravated now by the conviction that he was totally to blame for their breakup. Ed accused himself of being a poor companion and lover, unable to understand and satisfy his wife's needs; he replayed scenes in which, he believed, he might have behaved differently and saved the relationship. Despite their frequent arguments, he refused to consider the possibility that he and his wife had been basically incompatible. He in no way blamed his wife for betraying him with his friend. To him the pertinent facts were these: In his wife he had found a source of self-confidence that he had lacked before. He had lost her, and with her his self-confidence. Therefore, his only chance of satisfaction in life was to get her back. He felt totally responsible for losing her.

There is not much difference between depression caused by inability to write off a loss and that caused by failure to achieve a self-imposed goal. The common link is poor appraisal of situations and the weakness of an individual's coping skills that are based on a quasi-magical construct of reality. Although in the second case, for example, the depression seemed to be the result of a sudden, traumatic event, the real source of Ed's problem lay in his mode of thinking.

In both cases, along with the depression (or underlying it) there is another basic feature: belief in absolute values. In the first case, Ms. M was unable to see any way to give meaning to her life except by becoming a successful actress; in the second case, Ed believed that his wife was irreplaceable, his only possible source of love and emotional gratification. In both cases, the high value attributed to the particular object-goal is not only unrealistic but destructive. The acting career and the wife were seen as supreme sources of happiness. These individuals' inability to reach or maintain this source of gratification threw them into despondency and a sense of helplessness and worthlessness.

Such absolute values operate with the power of belief, beyond any considerations of logic. They have the power to permeate all aspects of an individual's life, controlling his view of the present and of the future, making him blind to any alternative possibilities for self-realization. Pursuit of these absolute values seems to the believer to be part of his destiny. Ed believed that the love of his wife had been a sort of divine gift; Ms. M felt that she *deserved* success. If things that are destined to happen do not happen, or if the cherished possession is taken away, then those who believe in such destiny think that the loss must be caused by supernatural forces or by their own inability to control events.

The depressed individual is apt to make self-accusatory statements about his own bad handling of situations (which makes him feel guilty); but often these statements are a means of seeking reassurance from others that he is not really responsible for what happened (so that he can stop feeling guilty). This reassurance brings him back to the underlying belief that his misfortune is part of an uncontrollable destiny. From time to time, particularly at the beginning of the depression, the individual feels angry at the lost love-object or at the fate that has placed him in what he feels to be a tragic situation. Yet the anger per se is not the cause of the depression, as psychoanalysts have suggested. Basically, the deeper the depression, the more the individual believes himself to be the victim of fate. But in fact he is the victim of his own set of beliefs that prevent him from developing coping skills to protect his interests. These beliefs reinforce his feelings of helplessness and hopelessness, which become beliefs in themselves.

Some theorists have attempted to describe a "depressed personality" by suggesting that some people during their development have acquired personality traits that make them react with depression to significant events in their lives. These traits are considered to include overseriousness, humorlessness, subservience, meticulousness, perfectionism, rigidity, and vulnerability to rejection. But though these traits may be found in those who suffer from depression, their presence certainly does not guarantee it. What is important is that behind a depressive reaction there is a certain mode of thinking, a certain style of appraising events.

The key is the interaction between an individual's mode of thinking and his pattern of reaction to a stressful event. When he is faced with a stressful event, the depressive person's thinking is apparently deficient in two ways: he incorrectly appraises the probable impact of the new situation, and he has difficulty in projecting alternatives for coping with the situation. But the individual would not fall into depression unless he had the additional problem of unrealistic expectations for himself and life. He becomes depressed not only because he is unable to accept the consequences of a stressful situation resulting from a loss but because he *believes* that his life is worthless without the lost object of love or value.

SUCCESS DEPRESSION

These conditions appear to be incongruous with the particular form of depression known as "success depression." This type of depression develops when an individual who has dedicated significant time and effort to achieving success in certain projects and ambitions becomes depressed after achieving this success. In fact the cause is not very different from the causes of the other types of depression, though in this case the individual has not in fact lost a valued object but has won it, absolutely. However, having won it, he finds that in fact it does not possess the value he had ascribed to it. Thus he has lost the valued object toward which he was striving, precisely by gaining it, since once he possesses it he can no longer deceive himself about its value.

Consider the case of Mel, a married businessman in his early fifties who had worked very hard to build up his family's business to the point where it was worth millions of dollars. In order to do this, he first had to acquire control of the business, which required that he remove his brother from a position of power. He did this, and afterward reorganized and expanded the business. In twelve years he had done everything he wanted to do. Then he lost interest in going to the office because, as he saw it, there was nothing for him to do there. He preferred to stay home and watch television. He lost interest in meeting friends and spent most of his time in bed. He complained of back pains, although repeated physical examinations failed to show anything wrong. Gradually he admitted that he had lost interest in things and that he felt depressed, but he did not know why. At the same time he started to drink heavily because, he claimed, he was unable to sleep otherwise. He also became worried about developing sexual dysfunction and lack of sexual interest.

The immediate explanation for this depression was that he had reached his goal and did not have anything else to do with himself. Yet on closer scrutiny it was apparent that he felt unhappy because, except for his desire to prove to his father (now deceased) that he could successfully run the family business, his interest in it had always been peripheral. He had always been primarily driven by the belief that his father had considered him less able than his brother to manage the business. After successfully saving the business from failure, Mel felt that he had treated his brother too harshly, and felt uncomfortable about this. Also, he feared that the business would not maintain its success, though he would have preferred to get out of it completely, but he felt that doing so would be unjust to his children, to whom he had promised positions.

But these would hardly be sufficient reasons for a prolonged depression if this man had not had a history of "irrational" beliefs about success. Success was connected so closely with his need for approval from his father that it lost its value after his father's death (though, interestingly enough, he had not been unduly upset by the death of his father). He attributed his current depression to his feeling of being bored with the organization of his life. The extent to which biochemical factors might have contributed to his depression is slight, particularly considering the fact that he was treated with antidepressants and did not respond to them.

In any event, the pattern of thinking leading to his depression was clear: an inability to separate the idea of adult success from the context of his childhood struggle for his father's approval. His expectation that financial success would make him happy had been illogical, because in obtaining success he had sacrificed his best years in long hours of hard work, instead of following his other interests. He felt stuck with his business and believed that it was too late for him to pursue his personal interests and learn to enjoy life, because he felt that he had lost the drive and the habit for it. His depression was caused by the loss of meaning and direction in his life; he now felt that the value of success had been imposed on him from outside. He had fought for the wrong values and cherished false ideals that did not give him any pleasure.

Generally, in "success depression" the individual's excessive concern with success causes him to neglect other aspects of his life. Sometimes the concern is itself only a compensatory expression related to some personal conflict from the developmental years and played out in adulthood, still with somewhat magical reasoning. Often this underlying conflict has to do with basic feelings of inadequacy.

Let us consider Sam, a bachelor in his mid-thirties who was extremely successful financially but became depressed about his relationships with women. He hoped to meet and marry an intelligent, extremely attractive woman. His social and financial success made him feel entitled to this. Unfortunately, he was admittedly socially detached and clumsy with words (if not boring). No woman was good enough for him unless she was beautiful and intelligent, but he had no success with such women. This caused him great anxiety and disappointment. Gradually he began to lose confidence in other matters. He questioned his ability to relate to all women, to the point of feeling rejected socially. At no time did he wonder about the reason for his lack of success with intelligent, attractive women. It never occurred to him that his manners and his reticent personality might have made him unattractive to such women.

Clearly, his need to conquer beautiful and intelligent women represented the need to affirm not merely his wealth and success but also his masculinity. In fact, since adolescence he had felt unsure about his masculinity and his ability to please a woman. He had felt unsuccessful in competing against other men in either sports or academics. Preoccupied with his maleness, he had begun to cultivate his clothes and his general demeanor in an attempt to present himself as a gallant, swaggering man, a man of elegance and refined taste: in short, a ladies' man. As he grew older he developed fast-moving relationships with women, but he was rarely able to establish meaningful emotional relationships, and he was never able to sustain them. He thought that this was due to the lack of excitement, of stimulating interaction in the relationships. He was always searching for the ideal woman, she who could give him a sense of security, of reassurance about his masculinity.

Why did Sam feel insecure about his manhood? The problem started with his father's death when he was eight years old. He had been forced to change neighborhoods, thus losing his playmates. In his new neighborhood he had been confronted with unfamiliar, rough boys who frightened him and made him feel weak. His mother's marriage to a man who was cold and unsupportive had increased his sense of insecurity. His stepfather had constantly criticized him for his awkwardness and timidity in social situations. At school he felt no more comfortable than at home, since he was neither a good student nor an outstanding athlete.

At various stages of his life Sam had attempted to cope with the conflict created by his interaction with his stepfather and with his peers according to the available coping possibilities of his age at the time. As a child he had become withdrawn and shy, and found shelter in daydreams. He dreamed about being an important figure respected by everyone, which compensated for his feelings of inadequacy. Later on, in adolescence, he had worn flamboyant clothes and gotten into indiscriminate relationships with girls. He had realized that girls were at least initially attracted to him, which gave him a sense of confidence and instant success. In adulthood the need to prove himself in business was a natural result of his competition with his stepfather; however, his eventual success in business did not alleviate his most serious problem: his sense of masculine insecurity. His success in business did not bring him the automatic success with outstanding women he had expected. As a seemingly self-confident young adult he had success with inexperienced young women, but when he grew older and was attracted to more mature sophisticated women, he had difficulty relating to them.

In fact, his coping mechanisms here were clearly inadequate. His appraisal of himself was wrong; his methods of alleviating his feelings of inadequacy were misguided. Sam felt that success in business would cure his problem. He believed that someday, as if by magic, he would meet a beautiful, intelligent woman who would fall in love with him, and this would confirm his masculinity. His distorted thinking about his maleness, as well as his obsessive preoccupation with unattainable women, inevitably led him to depression.

Sam's attempt, as an adult, to use the same kinds of compensatory psychological mechanisms as those he had used as a child, was inadequate to solve his problems. Magical thinking about changing reality to suit his needs, discounting the true realities of his life, could no longer give him solace. The depression caused by disappointment about his inability to overcome his poor sense of manhood reinforced his low self-esteem and his inability to enjoy success.

DEPRESSION AND ANXIETY CONTINUUM

It is common knowledge that an individual, while depressed, has frequent attacks of anxiety. As discussed in chapter 4, anxiety is produced when he is afraid that he will not be able to control all the contingencies of a situation he perceives as a threat. The depressed individual not only feels unable to find another meaningful object to replace the one he has lost but becomes anxious because he perceives all other new possibilities as overwhelming and frightening. For him significant new events present indeterminate, even negative, possibilities that appear uncontrollable; hence he retains his fear. This fear is aggravated by the already present feeling of distress caused by the loss of the valued object. In his state of mourning he is very vulnerable to any situation perceived as a potential rejection or failure. Remembering the experiences of the past and believing that new ones will end in the same way, he becomes paralyzed with inaction.

This state of mind gradually leads to chronic depression. If the depressed person is unable to overcome his obsessional fixation on the lost object and is unmotivated to look for alternative means of gratification, he will continue to feel depressed. Yet this is only one aspect of his problem.

Additional psychological factors contribute to making depression chronic if untreated. While depressed, the individual has a different qualitative and quantitative experience of events than normally. Because of his mental state and mood he processes, interprets, and stores experiences in an altered manner. His learning-memory processes process information somewhat inefficiently, with the result that he experiences events in a partially dissociated manner, which further increases his sense of inadequacy, failure, and hopelessness.

Further, we now know that psychological changes set in motion chemical changes in the brain that also activate depression. The circle is closed: the cognitive dysfunction brings affective changes, which together bring further cognitive and mood changes, at the same time chemical changes maintain and aggravate the depressive condition.

In this context it seems that the differences between the two basic types of depression—external-reactive and internal-endogenous—can be reduced to this basic distinction. In the reactive type the cognitive dysfunction leads to chemical changes in the brain; in the endogenous type the genetic chemical vulnerability of the brain makes an individual sensitive to stressful external events, causing a change in his cognition.

In fact, the interaction between chemical processes and the premorbid type of thinking can trigger either type of depression, though the genetic predisposition will separate them. For instance, a study showed that 35 percent of reactively depressed persons in a period of mourning had developed, in one month, typical signs of psychotic depression. Apparently they had been sensitized to emotional losses since childhood, thus reacting more strongly to losses in adulthood.

What all types of depressives have in common is their sensitivity to societal and cultural values, which, when perceived as stressful, can trigger, activate, or aggravate their symptoms. Cultural and social values, like personal values, can create a background for powerful depressive reactions when the individual attaches great importance to them or when society unduly emphasizes their importance for the individual's self-esteem or sense of well-being.

As we know, the overestimation of a given societal value, the belief that money, love, social status, or power will give complete meaning and stabilization to one's life, can lead to frustration and unrealistic expectations of oneself or of others. This type of thinking amounts to a naïve conceptualization of human nature and society. While social values, as part of the cultural determinants of personality, play a major role in shaping the individual's behavioral responses to his environment, total identification with any particular social value or social role can induce powerful emotional responses if the individual does not have other means of gratification.

For instance, during periods of history when the exaltation of love was seen as the highest happiness, an inability to consummate or to consecrate the relationship with the beloved one was a cause of deep depression and even of suicide. It is hard to conceive, in modern society, of another Romeo and Juliet, Paul and Virginie, or Tristan and Isolde. It is unthinkable that a book like Goethe's *Sorrows of Young Werther*, which led to a wave of suicides throughout Europe at the time of its publication, would do the same today. The new sexual code has affected the individual's response to lovemaking, dispelling some of the mystique of sexual intercourse and causing him to see that there are replacements for his lost lover. The loss of the beloved may create temporary disappointment, frustration, and sadness, but suicide results only in unusual instances. The relativity of the importance of love is further demonstrated by the high rate of American marriages ended by divorce (46 percent), particularly when most marriages are supposedly based on mutual love. In the past, the inability to possess a loved one forever and to consummate the love relationship was a blow to the individual's sense of self. Now "love relationships" are often conceived as temporary liaisons in which both parties should enjoy each other only as long as they mutually decide to do so. With the mystique of the sexes dispelled, people should ideally be able to judge, understand, and accept or reject each other, based on greater understanding of each other's qualities, without extreme societal pressure to strive for an unattainable ideal.

The association between depression and social values cannot be better demonstrated than by the observation of the varying amounts of depression evident in different cultures. For instance, some cultures impose rigid patterns of acceptable social behavior and high expectations of achievement on the individual from an early age. Any inability to reach the proposed goal brings a sense of failure, and with it a state of depression. For instance, the Hutterites, a religious group with communities in Montana, Dakota, and Canada, have a high incidence of manic-depressive illness and a low incidence of schizophrenia, contrary to statistics in the general U.S. population. (Although manic-depressive illness is a condition with a genetic predisposition and transmission, stressful cultural factors also contribute to its appearance.) The Hutterite religion encourages control of the expression of emotion and obedience to strict moral and social codes of behavior. Those individuals who are unable to conform are considered to have failed miserably. The code of behavior, imposed with the authority of divine sanction and supported by parental rewards and punishments, is likely to create low self-esteem and despair in people who are unable to live up to it. Any rebellion against the code is likely to bring with it anxiety and depression.

In other societies, particularly African ones, which have freer attitudes toward the expression of emotion and in which the responsibility for human failures is ascribed to fate, there is less incidence of depression. In these societies people do not feel guilty or remorseful about their inability to meet the social expectations of others. Instead of becoming depressed and experiencing remorse, low self-esteem, and self-incriminatory feelings, they tend to develop persecutory feelings, somatic complaints, or delusions, symptoms hardly typical of depression as defined by Western culture. The difference lies in cultural backgrounds that emphasize different values carrying specific affective connotations and meanings. The same cultural influences are responsible for the differences in the frequency of suicide in various societies.

THE "LOGIC" OF SUICIDE

Suicide is one of the most puzzling negative human responses. An individual who has heretofore accepted life, sometimes enjoying it, sometimes disliking it, is struck by an adverse event that throws him into such despair that he rejects life in favor of death. Suicide seems to represent, to those people who resort to it, the ultimate solution to difficulties that they see as unbearable. Suicide is usually, but not always, the result of depression. A person who commits suicide generally feels that the loss of someone loved, or of some social or financial asset, has rendered his existence meaningless.

The suicidal act is interpreted by psychoanalysts as the final result of aggressiveness turned inward. It represents the final revenge on the love object, who becomes responsible, in the suicide's mind, for his death. (According to psychoanalysts, this is part of the dynamic of the narcissistic oral structure of personality, which incorporates the image of the lost love object, toward which the suicide has ambivalent feelings.) What is important about this theory is that it relates suicide to a sense of childish dependency on the love object; the suicide is unable to replace a source of gratification that he believes essential to his life and responsible for it.

The potential suicide sees himself as weak, dependent, and ineffectual when confronted with difficult situations. Unable to see any prospect for relief of his distress, he feels hopeless and helpless. Obsessed by his loss, he cannot envision any exit but death. Death is viewed as the only possible escape from tormenting, intractable mental pain.

This solution to his difficulties actually has its roots in the childhood fantasy of "disappearing" in order to escape unpleasant situations or to punish others for alleged or real hurts. The child, in his prelogical thinking, conceives of death as a temporary withdrawal from a painful situation, a reversible process (just "playing dead" and ignoring reality). As a fantasy, death relieves the child of accumulated frustrations toward others. This way of thinking about death can survive throughout childhood and even into adulthood. The magic of childhood, as expressed in the fantasy of death, can become so integral to the thought processes of the adult that it is resorted to as a means of relieving the hurt induced by adverse events. If a given hurt cannot be alleviated by suicidal fantasy, and if the individual has not developed other coping skills to deal with significant losses, then he may find actual suicide the only prospect for terminating the torture in his mind.

The potential suicide sees himself as disconnected from others, alienated from his surroundings, without any support for the continuation of his life. The adjusted individual may feel blocked or hindered in meeting his goals; he may have setbacks or be forced to postpone his deadline for achievement; but he still hopes to reach his objectives, and this makes him able to sustain his effort and gives meaning to his life. Life must have meaning to an individual, regardless of how unrealistic or purposeless it may appear to others; when this meaning is lost, the structure of life collapses, and with it the individual himself.

To arrive at the conclusion that all is lost the individual must either realize that his ability to continue his life is minimal, or believe that his loss leaves him little chance to find acceptable alternatives for gratification in life. His life comes to a standstill, while the idea of escape from the world becomes an all-consuming desire beyond control. What at first appears to be an irrational act fits perfectly into the potential suicide's view of the world and himself at the time. Within his system of values, his concept of life, the priorities with which he operates, his loss means the loss of his place in life. But the values for which he is ready to die are values instilled in his mind from childhood through the process of socialization. The familial and societal values assimilated during the early developmental years become the most entrenched; the social values acquired in later years only reinforce those norms of conduct. Since these basic norms are his major point of reference for the organization of life, any disequilibrium can produce turmoil in an otherwise unstable, weak, dependent personality who depends on them highly.

Statistical evidence shows that at certain critical age periods the inability of an individual to adapt to new social demands may lead to suicide. Between the ages of fifteen and nineteen, suicide is the third most common cause of death; among college students it is the second, with the rates for boys twice as high as for girls. The clash between their expectations of themselves and the societal realities that confront them become too hard for some young people to handle. Under this pressure they have to make compromises in either values or expectations of life. When unable to do so they collapse emotionally. With their confidence shattered, with their hopes disintegrated, life appears senseless and purposeless. The fantasy of evading reality by death becomes attractive.

The second highest suicide rate is found in the age group between forty and fifty-nine, the period of middle-age crisis. During this period people are reevaluating their lives in view of their fulfilled goals and unmet expectations. Sometimes, when their achievement appears to them mediocre as compared to their ambitions, they see themselves as failures. They question their ability to further their goals against the competition of others; they feel too old to start new careers and unwanted by those close to them or by society. Dissatisfied with their performance at work or at home, they feel ineffectual, inadequate, and useless. Unable to rid themselves of their negative feelings about themselves and life, expecting future setbacks, if not catastrophes, they see the only solution to their misery in death.

A skilled worker, laid off from his job and unable to find another one, attempts suicide because he feels "washed out" and does not want to be supported by his wife; a housewife in her late forties feels the gradual withdrawal of her husband's affection and finds her life without purpose after the departure of her grown-up children, and becomes depressed to the point of attempting suicide; a businessman suffers a serious reverse leading to bankruptcy and attempts suicide. The people who commit or attempt suicide all have in common the inability to see any exit from the frustrating, uncomfortable position in which they have placed themselves. The discrepancy between their beliefs about what life should offer them and the unpleasant realities they experience makes them unable to cope with their real possibilities. Their unreal assumptions about what life should be lead them to the conclusion that their lives are wasted and that it is too late to make any attempt to change them. They are ready to die for their belief in an ideal world.

An intriguing issue is the suicide of the rebel-martyr. From this point of view, there is some broad similarity between the suicidal person who wants to die because his ideal world has failed to materialize, and the rebel-martyr who is ready to die when his cause is defeated. Both feel rejected by the world as it is, both want to be accepted by society on their own terms, both believe that death is the only solution to what we otherwise perceive as their maladapted thinking and self-destructive behavior. The difference between them is only one, the rebel-martyr in his flight from life secretly believes in a compensatory, more endurable future triumph of his ideas while the commoner suicide dies with a sense of the total failure of the project of his life.

Certainly, one might argue from the existentialist position that sometimes suicide is the logical decision, the only valid solution to problems perceived as intolerable. The individual may be unwilling to accept the terms of his life because of physical or mental suffering, or for purely intellectual reasons. According to the existentialist concept, life is a project that can be terminated by the individual when he believes that future experiences or events will be either meaningless or undesirable. Such an individual does not feel depressed or hopeless; he is simply unwilling to experience whatever future life may offer him.

This philosophical position raises a few unanswerable questions. For instance, if the individual is ready to terminate the project of life by exercising his option to die, does he not make a decision based on his evaluation of himself versus society, and must he not make that decision according to the conditions of that relationship at that time? And is he not even influenced in his decision by his cognitive-affective state, which may change from day to day, from event to event? If this is so, then his decision is a personal, subjective one, based on his view of reality at a certain period of time and in the context of his rational *and irrational* beliefs about what life should be in order to satisfy his needs. Even if he is not depressed because of a particular loss, his view of the world is negative and is intellectually alienated.

Clearly, suicide is the ultimate mechanism for handling the reality of a life that has lost its focus because of irrational attitudes and expectations. Suicide is a final statement to the effect that all of the irrational magical beliefs held by the individual are real to him. These beliefs are the decisive factor in his decision to terminate his life.

6

PARANOID THINKING

Fighting a
Conspiratorial World

IAGO:
O monstrous world! Take note, take note, O world,
To be direct and honest is not safe.—
I thank you for this profit; and from hence
I'll love no friend, sith love breeds such offense.
                        —WILLIAM SHAKESPEARE, *Othello*, III, 3

OTHELLO:
Even so my bloody thoughts, with violent pace,
Shall ne'er look back, ne'er ebb to humble love,
Till that a capable and wide revenge
Swallow them up.
                        —WILLIAM SHAKESPEARE, *Othello*, III, 3

THE DEVELOPMENT OF PARANOID THINKING

Whereas the depressed individual sees the world as offering him no chance of gratification, the paranoid individual sees it as a hostile and antagonistic place where he can get neither the acceptance nor the recognition he deserves. The depressed individual feels impotent and helpless in confronting the world; the paranoid individual is belligerent, argumentative, and uncompromising. The depressed individual withdraws from his environment; the paranoid individual fights it in the name of his beliefs or rights.

Both of these conditions involve distorted, maladaptive thinking processes. The depressed individual attributes a catastrophic importance to some stressful event resulting from irreparable losses; the paranoid individual interprets a negative experience, such as being passed over for promotion in his career, as part of a conspiracy to attack and destroy him. Whereas a nonparanoid person would not suspect such a conspiracy against him unless he observed evidence to suggest one, the paranoid* seeks no further evidence beyond the negative experience itself; he can see no explanation for his own setbacks and failures that does not involve the malicious motives of others toward him.

Since Freud, the classical theory describing paranoid thinking has involved the paranoid's projection of his own personal shortcomings onto others. The projection, according to this theory, springs from the individual's anxiety about his own latent or expressed homosexuality. The individual's attitude toward others takes the form of denying his homosexual interest in them: "I do not love him, I hate him," followed by the projection, "He hates me," rather than the admission, "I hate him because he might reject me." According to this hypothesis, the paranoid defends himself against homosexual impulses by assuming that others will persecute him. This theory fails for at least two reasons: first, if the individual really is homosexual, then in many societies his fears of persecution are apt to be perfectly reasonable; second, if the individual is not homosexual, which is most often the case, then even if a psychoanalyst could convince him that he is, at least latently, the therapy still would not really solve his problems. The theory's significance lies in its recognition of the paranoid's tendency to project his own negative views onto others. However, the problem of paranoia is more complicated than this.

If the paranoid personality does not result from a partial suppression of latent homosexual impulses, what mechanism of thinking is responsible for its development? To reach his erroneous conclusions about reality, the paranoid individual must approach his experiences in life in a different judgmental manner from other individuals. Paranoia develops out of his experiences, his expectations about human nature and human relationships, and certain special convictions based on his rigid assumptions and how they relate to others. The basic assumption guiding the paranoid individual in his interactions with others is that he will be abused and mistreated by them. This in exchange determines him to act in a particular hostile manner. This aggression and hostility toward others is defined by others as paranoid thinking. The difference between the paranoid assumption and the cautious suspicion is one of degree of conviction and intensity. Imagine if someone feels that people should not be trusted, he then relates to them with extreme reserve, caution, and suspicion about their intentions toward him. Inevitably, bringing particular assumptions to a situation indirectly influences its outcome. The paranoid individual goes a step further and makes another assumption that the other people are out to hurt him.

Paranoid is used here to mean "paranoid personality."

Where do these assumptions come from? They are primarily learned in the child's developmental years, from his family, when they are used to serve the purpose of supporting his self-esteem from the probable consequences of an undesirable event. This type of evaluation inevitably colors his perception and may distort it slightly or grossly. Invariably these assumptions affect the judgment of the child, giving him the illusion of being right and doing no wrong; the responsibility for his failure is placed on others. These assumptions when internalized become integrated into his system of thinking and later on become the basis for his adult concept of reality. It will be shown later how this helps in the development of paranoid thinking.

Other times, the specific meanings given by a paranoid individual in his developmental years to various classes of events or persons is due to harsh treatment experienced from adults, which makes him believe that the world is a conspiratorial place.

Let us consider, for example, the development of a child's concept of authority. The concept evolves gradually from the child's relationship with his parents, teachers, or other significant people in his life. Authority is understood by the child as an act of submission and obedience by him and of power and control over him. It always contains an anxiety-creating component related to the fear of punishment or of the withdrawal of interest or love. But at the same time compliance with authority may also produce an element of frustration, resentment, or open anger.

The concept of authority is not abstract or neutral to the child; it has a specific emotional connotation based on his experiences. If he has been abused by an authority figure, he may either have rebelled or, on the contrary, he may have become passive and frightened. In adult life a rebellious person, will tend to interpret authority as deprivation of his liberty, and may react violently; a passive person will tend to accept the authority but attempt to manipulate it to his own advantage.

Should the rebellious attitude be considered paranoid thinking? Not necessarily, because another factor must be added to this equation in order to create the conditions for the paranoid organization of thought: the individual's unyielding belief that he is special or important, or has a personality trait that is resented by other people, who attempt to suppress or oppress him because of it. Even if there is no evidence to support his contention of his special virtues or evidence of a deliberate attempt by other people to deny him his rights, the paranoid will inflexibly persist in his belief.

The paranoid's belief in his superiority and talent starts in childhood. His parents or others important to him gradually instill in his mind this notion of superiority. Regardless of how unrealistic and unproven it may be: as long as the notion is supported by his family, the child remains convinced of it. Proof to the contrary will not affect him to the extent that he and his parents can justify his failures as the fault of others. Later, unable to accept his intellectual limitations, he continues to believe that "others" are trying to undermine his efforts to achieve his goals and are setting obstacles in his path to success. For him, the explanation is obvious: the others feel threatened by his great talent, his singular values. Often he feels that he is persecuted because he stands for a set of values that his persecutors dislike or cannot live up to. Other people are corrupt and incompetent, while he is fair-minded, highly skilled, and clearly superior to them.

While his logic, on superficial examination, appears to be persuasive and convincing, after careful scrutiny we can see its inconsistency and irrelevance. His argument follows along these syllogistic formulations:

1. Superior qualities create envy and resentment.
2. I possess superior qualities.
3. Therefore, I am envied by others.

At times the minor premise and the conclusion are reversed:

1. Superior qualities create envy and resentment.
2. People resent me or are against me.
3. Therefore, I am superior to them.

Regardless of the syllogistic variant that attempts to document the superiority of his actions over those of others, the result is always the same, he must defend himself against them by whatever means are available to him. This thinking is pseudological, based on inferences, partial evidence, and unsupported beliefs.

In general terms, one of the difficulties of the paranoid appears to stem from his self-image and the image he conveys to others. The discrepancy between his ideal image—the one learned in childhood—and the real image perceived by others is the source of this conflict with others. Unable to accept the incongruity with reality of his talents or behavior, he makes others responsible for his lack of achievement. He learns this from parents who blame any failure of the child to live up to their expectations on institutions and on other people. If such a view of the child's interaction with society is expressed frequently, it may be integrated into the child's evaluation of reality, already based on precausal, prelogical thinking patterns, and can become a guiding principle in his view of the world and in his attempts to cope with favorable and unfavorable events.

The following example may clarify this paranoid approach to one's environment. Jon, a young physician, originally from Eastern Europe, completed his medical studies in Western Europe and came to the United States at around the age of thirty. In order to complete his medical studies, he had experienced extreme hardship. He had had to work at menial jobs in which he was abused by his bosses and mistreated by his co-workers because he was an immigrant, as well as far more educated than they. He felt justifiably proud that he had been able to overcome all these obstacles and complete his medical studies. Armed with a diploma but not an M.D. degree, he came to the United States to begin an internship. To his dismay, he found himself in almost the same situation he had endured in Western Europe—that of feeling "an incompetent immigrant," mainly because of language difficulties. He thought that he was treated abusively by the hospital administration and by the attendants. In return, he expressed his disdain for them, their medical knowledge, and their manners. The result was a very hard internship that increased his feelings of being mistreated, particularly because he considered himself superior to the attendant physician at the hospital. He changed hospitals for his residency, but his feelings of persecution only grew stronger. He became more hostile and resentful about his lack of recognition by other physicians.

He decided to go back to Europe to take his medical degree and then to obtain an American medical license. However, on his return to Europe, he felt that the European medical system was less technologically advanced than the American. During his final examinations he shocked his professors by disputing their medical judgment on the basis of what he claimed to have learned in the United States. The confrontation resulted in his failing his finals and in his inability to get a degree. Though he had the right to repeat the examinations, he refused to do so on the ground that again submitting to the professional evaluation of those professors was pointless and humiliating, as his knowledge was superior to theirs.

After a period of soul-searching Jon decided to come back to the United States and pursue a research career, in order to prove his talent and superior knowledge. But again he felt frustrated because he could only get a job as a technician, without any opportunity for creativity or for a part in the process of deciding what research was to be undertaken. He thought that the research he was involved in was insignificant and would not give him a chance to grow as he wanted to.

At the same time, Jon developed some clinical theories of his own, which in his opinion were revolutionary and would change the field of cardiology. He started to treat his superior condescendingly and to spend most of his time on his own work, which became all-consuming. When his personal project was finished, he showed it to a few scientists in the field of cardiology, and to his dismay it was rejected as worthless. The scientists' response convinced him of two things: that they were envious of his great achievement and that he was superior to them. He had been rejected by them, he believed, because they were afraid of his talent.

From that time on he was convinced that his future research would be blocked by "them" because of his outstanding creativity. Without any hope of pursuing a medical career, he started to drift from hospital to hospital, working as a technician, convinced that "they" would interfere with his ability to obtain his license. His co-workers annoyed him; they treated him disrespectfully and made cruel jokes about him. Moreover, he came to feel rejected by his acquaintances and even his friends. In all their actions he read special meanings and references to his failures and difficulties. He came to believe that his friends were unable to appreciate his talent and knowledge. He began to think that other people were making disparaging remarks about him in his absence, laughing behind his back because he was a failure. Suspicious of others, and now distrustful of his friends, he became progressively more isolated and withdrawn. From time to time he had outbursts of anger and virulent arguments with authorities, which on one occasion landed him in court.

A closer study of Jon's life history provides some clues to the source of his emotional difficulties. The youngest of three children and the only boy in his family, he was pampered by his mother. His father, a high school teacher who had dreamed of greater achievements, expected his son to fulfill his own unrealized dreams. The family's financial means were meager, but the boy was a good student, so he was sent to military school on scholarship. After graduation, he decided to go to medical school.

At military school he was a good student. This caused him to feel superior to his fellow students and to treat them condescendingly. His parents fed this sense of superiority by continual praise and support. Though he had various conflicts and arguments with either his peers or his superiors, they were usually resolved amicably because of his scholastic record. There were occasional punishments, but he was able to cope with them because he felt compensated by the praise he received for his achievements.

In school he was known to be very sensitive to the actions or statements of others. He refused to have anything to do with anyone who, in his opinion, did not treat him with sufficient respect. If he felt that people were inferior to him, he related to them arrogantly; if such people had higher military rank than he, he accepted their authority resentfully. He was intolerant with people who did not meet his standards of behavior, looking down on them as ignoramuses.

Jon's sense of superiority was also supported at this point by the closed environment of the military school, where the majority of the students were not intellectually oriented. When he left the school, he discovered that things were somewhat different outside. In medical school he was not an outstanding student. He blamed this on the hardships of postwar life in his country, which prevented him from dedicating enough time to his studies. After his emigration to Western Europe, things became even more difficult because of the meagerness of his income and his difficulties with the language—but even then he went on constructing grandiose dreams about his future. He imagined himself as a rich, famous clinician and researcher who had discovered the causes of various incurable diseases; he fantasized that he would return to his native land in triumph and be celebrated for his great accomplishments. This daydreaming helped him survive the miserable existence he had to endure at the time, but it also established unrealistic expectations with little chance of realization.

When he moved to the United States, he believed that he was at last taking the first step toward the achievement of his great future. His expectations were high; adjusting to the new country was difficult; and the disappointments were endless. Unable to accept another round of setbacks and attacks on his pride, he came to see himself as functioning in an antagonistic environment. The trials of internship, a difficult experience for any physician, became evidence of a conspiracy to destroy his self-esteem and superior talents.

Now the picture of the development of his paranoid personality emerges more clearly. Overprotected as a child, overpraised by his parents, convinced by his father that he would someday become an important person, he grew up with high expectations that might never have been fulfilled even under normal conditions. However, when his life required drastic readjustments because of his émigré status in a foreign country, these defects of personality became a major handicap. His arrogance, his lack of flexibility, his intolerance of others all contributed to his inability to adapt. In his appraisal of reality he relied on an old evaluation of himself that was incongruous with the new situation. Instead of developing new coping mechanisms to counteract stressful situations, he counted on his past style of now worthless defenses. He was unable to readjust his view of interpersonal relationships to the new circumstances of his life. Had he been less attached to his sense of superiority, he would have been more flexible and realistic about his true position and expectations in relation to his environment.

Traits developed in childhood remained with him, interfering with his ability to respond properly to new events. For instance, he was unable to accept responsibility for mistakes. Instead of learning from his mishandling of interpersonal relationships and professional situations, he simply refused to recognize his errors. Rather than admit that he might have made mistakes, he told himself that he was being persecuted. Belief in persecution by others in order to protect one's self-esteem is a fundamental aspect of most paranoid thinking. The inability to be objective about one's own errors is typical of the child's egotistical approach to reality. Another childish character trait that Jon maintained in adulthood was his need for instant, unqualified recognition and appreciation: for instance, he expected praise for and acceptance of his cardiology theories even though they were not based on true research. In fact, they were the result of interpolations and deductions from other works that he put together while ignoring some basic principles of physiology. Nevertheless, he was convinced that his work was a major contribution to the field of cardiology. His denial, despite his professional background, of the need for experimental verification of his theories further reflected his unrealistic thinking. His need to succeed was so great, and his failures were so painful, that the distinction between fantasy and reality became blurred. He replaced the real world of research with his own magical theory-making.

Furthermore, once he came to the conclusion that others were against him, he began to defend his ideas and his identity by using the special talents he believed he possessed, talents for detecting the hidden meanings behind the apparently neutral gestures and expressions of those around him. He came to assume that the things he perceived in this way carried the weight of final truth. All these aspects of childlike thinking invaded the operations of his adult logic and worked to reinforce his distorted perception of reality.

By thinking in these terms he came to feel even more frustrated, and this increased his sense of isolation and his distrust of others. His life became progressively a struggle for professional and social survival against the "others" who were working against him. The style of his interactions with institutions and people was dictated by the need to preserve the constancy of his self-image, which would have been badly hurt by his professional failure had he not been able to blame this failure on the persecution of others.

LEARNED MISTRUST AS A SOURCE OF PARANOID THINKING

Another type of paranoid thinking is based on the belief that people are wicked and bad. In this case the child is brought up by his parents or significant others in an atmosphere of suspiciousness and mistrust. He is taught to believe that people are basically untrustworthy, that everybody has to watch out for himself because the world is cruel and evil-minded. This negative concept of the world is further reinforced by whatever unfavorable experiences the individual has in the process of his socialization. He is likely to harbor even more feelings of hostility toward others if he believes that he has special qualities that cannot be realized because of the "others." The stronger his desire for acceptance, the more resentful and unfriendly he becomes toward people he feels are critical of him. Unable to impress other people, he assumes an aloof attitude of superiority, looking down on them, meanwhile searching for clues to prove that they have slighted him. His defensiveness enables him to maintain his self-esteem regardless of others' negative attitudes toward him.

Consider the case of Judy, an attractive housewife in her thirties who sought psychiatric attention because she felt anxious about and discontented with her life. She was well-off in many ways. Her household duties and her social life were those of an upper-class woman; yet she was uneasy about her social life because she disliked her friends' snobbery and their life-styles. In addition, she felt that her own life lacked direction.

Judy had been born into a relatively poor family oriented toward the arts and not toward the accumulation of material goods. As a child she came to believe that people were generally mischievous, wicked, and not to be trusted. This belief was instilled by her mother, who was distrustful of and hostile to other people. Her mother, Judy believed, protected her from this world of danger, from the people who would otherwise take advantage of her. Judy used to imagine that neighbors and other people somehow wished to harm her. She came to feel that the only way to protect herself was to relate to them as little as possible.

As a teen-ager, she thought of herself as an artist and was intensely involved in the pursuit of artistic activities. She played the violin and wanted to become a musician. Her parents encouraged her artistic expression, and she accepted their judgment that she should become an artist, though she had periods of doubts about her talents. In school she was detached from and suspicious of her peers; she had little interaction with them because of her fear that she would be derided. She was afraid that if other people really knew who she was, if they could see her "inner self," they would be jealous and try to hurt her. Her "inner self," she believed, sheltered her unique talents, which, if exposed, would create such envy that those who recognized them would feel compelled to destroy her. She was proud of this hidden knowledge of herself. It gave her a sense of distinction. She could withstand the derision of other people as long as she knew that she possessed something special that they did not have.

She eventually got married, and as she grew older she carried with her this secret, which made her look down on the artistic or social qualifications of others. She claimed that she was working alone on some indefinable artistic expression that, though she felt it was revolutionary, she did not care to share with others because they would not understand it. She was basically content in her little world, though suspicious of any attempt by others to penetrate her secret. She treated others with a benign air of superiority because she believed that they did not have as much talent or substance as she did.

However, a gnawing question was bothering her. Why, she wondered, was her family able to freely produce artistically instead of sheltering their artistic talents as she was doing? Her brother was creating and producing, while she was not; moreover, he seemed to look down on her life as a housewife. Gradually, a feeling of apprehension and doubt started to creep in. She wondered whether what she was holding inside as a creative treasure might in fact be nothing at all. Now, when friends asked her about her artistic work, she would get upset, if not hostile. She interpreted their questions as maliciously motivated, as making fun of her and disputing her talent. Yet she was still afraid to reveal her artistic preoccupations.

As if this were not enough to interfere with her peace of mind, her relationship with her husband was also becoming unsettling. She always tried to appear more educated, more knowledgeable than her husband, who was "just a businessman." However, he became more successful and more culturally informed, while she had not yet produced anything. In addition, a former girl friend of his was continually involved in their life. She was afraid that he might go back to her, or that at least he would make unfavorable comparisons between them. She felt that the other woman was conspiring, if not to convince her husband to divorce her, at least to make her life miserable. Though there was no evidence of this, she was convinced that somehow her husband's former girl friend would "get her." The last straw in this struggle came when the other woman succeeded in becoming very friendly with one of Judy's best friends. Judy not only became uncomfortable about her friend but feared that something further might happen to her as a result of her enemy's plotting.

She started to wonder about the sincerity of her friends, about the substance of her social relationships with her acquaintances, considering all of them either "phonies" or "hypocrites." She felt estranged from her social environment. She believed that the world was weird and senseless, and that her talents could not possibly be appreciated under these circumstances. Her inner drama led her sometimes to react condescendingly toward others, while at other times she felt weak and worthless. Her inner and external worlds did not fit together. The gap between them was full of anxiety, suspicion, and depressive thoughts, mixed with fantasies of fame and success.

By her own admission, she was still a child at heart. Reality was too frightening and confusing for her, and she escaped into fantasy and magic, as she always had. In that world she felt secure. In her fantasy world she could have full recognition and admiration from others; she could magically dismiss her critics and her enemies; she could make herself desired, loved, and famous. She had learned to derive real gratification from this world and this made it harder for her to face her daily interaction with others.

Certainly, something was wrong with her perception of reality. She could not accept herself as a comfortable housewife without high artistic or intellectual aspirations. Her attempts to hide her sense of inferiority made her magnify her moderate talents. To defend herself against a true evaluation of her talent, she never seriously tried to express it. At the same time, she defensively adopted the view that the world was malevolent and unfriendly, a view with which she had become comfortable as a child. She generalized her resentment toward those who attempted to criticize her and projected her own hostility onto others, seeing it as their hostility toward her.

Judy had developed this style of approaching reality gradually, in the years since childhood. Her perception of her experiences had become distorted by her tendency to observe only those aspects of her environment that would tend to confirm her suspicion that other people were treating her unfairly, maliciously, and disrespectfully. She was extremely aware of any criticism directed toward her and magnified it beyond the proportions of its objective significance.

Her thinking became an instrument to rationalize and justify a view of the world that supported her shaky self-esteem. The set of attitudes that she had developed in childhood, based on her prelogical thinking, continued to persist in her adult life, disguised by superficial pseudologic.

To correct her unbalanced evaluation of reality would require a basic change in her appraisal of herself; that is, accepting herself at her true value. This might also have helped her feel less competitive with and less inferior to her brother. By not trying to know herself better and to be realistic about her abilities over the years, she had become jealous of the talent of her brother, with whom she could hardly compete artistically. The more pressure she felt to prove herself and the more defensive she became, the less able she was realistically to compete with others or achieve her aspirations. Thus, her self-esteem fell still further. The organization of her thought processes was focused on daily confrontation with others instead of on maintaining a sense of herself. Her inability to resolve the conflict between the external and internal images of herself made her progressively more frustrated, to the point of occasional rage over insignificant events, making others responsible for her faults or failures. This frustration brought on further fear of losing complete control over her anger when dealing with antagonistic situations.

Judy had developed a pattern of behavior in her interaction with others that was only reinforcing her paranoid thinking. As we have seen, the inculcation of a negative concept of the world during the child's developmental years can create a personality oriented toward paranoia. Even an unrealistic overemphasis on positive values may induce the same problems, as long as the other personality factors already mentioned are present.

NAÏVETÉ AS A SOURCE OF PARANOID THINKING

If a child, in his early years of development, evolves a concept of human relationships based on such highly unrealistic values as: "People are always good to each other," "People always tell the truth," or "People are rewarded for good deeds and punished for bad ones," when he grows older and is confronted with a different reality, he will experience conflict. In adulthood he may appear socially naïve to others and find his dealings with them often frustrating. He will find it hard to accept the fact that human interaction is usually governed by egotistic and self-serving motives. The naïve individual still believes in his childhood world, where good always triumphed over evil. His parents taught him that truth, honesty, and dignity should govern human interaction. With shock and disbelief he discovers that human values are too unstable to assure that his learned norms of conduct will be respected in all circumstances; he becomes confused and disappointed, and feels deceived by others.

If a child's social expectations are very high but his qualifications to fulfill them are insufficient, his difficulties in adjusting to the real world in adulthood will be great. When his anticipated success does not occur, he wonders what went wrong. He does not understand that there is only a circumstantial relationship between effort and success. If he naïvely believes that only good work will bring success, he feels cheated when, for instance, he is bypassed for promotion because he was not annually contributing for his supervisor's birthday gift. If his self-esteem is high, he starts to brood and then to suspect that the pernicious influence of others is responsible for his professional failures and his social difficulties. His self-esteem does not permit him to accept his own responsibility for improperly handling critical events in his life.

His beliefs about the social system, based on his moral principles, make him appraise significant events of his life in a distorted manner. His conclusions are obvious: he is being treated unfairly and his basic rights are being denied. And, of course, at times he is right. Such occasions reinforce his belief that he is mistreated in all situations. (This tendency to generalize from particular situations is a remnant of prelogical thinking.) It becomes difficult for him to distinguish between events in which he has indeed been unfairly treated and those in which he imagines or assumes that he has been.

From this point of view, any combination of naïveté and drive for success could produce paranoid thinking. For instance, a low achiever may rationalize his lack of success as the result of persecution by those who are more powerful, whereas a high achiever may develop the conviction that there is a conspiracy to topple him. Both are suspicious of the intentions of others toward them. The low achiever believes that, had he not trusted others, he would have fared better; the high achiever suspects the intentions of others because he knows that he has reached power by manipulating others. Yet in both cases, there is an element of naïveté. While the low achiever refuses to acknowledge his own social incompetence, the high achiever believes that he can read the hidden meanings in the actions of those who conspire to destroy him.

PARANOID AND NORMAL THINKING

Why are such individuals considered to have paranoid personalities, when there may be a great deal of truth in their assumptions about their interactions with others? Is it not true that someone who handles situations naïvely will be exploited and that someone who reaches the pinnacle of power is envied and marked for downfall? In general, it is not uncommon for someone to be deceived or exploited by others posing as friendly to him, neither is it unheard of for a person's career or social standing to be maliciously undermined. What is the dividing line between normal coping and paranoid responses? The dividing line between a prudent cautiousness with respect to such possibilities and a paranoid preoccupation with them is defined by an individual's ability or inability to distinguish real from imaginary hostility and antagonism, to discriminate between the intentions one has attributed to others in a situation and their real intentions as those become apparent.

In order to understand better the differences between these two modes of coping, let us compare the underlying perceptions of reality in both cases. To begin with, all behavior reflects the individual's self-appraisal, which is based on his perception of himself and on the critical feedback he receives from friends, members of his family, authority figures in his life, and on his appraisal of a particular situation. While the normal individual tries to maintain consistency in his behavior, environmental forces and life events occasionally force him to reappraise his patterns of reaction. At such times the individual must modify his priorities and his views in order to meet the challenge of a new situation. The paranoid's perception of reality, however, does not permit him to respond in new ways to new situations that relate to his difficulties with people. Because of his biased way of processing information and reaching conclusions, he approaches the interaction with others with a rigid framework of preconceived expectations as to their attitudes and responses toward him. When these responses are not produced, he automatically categorizes any interaction as unpleasant, as an experience of rejection. His reactions are highly charged emotionally because of his preconceptions, which distort the meaning of any given interaction into a confrontation.

The paranoid individual is ambivalent in his approach to human relationships. This approach appears to be dictated by the interpretation of past experiences in the context of prelogical thinking. He is ambivalent, needing on the one hand to be close to others and on the other to avoid being hurt, as perhaps he has been in the past. Often these choices become so confused that he unwittingly behaves in such a way as to ensure his rejection.

Consider the example of Rachel, a career woman in her early thirties who was very frustrated with both her job and her personal life. She considered her job beneath her qualifications and found herself in constant conflict with her superiors and co-workers. Her conflicts with her superiors were over such things as their insistence that she arrive at work punctually and that she not read or talk excessively. She felt entitled to do these things because she was getting all her work done anyway. Conflict with her co-workers often stemmed from the fact that they would not support her in these arguments with the boss.

This was not the first job in which she had experienced this type of difficulty. In the past she had ascribed her difficulty to her preoccupation with the completion of her education or with family problems related to the long-term, incurable illness of her mother. Now, however, she felt that she was making a complete effort on behalf of her career; and yet in her last two jobs she had been totally unsuccessful, mainly, she believed, because the people she worked with had been mean and unfair. They had rejected her plans for reorganizing the office, responding coldly to her enthusiasm. She thought that her current supervisor was afraid of her because she was more intelligent and creative than he was, and because she had dared to challenge his judgment with regard to the management of the workplace.

Her private life was no better than her career. According to her, because she was so intelligent, so talented, and such a good lover, men were afraid of getting deeply involved with her. After several short-lived affairs terminated by the men because, she believed, her superiority to them made them insecure, she had recently met a man she liked very much. He was successful, intelligent, and kind to her. Though she did not have much information about his private life, she was under the impression that he was in the process of separating from his wife. After a short time, however, she discovered that he was solidly married, had four children, and was interested only in a "relaxing affair." Though the affair was at its beginning, she became very demanding of his time. He became angry and broke off the relationship.

Rachel felt betrayed and abused by this man, who, she believed, should not have gotten involved with her unless he meant to leave his wife and children. In her opinion, he had taken advantage of her sincere love for him. She overlooked the fact that after their third date she had known perfectly well that he was married, but that she had continued the relationship because she enjoyed it and because she hoped to win him from his wife. In fact, he had never made any commitment to live with her; he had not even told her that he loved her. But she had perceived the situation differently. She felt that he had become emotionally committed to her because he enjoyed being with her so much, and had told her so. Thus, in her eyes, he had proved to be deceitful.

Her relationships with other men had terminated with the same sense of frustration and bitterness. She took vehement issue with some of her lovers' attitudes, which she believed were sexist, arrogant, or downright antipathetic toward women. She loathed the thought that she might be used as a sexual object, although at the same time she was very demanding sexually. Nevertheless, she felt that it was the man's responsibility to pay the expenses involved in the relationship (she rationalized that this was because in our society men can earn more than women). She felt that her charm and her good company were enough to repay the man's financial investment in the relationship. In her relationships with men, as well as in her work, she expected to be treated on her own terms because of the value of what she had to offer. If she was not treated accordingly, she felt misunderstood or abused.

Her attitude was a mixture of naïveté and suspicion. Her naïveté mixed with magical thinking was expressed in her assumption that her last lover would leave his wife and children because he was happy with her sexually in their three-month affair, and in her belief that her innovative attitude toward the job would be highly appreciated by her boss and co-workers. Proceeding from these assumptions, she naturally was angry about the reactions of her lover and co-workers, whom she perceived as deceitful and hostile. In reality they were simply bewildered by her behavior and actions, which they considered utterly inappropriate.

At the same time, Rachel was suspicious of others. She felt that people took advantage of her because she was good-hearted and uninterested in social manipulation. Unable to see her own manipulation of others, she instead saw them as manipulative of her. She was very sensitive to remarks about her, always assuming that others were trying to put her down. She was convinced that her co-workers were talking behind her back and attempting to exploit her good nature. She believed that only by fighting hard for what she took to be her rights could she hope to hold her own against a world that was mistreating her. Meanwhile, she had come to feel miserable, hostile, and belligerent.

The combination of her naïveté–magical thinking about human interaction with her high drive for achievement generated conflict with others. Frustrated by her lack of achievement, she blamed other people and became suspicious of their intentions toward her. Gradually her thinking became paranoid whenever others failed to behave according to her naïve expectations or to treat her according to her own high valuation of her qualities. Her suspiciousness caused her to conclude that they were in fact acting willfully against her. The more she was unable to reach her goals, the more she sought the cause of her failure not in her own shortcomings but in the malicious machinations of others.

This way of looking at the world had its origin in Rachel's childhood. The younger of two daughters, she was the darling of her mother, who gave her ample attention and support. Her father, however, preferred her sister, though he did not ignore her. Her mother felt that she was the more intelligent of her daughters, while her sister was more attractive. She did better than her sister scholastically, but her sister was better in social situations. Gradually Rachel developed an attitude that was aloof and intellectually oriented; she became detached from and sometimes arrogant toward her peers, yet she was very sensitive to their remarks about her and felt deeply hurt when she believed that she was being improperly treated. As a child she had often become upset if she did not get something she believed she deserved, or if she felt that her sister was being treated better than she; in her teens she believed that other people did not like her.

When, around the time she obtained her master's degree, her mother died, she felt alone and unprotected. Her mother had been her main support, her source of reassurance that she might in fact be able to fulfill her dreams, and that her talents were indeed special. Around the same time her sister got married to an extremely successful man. The success of her sister made it even harder for Rachel to accept any lowering of her own social and emotional goals. Yet she was having a rather difficult time in both her professional and personal life. Rather than take responsibility for her failures, she blamed others for her problems. She defended her negative feelings toward others by observing that in general women have been oppressed by men, and that in general people manipulate and abuse each other if they can. She felt victimized by people because she thought of herself as inexperienced in social manipulation; in addition, she believed that being a woman made things worse for her. In reality, her aspirations were higher than her true possibilities: instead of realistically reevaluating her goals and her social interactions she justified her failures by blaming, accusing, and being hostile to her environment.

All of the cases presented in this chapter demonstrate the relationship between adult paranoid thinking and the contributing developmental experiences of childhood. These childhood experiences, interpreted and stored by the individuals in terms of the child's prelogical thinking, become the point of reference for interpreting subsequent similar experiences in adult life.

ADOLESCENT TRANSIENT PARANOID THINKING

Superficially, the paranoid's thinking and the child's prelogical thinking appear to be quite different, but in reality the similarity between them is striking. Though on a more subtle level, the paranoid, like the child, makes undocumented connections between things, disregarding of the laws of cause and effect, he builds a world of meaningful, subjective links in which events and people interact according to his own way of perceiving them. The gap between otherwise unrelated phenomena is thereby filled by conjecture and fantasy. General social observations about the competitive, ruthless structure of the world are internalized by the paranoid and applied to his own situation, regardless of their applicability to his case. While he admits that our society permits injustices that can cause setbacks in a person's career, for example, the paranoid is convinced that he, in particular, is the target of social injustice.

Another aspect of childlike thinking is the paranoid's peculiar sense of importance. It is because of his great importance, he believes, that others attempt to destroy him. Like the child, the paranoid feels that the world revolves around himself, its main purpose being his victimization. His failures are blamed on the actions of others who conspire to bring about his demise. This attitude usually starts to become structured as a pattern of thinking in adolescence, the time when the transition from childhood to adulthood brings with it a crisis related to the formation of adult identity. In fact, as part of the process most adolescents normally show some paranoid trends in their thinking.

In adolescence, the defining of self takes place under the most threatening of conditions: social acceptance or rejection. If the adolescent is unable to succeed in feeling accepted socially because he has developed inappropriate coping skills, this entire experience will only reinforce his negative attitudes toward others. In addition, integration into a typical adolescent social group, while strengthening his identity, will almost certainly involve a paranoid component of joining the rebellion against the values that the group rejects and against such adherents of those rejected values as parents and social institutions. Adolescent turmoil contains all of the elements of paranoid projection, denial, and rebellion against conformity and control. Any further inability to reach a balance with society increases the adolescent's sense of frustration and reinforces his paranoid thinking. If the individual emerges from adolescence with an unresolved conflict between his sense of self and his social acceptance, he may continue to be controlled by the paranoid but protective thinking patterns of his childhood (the very patterns adolescence should work through) and he may retain these patterns into adulthood.

But can we say that adult paranoid thinking duplicates the child's pre-logical thinking? Certainly not, although its formulation is not too different, in spite of the fact that it is layered with loose logic that may appear to give it an independent validity.

The paranoid, because of his preconceived view of human interaction, has lost the ability to discriminate between potentially threatening situations and those that are not. His generalization of past experiences leads him to the conclusion that he is surrounded by a hostile world in which people are either deceitful or outright persecutors. Unlike a normal individual, who may at one time or another feel harassed, hindered, or oppressed by other people, the paranoid automatically assumes that this is happening. Any perceived infringement of his rights is interpreted as an intentional threat to his self-esteem and leads, as previously discussed, to hostile behavior on his part. Instead of documentation of his mistreatment, abuse, or persecution, the paranoid relies on presumptive evidence introduced into his "logical argument" as clear-cut, proven facts. In this way his failures or negative experiences are denied, unless they reinforce this type of thinking. As a by-product, he must overcome the consequences of his negative interaction with others by continually compensating if he wants to achieve his goals.

In fact, many paranoid personalities are so determined to prove themselves that they become outstanding achievers and skillful manipulators of the environment. The price they pay for their success is directly related to the amount of effort and frustration required to control others. An example of a successful paranoid personality will document this point.

Mr. S was a businessman in his forties who was very successful in his field but had extreme difficulty in interpersonal relationships because he perceived anyone who did not accept him on his terms as defiant or hostile. In reality, it was he who was verbally abusive and insulting; yet he interpreted any disagreement as a personal offense and reflexively reacted to it with anger. Although he frequently had to go through great difficulties in order to mitigate the harm done by his outbursts, he was unable to find a way to control them. His business acumen enabled him to maintain his professional relationships, but his personal life was severely affected by his hostile, aggressive attitude.

He was often suspicious of the intentions of others and felt most of the time that they wanted to take advantage of him. Mr. S. took unusual measures to assure himself beyond doubt that he was not being either misrepresented or cheated. For instance, in order to make sure that his close associates did not misrepresent him at any meeting he could not attend, they were directed to attend all meetings only in teams, as assigned by him, and whenever possible to register the proceedings on tape. Furthermore, in each section of his business he planted his own loyal man to check on others and to report confidentially to him not only about work but also about any talk regarding him. He rationalized this behavior as being part of work efficiency.

Mr. S. did not trust anybody, and at the same time he took advantage of all the people surrounding him. His suspiciousness was combined with naïve expectations of other people. He expected loyalty from his staff in spite of the abuse he dealt out to them; he expected others to be truthful and even self-sacrificing in the interests of his business and his rights, while he took advantage of them to promote his own interests.

Mr. S. also felt a continual need to assert himself, which he expressed by disregarding the rules of institutions, organizations, and corporations. This tendency created endless conflicts between himself and other corporations, and occasionally resulted in his being barred from doing business with certain customers. In order to maintain his self-image, he interpreted these consequences as reflections either of lack of understanding of his intentions or of unreasonable hostility toward him. This vicious circle was repeated often enough to support his impression that people slighted him, while he perceived his own provocations toward others as only reasonable assertions of his own rights, which otherwise might not be recognized. He thus dismissed any inconsistency in his own actions as temporary and necessary.

His abusiveness and suspicion toward others was essentially an over-reaction to his own fear of being abused and cheated by them. However, ultimately he despaired of conveying a positive image in his interaction with others and met any antagonism he perceived with verbal abusiveness and reprimands in order to remain in control.

Mr. S's pattern of negative interpersonal relationships started long before he became a business success. It began in his childhood as a defense against the other members of his family, who either mistreated him or refused to recognize his independent identity. His father felt that his son would not be able to achieve much in life because of his lack of interest in the family business; he considered him lazy, unreliable, and undisciplined. To his mother, on the other hand, he seemed intelligent, sensitive, and responsive to her needs. But his father's lack of acceptance and continuous friction with his older brother affected his self-esteem. His lack of athletic ability undermined his masculine image to the point that he was compelled to compensate for it. One way was to provoke arguments with his teachers and with students older than himself in the hope of impressing them with his intelligence and aggression. But if, instead of impressing them, he felt slighted by them, he would become extremely angry and could hold off his rage only with difficulty. In addition, he grew up in an atmosphere of suspicion and mistrust. In his family everyone was for himself and tried to get whatever he could even at the expense of another. Later, when he started to work, his image of human interaction did not change. He found it progressively more difficult to suppress his anger at the feeling that he was abused and "pushed around" by others. In fact, it took him several years, after changing jobs numerous times, to realize that he could not work for anybody else. He then decided to start his own business, which became a success. His need for self-assertion made him particularly vulnerable to conflict with other men who, he believed, were minimizing his importance. His life was governed by his fragile sense of self-esteem, which created the need to reaffirm his power, often inappropriately.

As in earlier examples, Mr. S's adult thinking resembled his prelogical childhood thinking. His logic was self-serving, designed to support his vulnerable ego. Logically, he was desperately attempting to reconcile contradictory beliefs, inconsistencies of behavior, and childish generalizations about unpleasant experiences for the sole purpose of making sure that he would not be hurt.

From the general premise that people are dishonest and distrustful in relating to each other, the distorted logic of Mr. S, like that of any other paranoid individual, followed these lines:

1. People try to outsmart each other by hiding the true meaning of their actions.
2. People try to outsmart me too.
3. Then I have to uncover the hidden meaning of their actions in order to protect myself.

Obviously, then, any gesture, act, or statement could be interpreted as proving that people were against him.

Logical rigor is absent because of the distorted use of premises in Mr. S's syllogistic approach. The inherent contradictions between the terms of the syllogism—the generalization of the minor premise and the particularizations of the major one—make the logic inconsistent. Mr. S was suspicious of the intentions of others toward him, while in reality he was reading his own paranoid script. Furthermore, though sometimes, for political reasons, he was conciliatory and accommodating, if the desired results were not achieved he would become even more angry and defiant. This convinced him that he was right in his assumption that "others" are devious, regardless how "good" he was to them.

This pattern of relating to others provided him with the necessary support to maintain his self-esteem. Without this approach, any slight setback in his ability to control his interaction with others would have thrown Mr. S. into a state of depression and left him with a sense of failure and impending disaster.

In Mr. S.'s behavior, as in all paranoid construction of reality, there was an important element of magic. There was magic in his ability to read the hidden meanings in the statements and actions of others, and in his belief that he could predict future actions. Like all paranoid individuals, he believed his assumptions without any doubt or need for factual confirmation. His lack of critical judgment about his own evaluation of events and his inability to distinguish between true and fortuitous causes of situations echo this magic element.

PARANOID PSYCHOSIS

Paranoid thinking helps the individual to resolve the contradiction between his own positive image of himself and the failures and setbacks he suffers in society. This style of thought enables the insecure person with a sense of inferiority, or the overconfident person who has been unable to reach his goals, to protect his self-esteem by transferring the blame for his failures to others. In fact, in his overprotectiveness the paranoid's defenses are over-alerted, his sensitivity becomes suspicion, his evaluation of an event magnifies it from a potential threat into a sinister plot against him. People around him who allegedly attempt to deny him his rights are seen as hostile, egotistical, potential or actual persecutors. Paradoxically, the paranoid's sense of himself rests on his sense of persecution. When his social predicament becomes so bad as to create a crisis of self-esteem, he may become truly delusional; under sufficiently stressful conditions he may become psychotic.

It is not uncommon, for instance, for a person to develop an acute paranoid psychosis after he has suffered some major physical trauma threatening to his self-esteem. The shift from neurotic paranoid thinking to psychotic paranoia is more direct in those cases in which the precipitating events are social. A typical example is Jon, the Eastern European immigrant described earlier. For him, the moment of critical stress was his failure to pass the French medical license. At that moment he came to believe that he was superior to his examiners and that they were persecuting him because they were afraid of his superior knowledge. Now everything began to make sense to him. He could clearly see that he had been mistreated for a long time because other people, envious of him and threatened by him, wanted to block his career. According to his reasoning everything appeared logical. He could establish a cause-and-effect relationship between the hostile actions of others and his own failures. He felt more confident after this delusive realization; his past doubts were replaced by certainty. Now he need not question any longer whether he might have made mistakes or might be less talented than others. Now he knew that he was the victim of a cruel and hostile environment. He felt, at least temporarily, secure.

Yet the transition from neurotic to psychotic paranoia cannot be explained only on the basis of environmentally unfavorable circumstances and rationalizations. Genetic personality factors may also play a part in determining an individual's pattern of responses. It has been suggested that the limbic system, that section of the human brain that is a vestige of the reptilian brain, might be involved in the development of paranoia, as part of the individual's primitive need to maintain a balance between his instinctive aggressive drive to control his environment and the restriction of that drive by outside forces. That there is a biological model for paranoia is also suggested by the paranoid state induced by amphetamine psychosis. However, these theories only lend support to the idea that paranoid thinking fulfills an adaptive function in the life of the individual: it is an overdefensive way of relating to the world.

In the final analysis, in order to avoid a paranoid orientation of thinking every individual must come to terms with the conflict between ideals and reality, between social values and social behavior, between expectations and achievements. It is ironic that society itself, with its competitive organization and relative values, is a major factor in the reinforcement of human hostility and aggression toward others.

Paranoid assumptions about social interaction can be easily developed in all of us. We may react in this way in situations that we find threatening to our sense of identity. In some cases social classes or organized groups become the collective matrices for the development of paranoid thinking. However, in general social conflict only maintains or brings out inherent characteristics of human nature (exploitation, discrimination, envy, greed for power, aggression). Operating within the realm of normality, each individual attempts to adapt to human reality by treating each situation on its own merits, sometimes absorbing losses of self-esteem, sometimes compromising in order to survive uncomfortable events, sometimes succeeding in the achievement of his goals. But the paranoid person, faced with social conflicts, is unable to adapt. His fragile sense of himself makes him too sensitive to these pressures to cope with the conflict without undue damage to that identity.

7

HYSTERICAL THINKING

The Denial of a Stressful Reality

The heart has its reasons, which reason knows not.
—BLAISE PASCAL, *Pensées*

To the hysterical individual, certain events can become so overwhelming a source of stress that he simply cannot acknowledge their existence as a cause of distress. Such denial may in fact succeed, at least temporarily, in driving the anxiety from the individual's conscious mind, but at a price. In reality the hysteric does react to the events with unusual physical symptoms or over-dramatized emotional behavior. The more difficult the conflict appears, the more impressive his symptoms will be, such as functional physical paralysis, amnesia, or loss of personal identity. These physical responses seem to take the person's mind off the problems he confronts; indeed the initial anxiety, the inner turmoil, the problem may at first have produced are gone. But how can an emotional conflict be so totally transformed into an apparent physical condition that the new condition becomes the only reality with which the individual has to deal? By what mental process can someone blot recent unpleasant events out of his memory as if they had never existed, or alter his state of consciousness to the point of temporarily losing his identity?

Though these responses are the most extreme forms of hysterical reaction, they are the result of a particular type of thinking typical of the hysteric. In most cases hysteria does not manifest itself in these forms, but only by great excitability and overdramatized displays of emotion. All types of hysterical behavior, however, originate in the same matrix of hysterical personality, characterized by emotional instability, suggestibility, need for attention, overreaction to events perceived as stressful, and a histrionic tendency.

Many of the same traits are part of the prelogical thinking of the child's developmental years. In adulthood a predominance of these traits raises doubt about whether the individual has ever matured cognitively and affectively to the adult level. The egocentrism, childish outbursts of emotion, need for immediate gratification, and bizarre attempts by the hysteric passively to control his environment (by means of his histrionic behavior) all suggest arrested development of the personality.

But if such a general arrest of personality development were true, as some theorists believe, it would cause the individual to approach all events and situations with the pseudologic of a child. This is not the case with the hysteric. The hysteric can make mature judgments about the organization of his life up to the point that he faces a serious threat to the gratification of some need he perceives as vital. Faced with a crisis, he reaches a state of anxiety, followed by a display of inappropriate emotionalism or overdramatic behavior, or by the sudden appearance of a physical symptom rendering him nonfunctional, which makes the original crisis moot as when, for instance, a soldier during a heavy artillery attack, surrounded by explosions and death, suddenly becomes deaf; or, after witnessing some shocking event, an individual may be suddenly stricken with loss of memory of the entire scene.

These reactions display the inability of the hysterical individual to cope with stressful or threatening situations. Under these conditions, he resorts to an unusual type of coping not used by the average person.

The relationship between a crisis and the bizarre behavioral response that results in the magical removal of emotional pain appears to the hysterical personality to be unexplainable coincidence but may be considered by others a convenient escape. It is important to emphasize that the hysteric does not take conscious responsibility for his act—for his "getting sick"—because he is not a malingerer, planning and scheming to avoid an unpleasant situation. For him the illness or loss of memory is just a fortuitous happening, a natural condition unrelated to the real problem.

The ability to react to an emotional crisis with a functional physical disturbance has long puzzled physicians. Understanding this type of response has become easier in the light of our present knowledge about the development of thinking in the child. At the child's level of intellectual and emotional development, it is normal for him to interpret events according to his egocentric view of the environment and his immediate need for gratification and attention, and to respond excessively to unpleasant experiences. When environmental conditions are difficult to cope with, the child often escapes them through fantasy, magic, and make-believe; in the game of

pretending to be something or someone else, he can imitate others and identify with the object of his imitation to the point where he begins to incorporate into his own personality aspects of that imitated object. On the child's
level of functioning can be found the roots of behavior later labeled hysterical. For instance, in symbolic play the child assimilates reality to his own
wants and suspends the need to adapt to the outside world; he enjoys a world
of his own, which he controls, understands, and finds pleasurable. He can
also create ways of behaving that may carry over into his behavior in real
situations.

At this early stage of intellectual development, symbolic thinking is
based almost entirely on imitation and assimilation. There is no critical
appraisal of reality, no logical reasoning; the child's judgment is a mixture of
beliefs, fantasy, and magical interpretations.

The child is supposed to outgrow this stage and reach the stage of logical
thinking; but he does not always do so. If he is faced with a stressful situation
for which he has no explanation and no available coping response, he is likely
to resort to the anxiety-controlling mechanisms that have worked for him in
the past. He may attempt to avoid any new encounter with the event and
become phobic; he may develop a ritual to control the anxiety provoked by
the event, becoming compulsive; or he may become hysterical, finding that,
unable to avoid the stressful conflict, he feels sick and believes that he is.

The most important factors that contribute to the development of a
hysterical personality (as opposed to, say, a compulsive or phobic personality) are specific familial influences and constitutional predisposition. Familial
influences involve the child's imitation and assimilation of the behavior of
others who act overemotionally or even hysterically, or who are superstitious
or mystical or simply sickly. Constitutional factors determine the degree of
arousal and the lability of the autonomic nervous system, and, in addition,
the individual's suggestibility and susceptibility to conditioning. This combination of factors can lead to a particular mode of consciousness, a specific
style of thinking about the environment that is typical of the hysterical
personality. A person who thinks in this way will perceive things as potentially frightening or anxiety creating, which must be warded off because they
interfere with his immediate gratification.

Hysterical reactions are attempts to offset anxiety caused by the extreme
lability and excitability of the hysteric's autonomic nervous system, which
tends to be easily aroused by external as well as internal stimuli. External and
internal stimuli are, in the final analysis, under the control of the cognitive
processes. In the case of hysteria, the cognitive apparatus poorly processes
these stimuli in terms of their significance or their appropriateness for release
in a particular situation. The hysteric incorrectly evaluates the situation,
concluding that it is beyond his ability to control it; the ensuing anxiety is
exacerbated by the oversensitivity of the autonomic nervous system, which
makes him to overreact to the event.

This appraisal system operates circularly, since his already distorted perception of past experience has in fact predetermined his response to this new experience. Certainly this represents only one part of the hysteric problem. The other part is the hysteric's impulsiveness, which makes him react to each new anxiety-creating situation. This condition belongs to the category described by behaviorists as *approach-avoidance conflict:* conflict induced by conditions that are equally appealing and discomfiting. For example, a young man wanted to enlist in the Marine Corps because of his desire to improve his self-image, yet he was afraid of the training and risky assignments. As a result, after enlisting he developed anxiety attacks and dizziness, which made him nonfunctional.

Another important aspect of hysterical thinking is the hysteric's high susceptibility to suggestion. This creates a certain state of consciousness resulting from the special meaning taken on by the perception and memories of an event. The hysteric is susceptible not only to others' opinion but to his own fantasies and daydreams. He sometimes has difficulty separating day-dreaming and fantasy from his real experiences. The invasion of wish-fulfilling fantasy into the reality of his daily life distorts his appraisal of events and his responses to them, and represents a secure escape route when external events become unbearable. Wish and reality are made one by the power of self-suggestion. In this process the hysteric shifts his attention from the mental pain of the traumatic event to the mental relief of a fantasy in which the event has been miraculously negated. Concentration on the fantasy attains a hypnotic quality and induces a state of consciousness in which the symptom that he imagined he would develop in the stressful situation becomes real for him. In this state he may perceive or, more correctly, imagine the symptoms of true illness (this is known as *hysterical conversion reaction* because the psychological stress that the hysteric was facing has been converted in his mind into a physical symptom). On the other hand, he may simply blot out awareness of certain events or circumstances by loss of memory (known as *hysterical dissociation*).

The difference between the symptoms of conversion reaction and true physical illness is that the physiological symptoms do not correspond to the anatomical structure affected by the illness. For instance, the individual may develop paralysis of the hand-glove type, in which the anaesthesia does not follow the distribution of the affected nerves. In this case it involves only the hand, up to a clearly defined line, above which the sensations are normal, whereas a true paralysis would follow the anatomical distribution of nerves. Furthermore, the anaesthesia may vary from one examination to another. The motor disturbances may follow a similar pattern; while the practical function itself is affected there is no physiological or anatomical damage because the symptoms follow the pattern of the individual's personal perception of how his bodily functions operate. All this is possible because fantasy magically takes over the reality of the traumatic event.

The similarity of both the hysterical conversion reaction and the dissociated state to the hypnotic state was recognized by physicians in the nineteenth century, and hypnotism has been used to treat hysterical conditions ever since. In fact, the treatment of hysteria with hypnosis that Freud studied with Charcot in Paris took into account the psychogenic (functional) nature of hysteria. The documentation of this was offered by Charcot, who by means of suggestions made to patients in the hypnotic state was able to produce a variety of hysterical symptoms. At Nancy, Hippolyte Bernheim taught Freud about posthypnotic suggestion, in which the individual is influenced in the hypnotic state to behave in a particular manner afterward, on a conscious level. In Bernheim's experiments the suggested act was performed as though it were a spontaneous realization. Freud integrated these findings into his theory of hysteria, which was related to repressed activity of a childhood sexual conflict. The anxiety experienced by hysterics he considered to be due to castration fear. However, this extension of the findings of Charcot, Bernheim, and his senior collaborator, Breuer, about sexual conflict to the general cause of all neurotic situations proved to be mistaken.

The discovery important to underscore is that phenomena of both hypnosis and hysteria have a similar underlying mechanism, that of suggestion. In hypnosis the suggestion is given by an authority figure; in hysteria the imitation or fantasy is internalized by a process of autosuggestion. The hysteric places himself in a state of partial hypnosis by focusing on any body activity that is related in his mind to the loathsome external event he would like magically to solve. In the same way, if the individual is faced with a conflict because he is very angry at someone he likes or respects but is afraid to say what he thinks (the "approach-avoidance" conflict, wherein the hysteric simultaneously wishes for something and wishes to avoid it), he may develop aphonia (an inability to speak). His anxiety about the possibility of offending the other person is thus converted into a physical disturbance, which nullifies the conflict and becomes the primary conscious problem with which he has to deal.

Most often hysteria manifests itself in the form of dramatized, overemotional responses to a situation. Hysterical behavior has been associated more with women than with men. In fact, the name of the illness comes from the Greek word for uterus, which was thought by ancient physicians to wander through the woman's body, producing hysteria. It seems that women, because of constitutional and cultural factors, are more prone than men to extreme emotional reactions and histrionic behavior. The nineteenth-century explanation for it, when hysterical behavior in women was particularly widespread, was related to the dependent, powerless position of women in society, which had blocked the expression of their true feelings. Other authors have linked hysteria to sex, the main tenet of Freud's theory.

In the light of this knowledge it is interesting to review the observations of some nineteenth-century British physicians. G. H. Napheys believed that hysteria was "a disease of the nerves to which girls about the age of puberty are very subject, particularly in higher circles of society where their emotions are over-educated and their organization delicate." Other physicians concluded that hysteria represented a socially tolerated outlet for an emotional conflict created by unacceptable demands that the individual did not know how to handle except through bodily expression—a form of nonverbal communication.

The dependent social position of women, combined with orgasmic difficulties, may well make them far more susceptible to hysterical reactions. Great tension is caused by the conflict between a woman's attempts to be herself and fears of being rejected and left helpless should she fail to meet the demands of her male partner. Many women today still perceive their situation in much the same terms. Often a woman copes with this by resorting to ways in which she learned to behave as a girl in relation to her father. This behavior persists more frequently in girls than in boys because society has historically tended to accept instability, moodiness, and higher displays of emotion more in women than in men.

But this would not be sufficient to cause hysteria without a particular type of personality. Eysenck theorized that the combination of high emotionality and high extroversion predisposed an individual toward histrionic behavior. In short, the hysterical behavior presupposed a hysterical thinking fostered by cultural and/or familial factors and a particular personality constellation.

However, the change in the cultural elements that in the past favored hysteria has resulted in the fact that hysteria in women in its more extravagant forms is not so common today as it was in the late nineteenth and early twentieth centuries; but this does not mean that it has disappeared as a result of women's changing role in society or the liberalization of sexual attitudes. Disappointments related to sex and to social ambitions still appear to be among the main causes of hysteria in women.

Consider the case of Gail, a young, college-educated woman who became chronically ill and nonfunctional after her husband left her and their two children without warning. According to her, he had not shown any intention to leave her prior to his actual departure, and the interaction between them had been comfortable during the three years of their married life. The major difficulty had been that he was a poor provider: she had to work to make ends meet while the children were left in the care of her mother. After the shock of realizing that her husband would not reconcile with her made her nonfunctional for a time, Gail was forced to leave her job and concentrate her energies on her children.

But she felt depressed about her situation and angry toward her former husband, who refused to have any contact with her or the children. Then she started to have difficulty meeting her financial obligations. Still, she struggled along and nearly two years later she started to complain of attacks of dizziness, nausea, and twitching of the facial muscles. She became afraid to walk on the street alone, or to ride subways or buses. Her attacks started suddenly, and she did not have any idea what might have triggered them— she simply felt sick and incapacitated.

Gail was the only child of a middle-class immigrant family that had come from Europe to the United States seeking a better life. Her parents were hard workers—her father an owner of a little shop and her mother a seamstress. They wanted their only child to have a better life than they had had. She was particularly spoiled by her father, who entertained grandiose plans for her. They encouraged her to go to college in order to get an education and upgrade her social status. She was attractive, and her parents advised her to look for a financially successful man to marry. She was led to believe that if she followed her parents' advice she would be able to reach the goals laid out for her.

Her mother was somewhat strict and discouraged her from getting involved with young men while she was in school. Her mother felt that because she was quite attractive it would be easy enough for her to find a suitable husband after graduation. As a result, the daughter rarely dated and had little experience relating to men. During her student years she was happy with herself, free of most major cares except those related to her academic performance. Her family provided all the emotional and financial support that she wanted, as long as she behaved according to their prescribed social and moral values. At times she wanted to rebel against her parents' restrictions on her social life, but her fear of rejection always prevailed. When she felt lonely and displeased with her life, she escaped into fantasy and daydreaming.

Sometimes she became absorbed in her fantasies to such an extent that when she stopped daydreaming she had difficulty in adjusting to her real surroundings. Her daydreams were about meeting a handsome, successful young man who would offer her an exciting, opulent social life. At other times she dreamed of becoming a famous actress, a celebrity. In high school or college, when she met a man in whom she was interested, she would often fabricate a story about her "true origin," claiming that she was the daughter of a wealthy European woman who had had an unfortunate love affair with a man who died while on a secret mission. She had been adopted by her present parents and brought to the United States with them as a child, she would claim, and now her true mother showed interest in getting her back. At home, after the date, she would feel ashamed of her made-up stories, but she was unable to resist her need for self-aggrandizement.

As a child she had always wanted to be admired and loved by everybody. Her parents described her as having been capricious and emotional, with tendencies to temper tantrums and impulsive behavior.

In adolescence the dream of becoming rich and successful became central to her life. Because she considered herself unusually attractive and intelligent, she felt entitled to wealth and success. When she graduated from college, she believed that she possessed all the requirements for success. But what she sorely lacked was experience with men. The first charming young man who pursued her with perseverance succeeded in capturing her total attention and her love. She believed in his claim that he was a successful businessman, although in reality he was only a boastful salesman, uncommitted to any type of work, emotionally unstable, unable to develop a lasting relationship or take responsibility for a family. He appeared to her to be charming, intelligent, and articulate, and she was impressed by his grandiose plans about getting rich quickly. In reality, he hoped that her family would put him in business and that she would work too.

Needless to say, things did not work out for either of them. Her family did not have the money to help him open a business, and she became pregnant. Suddenly he was forced to work hard to support a wife and child, a situation that he had never wanted. After the birth of his second child, conceived accidentally, the responsibilities of family life became unbearable, and he ran away.

Gail's shock was indescribable. She literally collapsed at the abrupt termination of their relationship. Her disbelief changed to anxiety, and ultimately to depression and feelings of helplessness mixed with confusion and self-pity. Her parents were extremely helpful throughout that painful period, but her self-esteem had been seriously damaged.

Her anxious, depressed state made her unable to concentrate on work, and she left her job. At home she felt more secure, but the presence of her children reminded her of her marital tragedy. She shunned any social activity, ashamed to have been deserted by her husband. She spent her free time reconsidering her past, fluctuating between self-recrimination and resentment toward her former husband.

Her dizziness began about two years later, when she was going out with a man who showed great interest in her. On her way home she suddenly became dizzy and almost fainted. She thought at the time that her condition might be related to drinking an alcoholic beverage to which she was not accustomed; but the next day she had another episode of dizziness and fainting while talking on the telephone to this man when he called her for a date. Afterward the attacks of dizziness became quite frequent and she consulted her family physician. He sent her to a neurologist who was unable to find anything wrong but prescribed some medication. She felt better for a few weeks, but afterward her condition became even worse. Eventually it was suggested that she consult a psychiatrist.

During her psychiatric sessions it became apparent that she had developed a strong resentment toward men, whom she believed to be untrustworthy, irresponsible, and only sexually motivated in all their interactions with women. But on first meeting the man she was dating, she had felt overpoweringly attracted to him. This was partly, she admitted, because he resembled her former husband, and that was upsetting her. In addition, since her divorce she had developed a strong attachment to a woman who was very supportive. This friend, who was divorced, had in the past had a sexual relationship with another woman. Gradually the relationship between Gail and her friend had become very intimate, with occasional sexual contact. Though she felt uneasy admitting the extent of their intimacy, she felt that it was acceptable, because she participated only for the sake of their close friendship. They had an understanding that they were free to pursue any relationship with a man if they so desired; but both of them nurtured the same negative feelings toward men. This had reduced their actual contact with men to practically none.

When Gail met the first man to whom she had felt attracted since her husband left her, she faced a painful dilemma. At the realization that the man was interested in her, she became anxious, but at the realization that dating him would mean changing her relationship with her friend, the anxiety became unbearable. She was faced with choosing between a man, who represented the heterosexuality that for her had become identified with insecurity and fear, and a woman, who represented security and a comfortable sexual outlet. Her solution was to internalize the conflict, following patterns of thinking that she had developed in the past in similar anxiety-producing situations that were evoked automatically in order to cope with situations: thus she was suddenly overcome by dizziness and the feeling that she was dying. Merely thinking of parting from her friend made her feel insecure, anxious, and upset; yet the desire to be with the man was strong, in terms of both reinforcing her self-confidence and staisfying instinctual needs while creating anxiety as well.

Her dilemma became even more pressing when the man began calling her and asking her out. The first time she had put him off by saying that she was not well. Unfortunately, this continued until he gave up. Meanwhile Gail felt it was unfortunate that she should have gotten sick just when she had the opportunity to date a man she liked. She did not see any connection between her emotional conflicts and her physical state. She believed that her dilemma would be solved as soon as she was healthy enough to develop a closer relationship with him.

In order to understand how and why Gail came to manifest this kind of hysterical response to her conflict, we must examine her previous experiences. In therapy Gail recalled that during childhood she had often heard one of her aunts, a single woman, complaining of dizziness, and would frequently see her leaning against furniture in order not to faint. This had impressed her greatly: her aunt had been treated with a great deal of attention by her parents because she seemed so sensitive to any type of commotion. The children were supposed to be silent and not bother their aunt because of her delicate constitution. She remembered also that between the ages of five and seven she had sometimes felt dizzy in unpleasant situations and had imagined that she might become sick like her aunt. Eventually, however, her episodes of dizziness had disappeared, probably because nobody had paid much attention to them.

But when, as an adult, she again became dizzy, she saw no connection with her childhood dizziness. She felt that it was only a temporary malady that would postpone her eventual dating of the man who was calling her. When, after a few months, he lost interest in her and stopped calling, the conflict that had precipitated her dizziness was eliminated. But she continued to have dizzy spells because the attention and care she had been receiving from her family and her friend boosted her self-esteem. This reinforcement of the hysterical behavior became a "secondary gain," which she had difficulty parting with.

The care lavished on her by her friend made her feel important and loved. Still, she saw her condition as a hindrance to her life. She could not see that her symptoms had developed as a protection against men, who had hurt her so much, and against the painful necessity of deciding between her need for her friend and her need to see the man who was calling her (which might even have required an admission to herself of her new homosexual orientation). The sudden onset of sickness magically negated her conflict. But it is interesting to note that her thinking in general functioned on an adult level.

With her conflict solved in an "honorable manner," Gail felt free to continue her emotional and sexual life with her friend, though other opportunities to meet men were available. But her problems were not solved, for she still had attacks of anxiety, particularly when a man appeared interested in her. She came to believe that her anxiety was caused by the fear that she might have an attack of dizziness while on a date. This kind of circular thinking is typical of the interaction between the childish, magical thinking of the hysteric and the more mature, rational thinking that coexists with it. The magical thinking creates an immediate response in order to offset the stress caused by certain situations; then the rational thinking seeks to integrate that response into the logical mainstream of adult consciousness.

FREUDIAN AND BEHAVIORIST EXPLANATIONS OF HYSTERIA

In Freudian terms Gail's anxiety would have been seen as a conscious expression of her feeling of being rejected by her father, for whom she had had "incestuous" feeling as a child. In this context her nausea was a symbolic representation of her disgust with men, while her homosexual behavior was confirming her unresolved Electra complex. But assumptions about her infantile sexuality hardly elucidate why, for instance, she had been able to relate sexually to her husband.

To assert that hysterical traits reflect Oedipal-genital conflict only introduces a hypothetical, unverifiable dimension into the understanding of the mental processes, further obfuscating the issue. Interestingly, in order to cover the gamut of hysterical reactions, the psychoanalytic theorists extended the sexual dynamic of conflict in hysteria from the Oedipal stage of conflict to that of oral fixation. Regardless of how alluring the psychosexual hypothesis may be to our imagination, the fact remains that fixation at the oral stage of psychosexual development is said to occur between the ages of two and three. A child of that age would not have an adequate neurological and mental level of maturation to formulate the connections that lead to hysterical behavior.

At the other end of the psychological spectrum, the behaviorists attempt to explain the hysterical response in terms of the traumatic avoidance response responsible for the development of anxiety. Yet this theory does not tell us why Gail had episodes of fainting and not other types of symptoms such as paralysis or aphonia.

The key to understanding hysteria lies in the organization of the thought processes. The inner experience represents an equally powerful source of affectively colored input, similar to the input from the external environment. By the process of focusing attention inward, the individual's daydreaming and fantasy activates a mental "action system," thereby mediating behavior. Apparently the inner experience works as an "action subsystem," underlying the ongoing thought processes and/or becoming loosely integrated into the mainstream of consciousness. This provides an immediate way of adapting to unpleasant, anxiety-arousing situations.

The same mechanism is responsible for the behavior of the hysterical personality. The most frequently encountered form of hysterical reaction is characterized by the exaggerated show of emotion, overreaction to events, outburst of uncontrollable anger, need to attract attention to oneself, and sexualization of behavior. These responses are present in various degrees in the hysteric's interaction with others. The hysteric is often egocentric, vain, superficial, dependent, demanding, and manipulative. An example might be in order.

Lucy, an attractive young woman, the daughter of a high-powered executive, sought psychiatric help for the third time in her life because of her difficulty in organizing her social and emotional life. She was particularly upset that her boyfriend, a rich but eccentric man, did not want to marry her. In fact, he had left the East Coast for the West and had joined an esoteric religious cult. She described their one-and-a-half-year relationship as having been quite stormy and questioned whether she should go to join him in his new ascetic life. She wondered whether he was still in love with her since he had become so deeply involved with the religious cult. She stated that she missed him very much, and while she talked about him in a very dramatic tone she started to cry and appeared to be despondent.

However, further discussion revealed that their relationship had been fragmented, often broken-off and mended again, with periods of separation when he had dated other men. Even now she was having an enjoyable affair. When the discussion focused on her new lover, she became cheerful and lively again.

In subsequent sessions Lucy unfolded a history of numerous love affairs that were ended by her because she felt that she did not get enough attention from her lovers. In addition, she considered most of her lovers sexually inadequate because they were unable either to arouse her or to bring her to orgasm. In fact, she rarely had an orgasm.

Her main satisfaction from interaction with men was being admired and desired by them. She was flirtatious and seductive; this had led to many conflicts with her various lovers, who had accused her of being too friendly toward other men in their presence. Lucy felt that she was only being charming and sociable and that their "jealousy fits" were unjustified. However, she admitted that since her adolescence she had wanted to get the attention of people, seeking to impress them with flamboyant clothing and a sensuous way of moving or talking. In conversations with men, she tended to be extremely friendly, to the point of casually touching them on the arms or legs. She admitted having been accused of flirtatiousness but denied any inappropriate or deliberately provocative behavior.

Looking back on her childhood, she recalled having had a great need to get the attention of her mother and father. Her mother had seemed aloof and detached, while her father had been warmer and more appreciative; he was very proud of her because she was attractive, intelligent, and "fun to be with."

She recalled that as a child she had gotten easily upset when she felt antagonized by others or frustrated in what she was doing. She would often cry and become irritable. She was apt to throw objects or stamp on the floor in rage. Her parents considered her a nervous, sensitive child who required a lot of attention, affection, and protection. She felt controlled and restricted by her parents with regard to her social life. This problem became acute in early adolescence, when she felt an irresistible desire to be close to boys.

Lucy developed into an attractive young woman quite early, and had a need to get full recognition of it. At thirteen she fell helplessly in love with a twenty-one-year-old student who lived in the neighborhood. She followed him whenever she could, trying to attract his attention. She had a fantasy that something terrible would happen to her and that he would save her. Sometimes she imagined that she would become sick and when she was close to death he would come to her deathbed and profess his love.

In general she wanted to be desired and surrounded by the most handsome and athletic boys. Her preoccupation with boys took a great deal of time and planning. It was reflected in her interest in clothes and cosmetics, and in her studied posture. By the time she was seventeen her whole person exuded provocative sensuality.

After graduating from high school she decided to become a model. Her career was short and unsuccessful because of her social ineptness. She was accused of being demanding, irritable, and overemotional. She became depressed for a while but "was saved" from her misery by an older man, a commercial artist, who fell in love with her. Eventually, however, the man found her difficult to relate to and terminated the relationship, accusing her of being unreliable, undisciplined, and unstable. She disregarded his criticism and pursued other relationships with men.

One of her disappointments with herself was her inability to hold a regular job for very long. The quality of the work, the hours, the tempo of working, the pettiness of co-workers, the freshness of her bosses all irritated her, and she was looking always for another job. Each new job, unfortunately, turned out to be not too different from the previous one. Under the influence of a friend she decided to pursue a theatrical career and started to take acting classes. She could identify with an acting career and for a while she was happy. She could justify not working at a regular job by defining herself as an actress. In order to support herself she became a waitress, hat-check girl, hostess, and so forth, stating emphatically that any sacrifice was justified in her struggle to become an actress; meanwhile, she was heavily subsidized by her lovers. In her acting career she never succeeded in getting beyond church plays. She was still reluctant to maintain a relationship with a man, however, because she was looking for someone young and rich to keep her in style.

Lucy finally felt that she had solved her problem when she met a rich young man to whom she felt attracted and who seemed to accept her unconditionally. It was difficult for her to realize that in reality he saw her as just a sexual companion; while his main preoccupation was with his mystical religious cult. In order to be accepted by him she decided to become a priestess of the cult. She was excited by this idea but afraid that the cult might harm her in some way. After her lover left for California to organize his cult, she became extremely depressed and reclusive. Dramatically she told everybody that life had lost all meaning; she refused to eat or even to get out of bed; she thought she would die. The old fantasy that her lover would come back to save her was revived. After two weeks of intensive attention from her friends and family (but lack of response from her lover) she became suicidal. When her lover failed to respond, she took a mild overdose of barbiturates. Her friends "saved her life." They found her in her apartment, drowsy after taking approximately five barbiturates. Afraid that she might attempt suicide again, her friends convinced her that her lover was callous, rude, and unreliable. She accepted this opinion totally and suddenly became hostile and vengeful toward him. She schemed for vengeance, wanting to destroy "this homosexual woman-hater." She thought of reporting him to the police for possession of marijuana and cocaine, or taking him to court and accusing him of raping her.

Her fantasies collapsed when he came to town unannounced and called her. He claimed to have been unaware of her efforts to contact him and laughed off her frenzied efforts to get him back. After a short interlude of renewed intimacy he left her as before, with vague promises of future contact. She continued to profess interest in him but now felt that he was getting "spaced out" by the use of drugs. Now she started to imagine herself as empowered by destiny with the noble cause of saving him from self-destruction. She was ready to go to California and valiantly overcome whatever obstacles might interfere with her mission of rescuing him. Although she had no knowledge of his whereabouts she felt confident that she could find him. This undertaking gave her a new direction in life. She felt that her sudden illumination gave a new meaning to her relationship with her estranged lover. The distinction between fact and fantasy become hopelessly blurred. She did not question her ability to redeem him and tried to appear undaunted in her intentions, while in fact she had no plan of action at all.

On closer scrutiny it was clear that the idea of this pursuit appealed to her more than its realization. She relished the sense of purpose it gave her, at the same time she hoped to be talked out of actually undertaking it. After a few sessions with the therapist she was ready to accept the futility of her mission. Now, with the same professed enthusiasm and conviction, she decided to direct her attention toward her relationship with her new lover.

Manipulative, suggestible, extremely emotional in her responses to men, with a low tolerance to frustration and an all-consuming need for recognition and attention—it was only normal for Lucy to go from crisis to crisis in the organization of her social and emotional life. Her difficulty resulted from her tendency to appraise reality from the narrow viewpoint of her immediate need for attention and acceptance from men. In the face of adverse events she resorted to infantile coping mechanisms based on wish-fulfilling fantasies. Her ability to think rationally collapsed and was replaced by the old magical mechanism of dealing with reality as learned in childhood. The sexual aspect of her behavior was her main modality of relating to the world. When this method of communication broke down, her world started to collapse as well, and then she took refuge in her fantasies of make-believe. This was her only way of dealing with overwhelming anxiety and depression.

DISSOCIATION AND MULTIPLE PERSONALITY

The wide gamut of hysterical reactions is not confined to histrionic behavior or conversion; in some cases it takes the form of altering the state of consciousness to the point that the individual changes his identity. Yet these conditions all represent different symptoms of the same basic mental pattern of response to the environment. The specific manifestations are determined by the degree of a given individual's tolerance to the stress he experiences and by the specific coping patterns embodied within his style of thinking. For instance, the dissociative reaction represents a disorganization of personality to the point that awareness of a stressful event is blotted out through a change in the state of consciousness. In this state there is loss of memory, either of a circumscribed span of time related to an unpleasant event or of a period when the individual discarded his true identity and assumed a fictional one. In both cases an altered state of consciousness is induced by a compelling need to deny either some event or deed from which the individual wishes to dissociate himself. In the case of multiple personality an individual can live two or more diverse lives under different names. Within each identity he denies the existence of the others. Change of identity is usually associated with the need to express suppressed desires that he cannot permit himself to fulfill within the context of his primary identity; he therefore "magically" transforms himself into someone different and believes that he is someone else when he satisfies these suppressed needs. This escape from reality into the world of another personality is typical of a childlike style of thinking wherein the boundaries between reality and fantasy are easily confounded and trespassed.

Consider the example of Carol, an attractive young college graduate who had been married for five years. She had been experiencing disturbing lapses of memory for the past two years. For instance, she would sometimes disappear from her home, only to find herself one to two days later in a hotel, wondering how she had gotten there. According to her husband, she would leave the apartment without notice and come back after one or more nights without explanation. She would have no memory of these absences. They usually occurred when her husband was out of town, on a business trip, or planning to come home very late. Her husband became alarmed and sought the advice of their family physician. After examining her and finding no abnormalities, he referred her to a neurologist for further testing and evaluation. The neurologist's findings were also negative; however, he placed her on anti-epileptic medication on a trial basis, on the theory that she might be suffering from psychomotor seizures. She did not respond to the medication, and she and her husband decided to consult a psychiatrist, on the advice of her physician.

The story of her condition was puzzling at first. She claimed to have been feeling perfectly well until the first episode, which came as a shock. She said that she had developed insomnia and had been taking sleeping pills for almost a year before the episode. Her insomnia was aggravated by the sporadic absences of her husband, who would go on business trips on short notice, leaving her alone. Further inquiry revealed that she was frustrated by his lack of attention to her and to her sexual needs in particular. In addition, her husband did not want her to go to work because he was afraid she would pay less attention to him if she did. Though she accepted this situation, she felt frustrated in her aspirations and relegated to the position of hostess and social showpiece.

During the lonely evenings when he was out of town, she developed a compulsive need to masturbate in order to satisfy her frustrations and to be able to go to sleep. Her fantasies were fed by sexual literature, which she read avidly, particularly that of a sadomasochistic nature. The sadomasochistic interaction was extremely stimulating to her. She could not explain why, for she had never had an experience of this nature, but the idea of being tied up and mildly hit appealed to her, stimulating her to the point of orgasm.

She described her husband as sexually detached, unimaginative, and clumsy; his unpassionate approach annoyed her so much that she had lost interest in having sex with him. She had started to avoid his sexual advances and had intercourse with him only when he became argumentative in his demands or totally withdrawn when she rejected him. He came to the conclusion that she was frigid.

In reality, she was attracted to men who were aggressive and well-built. She imagined having an affair with such a man; these thoughts aroused her to a real state of desire. Yet her upbringing, her moral background, did not permit her to take the steps that might lead to an affair. The conflict between her need for a satisfying sexual experience and the moral constraints against betraying her husband gradually became unbearable. Masturbation was not enough to satisfy her now-compelling desire for aggressive, even masochistic sex. Her frustration about resisting the desire for an affair was as excruciating as her anxiety while contemplating one.

In this state of mind, one evening she decided to go to a party alone because her husband was out of town. At the party she met one of her fantasy lovers, and he invited her out for dinner. All she remembered afterward was that she drank too much, flirted, and woke up the next morning in her apartment half-dressed. She was afraid to ask the man what had happened the night before. He himself was married and did not pursue the relationship.

One week later, while her husband was out of town, she left her apartment in the evening, only to find herself early the next morning checking out of a hotel. On being questioned by the desk clerk she said that she did not know how she had gotten there. It dawned on her that she might have suffered a blackout like one she had read about in a novel not long before.

She did not mention this incident to her husband until he confronted her at the time of another blackout, when he called her from out of town all night long and she had not answered the telephone. He insisted on an explanation. She told him about her blackouts.

At first the blackouts took place only when her husband was out of town; but after she told him about them, they began taking place when he was in town as well. He might come home late from work to discover that she had gone out without leaving any message about her whereabouts. When she would come home later, tired out, sometimes with bruises on her arms or legs, she could offer no information about what had happened to her. She was tired and wanted to go to sleep. Her husband was angry, baffled, and suspicious, but could do nothing.

Carol stated that the episodes always started with a sensation of feverish restlessness, a light dizziness, and a compelling need to walk. Afterward she did not remember anything. Under sodium amytal, however, her memory of these episodes came back, revealing an entire new dimension of her life. In the state of internal agitation she described as preceding each episode, a strong urge to experience masochistic sex would take over. After leaving home she would wander in the street, going into bars in the hopes of meeting a man who would satisfy her needs. During each of her episodes she would have sex with one or two men, always with the understanding that he was to tie her up and abuse her. Under these circumstances she could have an orgasm. Sometimes the sexual encounter would take place in a hotel, where she would check in under the assumed identity of a free-lance writer or an actress who was in town on business.

In her dissociative state of consciousness she was vaguely aware of her other, real identity, but at the time it appeared to her to belong to the past. It was as if she had once been married, had once lived in a different place during some blurred, almost-forgotten period. What was real for her was the sexual experience; everything else was blotted out. Fantasy became reality, consummated in the fervor of the sadomasochistic interaction, of the un-chained instinctual need that could not find an expression in the regular channels of sexual interaction with her husband. The frenzy of the moment, expressed by the harsh words and the brutal touch, dramatized by the tying of her hands and legs, gave meaning to her new identity. This was a total abandonment to her carnal pleasure, shutting out any self-control. It was a complete reversal of her other identity, controlled by moderation, concern for the opinion of others, and devotion to marital duties.

The conflict of her needs was obvious. Two different aspects of her personality were fighting to express themselves, each at the expense of the other. She was unable to accept or understand her sexual urges, and she considered the masochistic urges she had developed alien to herself. Whenever they surged to the surface, demanding gratification, she would feel a strange sensation in her body and mind, which she interpreted as the sign of a physical ailment. Finally, she would become her new personality, free to pursue sexual gratification and able to integrate her sexual drives into her real life.

In fact, she was enacting the fantasy she had actually read about, of a woman who changed her personality into a different one in order to have the freedom to do what she was unable to do otherwise. Carol's strong sexual feelings, combined with the power of the autosuggestion that she might suffer from the same condition as the woman she had read about, made the condition real for her. With a new identity she was not responsible for what she was doing; she could not even remember having done anything. Memories of the events were disconnected from the mainstream of her consciousness. The forbidden needs had found an acceptable expression: the anxiety-arousing situation was resolved magically by the sheer power of autosuggestion.

There have been many attempts to explain the mental mechanism that produces the dissociative state of consciousness. Pierre Janet thought that dissociation was a spontaneous phenomenon that occurred when a sudden lowering of psychological tension caused certain events to be dissociated from the conscious personality. According to Freud, dissociation is a solution to two opposing urges, one attempting to satisfy some sexual impulse, the other striving to repress it. Freud appears to have been on the right track initially, but the rest of his explanation relied on the universality of the Oedipus complex and on his concept of the unconscious. As such, it did little to further our understanding of the actual behavioral manifestation of the hysterical dissociative mechanism.

Two types of thinking processes are central to the dissociative state: first, the process of suggestion; second, the attitude of magical expectation. Both of these mechanisms are part of the prelogical stage of childish thinking. If a susceptibility toward these types of thinking is combined with a constitutional predisposition to high emotionalism and extroversion, the individual's response to a powerful, stressful situation may reach the level of dissociative reaction. This is a form of escape in which the functions of thinking are oriented to a prelogical level by the power of suggestion, making possible the fulfillment of hitherto controlled needs. The individual's perception of reality is progressively impaired, with the result that the distinction between reality and fantasy is obscured; cause-and-effect relationships are thereby transformed to meet the needs of the hysteric.

There are other forms of dissociative reaction, such as the state in which the individual doubts the reality of his personal identity. In such a case his consciousness is befogged and his feelings shift continually, while his perception of his surroundings fluctuates between reality and fantasy. In other, milder, forms of dissociation of consciousness, like automatic writing or speech, or somnambulism, only a discrete system of ideas becomes detached from the mainstream of consciousness, functioning at the periphery of the consciousness yet independent of it. The main portion of the consciousness is not aware of what is going on in this marginal area of activity.

An insight into the mechanism of this mild dissociated state is offered by the observations of Milton H. Erickson and Aldous Huxley about what they called *deep-reflection state*. In this state Huxley was able to pursue two different activities in the same period of time and be totally unaware of them. Erickson explained this as the result of an intense state of concentration that made Huxley oblivious to external reality yet able to respond to stimuli from it.

These various altered states of consciousness, though they have a common neurophysiological mechanism, are triggered by a variety of psychological conditions not all of which are hysterical in nature. For instance, the hypnotic trance and the mystic experience are both dissociated states of consciousness produced by suggestion or autosuggestion, but they appear in a context quite different from that of the hysterical experience.

. What distinguishes hysterical dissociation is that it is a special state of alteration of consciousness operating beyond the control of the individual and allowing the expression of suppressed parts of his personality. It is an attempt to adapt to an undesirable situation by a kind of self-hypnosis that has no rational or controlling elements. When hypnosis is used to treat hysterics, it involves the induction of an altered state in order to replace another altered state of consciousness induced by the subject himself.

8

THE THINKING
PROCESSES
IN SEXUAL DEVIATION

To return the word to the flesh, to make knowledge carnal
again: not by deduction but immediate by perception or
sense at once: the bodily senses.
　　　—WILLIAM BLAKE, *Annotations to Berkeley's "Siris"*

SEXUAL DYSFUNCTION

The expression of sexual behavior obviously has an emotional component,
but it actually is a complex process in which the individual's thought processes and concept of self play major roles.

As previously discussed, Freud was convinced that the entire development of personality was based on infantile psychosexual development.
He believed that each stage in a child's psychological growth was determined
by the way the child resolved each sexual conflict he experienced. For Freud,
it was this libidinal energy that controlled the child's development, and
fixation at either the oral, anal, or genital level determined the type of
neurotic conflict he would face as an adult. In this way Freud formulated the
law of *psychic determinism* caused by the unconscious repression of childhood
sexual conflict. Psychic determinism became highly controversial because
researchers were unable to develop the means to test its validity. But even so,
a new approach to understanding the psychological life of the individual
emerged from it, becoming a basic tenet of modern psychology: the fact that
there was continuity in the mental life of the individual from childhood to
adulthood to which we should add now that the specific patterns of adult
thinking are rooted in childhood thinking.

This principle holds true in the formation of sexual behavior more than in any other area of human psychology. The development of most deviant sexual behavior is triggered by association with a particular individual or object presented intentionally or accidentally at a critical period of a child's rudimentary sexual development. This individual or object then becomes a source of sexual arousal that induces the need for immediate physical gratification. The binding of the child's mental representation of this individual or object with his expression of sexuality is reinforced if the child, and later the adult, finds that sexual gratification is continually derived from the use of the particular association.

There is general agreement that most sexual dysfunctions are produced by the assignment of sexual importance to a particular experience; yet various schools of thought have remarkably different views on how to identify their specific psychological cause.

If the child, in interaction with his family, friends, and others, develops a misconception about his sexual role and sexual identity, this often is reflected in his later sexual behavior on the most basic level of sexual dysfunction. It may be these misconceptions that affect the individual's performance in adulthood. Various dysfunctions of erection or ejaculation in men, or of orgasm in women, are related to a faulty conceptualization of the sexual relationship or to the individual's unrealistic sexual expectations.

If a young man, for instance, has developed a sense of sexual inferiority or doubt about his ability to interact sexually with a woman, these feelings may affect his performance. His feelings of sexual inferiority may inhibit him from freely expressing his emotions or physically relating to his partner, and these are important aspects of arousal. The sexual act, if it comes to pass at all, is likely to be permeated with an anxiety that may disrupt or ruin his performance.

The inability to attain or sustain an erection or premature ejaculation are dysfunctions arising from the male's sense of sexual inferiority and/or misguided conceptions about sexual functions and intercourse. Preconceived ideas often exist in such individuals, attitudes toward the body, an inferior sexual image that makes him feel inadequate and unattractive, or even a general discomfort with sex itself, seen as dirty and animallike, a cause of guilt.

An inferior sexual image is formulated gradually during an individual's development and is often a mixture of misinterpreted facts and infantile experiences related to sex. If uncorrected, particularly in introverted boys who have difficulty initiating sexual relationships, these misconceptions may reinforce the fear of rejection and the inability to perform sexually. They may produce such a high level of anxiety that even when the individual is faced with a willing partner, any attempt at normal performance is sabotaged.

Another problem, that of sexual guilt, is basically the inability to integrate sex into the total framework of the personality. Men, for example, may operate with the concept of sexual women and nonsexual women, and equate this to bad women and good women. This is often a remnant of the incest taboo, instilled in a boy in childhood in relation to his mother and transferred later on to all women. If in the child's family, sexual expression is suppressed, a sense of guilt may come to be associated with sex, even when it is secretly enjoyed. The more moralistic and unable to express love the parents are, the more difficulty the child will have in handling a sexual relationship later. One way or another, the result is often sexual conflict in the young man. Biologically, he is ready to express his sexual impulses; psychologically, he is handicapped by his misinterpretation of sex and of his sexual role. Unable to accept his own sexuality, uncertain of his ability to satisfy his partner, he projects anxiety into the situation. This affects his performance, which becomes the basis for a new experience and begins to set a pattern of attitudes and beliefs.

In psychological terms, the individual's inability to attain erection results from the blocking of arousal by anxiety. Inability to sustain erection and premature ejaculation are caused by the same anxiety acting at different phases of sexual excitement and intercourse. The almost certain result—negative conditioning to the sexual act—projects further anxiety into future experiences. The pattern of sexual dysfunction, once established, is reinforced by every new anxiety projected onto the sexual act.

In a woman, sexual performance may be affected by a feeling of sexual unattractiveness or inadequacy that may make her less responsive to sexual gratification and less able to achieve orgasm. By the same token, any guilt she may have developed at the prelogical level of understanding sexual relationships may induce anxiety to such a degree that it will interfere with her ability to function sexually. The problem is complicated by the fact that biologically only approximately 30 percent of all women achieve orgasm by penetration alone, without extensive foreplay and clitoral manipulation. The inability to achieve orgasm makes some women feel sexually inadequate and is further inhibitive.

CHILDHOOD SOURCES OF DEVIANT SEXUALITY

Childhood sexual experiences, misconceptions, and attitudes may become integrated into the child's concept of sexuality, however, if, as a young adult, he learns about and better understands the dynamics and mechanics of sexuality, then why is the adult sometimes unable to free himself from his childhood sexual misconceptions? Apparently, once arousal has been triggered or inhibited in a particular way, the individual becomes easily conditioned to it and has great difficulty freeing himself from it. When a particular arousal leads to gratification, the positive reinforcement precludes other normal forms of sexual expression. When arousal is inhibited by anticipatory anxiety, any attempt at normal performance is affected.

Certainly the majority of sexual deviations or dysfunctions are not based on just one isolated experience that triggers and distorts the entire organization of sexuality. Rather the experience itself is perceived within the context of the child's relationship to others, his personality makeup, his degree of neuroticism, the development of his relations with others and with society—within the framework of a whole range of factors. This explains why, although a group of children may undergo the same homosexual or even sadomasochistic experiences, only a small number of them remain firmly established in these patterns.

The crucial period for the crystallization of sexual orientation and identity is adolescence, when the socialization process, with its norms and values, becomes gradually integrated into personality needs. In this stormy and stressful period of adjustment to social reality, an important element is the emergence of mature sexuality, with its conflicting problems of expression. The sexual adjustment of the individual, the choice of sexual role and expression, will be largely determined by the makeup of the child's preexisting pattern of latent sexuality.

It is important to emphasize that any premature interference with the maturation of sexual instinct can affect its adult manifestations. Such interference can lead to any one or any combination of these forms of maladapted sexual expression: replacing the sexual act with a partner by the symbolic representation of an object that triggers the sexual arousal, resulting in fetishism; altering the direction of the sexual identity from heterosexuality to homosexuality or bisexuality; or identifying with the opposite sex only by dressing in its clothes in order to achieve the arousal necessary for sexual gratification with or without a partner. All these forms of sexual expression can combine with pain/punishment activity, which itself has symbolic meaning in the process of sexual gratification.

A common denominator of all these types of sexual behavior is the element of fantasy, which magically changes reality according to the individual's need to replace the partner with a symbolic image or to deny his own sexual identity. The second common aspect of all these sexual behaviors is their fetishlike quality. In this context fetishism is the vehicle that permits sexual gratification through a symbolic substitute for the partner or as an added stimulant to the sexual performance.

FETISHISM

In various degrees, all men and women operate sexually with a degree of fetishism. For instance, any part of a woman's anatomy or clothing that becomes a constant source of sexual arousal for a man takes on a fetishistic quality. Fashion, by emphasizing a specific part of the body, attempts to focus erotic interest as a source of sexual arousal. This, of course, is not considered pathological because it is not a substitute for sexual intercourse. Fetishism becomes a sexual deviation only when an object connected with a person or a particular action performed by a person is used for arousal to the point of bringing sexual gratification. The fetishist's attraction to the object is based on a particular type of thinking developed in relationship to sexual activity. In his thinking the fetishist endows the object of his sexual fascination with the magical quality of representing a sexual partner. Many explanations have been offered for this type of sexual behavior.

Psychoanalysts believe that male fetishism is caused by regression to an infantile sexual level, which is seen as a defense against the male's fear of castration. In this sense most male fetishes are said to represent symbols of a penis possessed by a woman, reassuring the fetishist that "women have penises too" and alleviating his fear of castration. Fascinating explanations have been elaborated in an attempt to interpret each specific type of fetish, from women's shoes to braids of hair; yet most of them lack scientific clarity, are contradictory and unconvincing. Furthermore, no explanation has been given for fetishes in homosexuals.

At the other end of the spectrum the behaviorists consider fetishism a deviant sexual behavior learned in response to a particular situation. They have shown that the fetish response can be replicated by simply conditioning the individual to associate, for example, an object identified with femininity and a picture of an attractive nude woman.

These differences in conceptualizing the nature of fetishism lead to such diametrically opposite therapeutic approaches as psychoanalysis and aversion therapy. The goal of psychoanalysis is to explain deviant sexual behavior within the context of a patient's repressed pregenital or genital conflict. Behaviorists, on the other hand, treat the deviant symptom by aversion therapy, independent of one's concept of sexuality or ability to interact emotionally with the opposite sex.

The fetishist's symbolization of the sexual act results in distorted concept of sexual interaction with a person, generally a woman, who is reduced to one eroticized object, body part, or act that arouses the same sexual feelings as the whole person. It is extremely difficult for the fetishist to achieve erection in response to the real body of a person. Usually any attempt at intercourse produces anxiety, unless accompanied by the fetish object. But therapists often confuse this anxiety, aroused by the fear of impotence, with an alleged anxiety hypothesized as related to the unconscious fear of castration. When the myth of castration anxiety is accepted by the patient, it only reinforces his sexual failures with woman.

In order to understand the origin and development of fetishism we have to go back to childhood, when the power of magical thinking could change reality according to the child's needs. The fetish, established as a sexual stimulus in early childhood, when the child does not have a clear notion of sexual intercourse, is maintained by the power of magical thinking and reinforced by the sexual gratification accompanying it. The reliance on masturbatory activity in adulthood is based on an individual's sense of sexual inadequacy or fear of impotence when faced with an actual partner in true sexual interaction. An example will illustrate this point.

Jan, a forty-year-old engineer, married and the father of two children, sought professional help because his wife had threatened to divorce him. His case is an example of a classic fetish and of the pitfalls of misguided treatment. The reason for his wife's dissatisfaction was his lack of sexual and emotional interest in her, which had become progressively worse during the six years of their marriage. According to Jan, this was the result of his compulsive need to masturbate. Gradually he lost all desire for her. Finally, at home in the evening after dinner, he retreated to his study three to four times a week, reading, working on drafts, and secretly masturbating.

This need to masturbate was triggered by thinking about or looking at women's long fingernails—in pictures, in magazines or real fingernails seen on women's hands. The sight of long, red, polished fingernails instantly induced a state of excitement, which he described as a sensation of feverishness, slight dizziness, and staring to the point of fixation. He would become restless and unable to concentrate seriously on whatever he was doing, and this could be relieved only by self-gratification. If he did not have the opportunity to admire fingernails for several days, the need to see them would become obsessive. Then he would lock himself in his study and look at nail advertisements in women's magazines while masturbating. Always after indulging in this sexual fantasy, Jan would become depressed, morose, and guilt-ridden, but this only made him even more detached and uninterested in his wife. He felt helplessly controlled by this fetish, and the problem appeared insoluble to him, which increased his despair and depression.

In order to understand Jan's condition it is necessary to examine the history of his psychosexual development. As the younger of two children he had been brought up in a highly moralistic home in which the Protestant ethic prevailed. He had rarely seen any expression of love between his parents. He had spent most of his time with his sister who was two years older. He had become aware of the physical differences between the sexes around the age of four or five. He had played doctor with his sister and was quite familiar with her sexual anatomy, and he accepted without anxiety the fact that boys were physically different from girls.

Between the ages of five and eleven his childhood was uneventful from the point of view of sexual development, except for one incident when some boys attempted unsuccessfully to convince him to masturbate with them. He was more interested in playing baseball than in any type of sexual activity.

After the age of eleven he started to change physically rapidly. By twelve he had become interested in girls, particularly his sister's friends. He felt shy, awkward, and unable to approach them for dates, although previously he had felt perfectly comfortable with them. Around this time he experienced his first erection. It was accompanied by pleasant sensations and related spontaneously to thoughts about a particular girl. He also had his first nocturnal emissions. He knew the meaning of these sexual responses from his friends. But in retrospect that time appeared to him to be one of great sexual preoccupation and turmoil. He recalled spending hours fantasizing about being close to girls. After reading some sexually oriented books he would become aroused to the point of fondling himself and ejaculating spontaneously. By thirteen he attempted to date one of his sister's friends, but she laughed off his awkward verbal advances.

It was during this period, he vividly remembered, that he was invited to the country to spend the weekend at the home of a friend of the family. There he became very friendly with a girl who was approximately eighteen. She was teaching him how to ride a horse when, to his embrarrassment, he experienced an erection. She said that the only way to be able to ride was to relieve himself by masturbation, and she proceeded to unzip his pants and took out his penis. As she fondled him, she told him that he was already a man, and he ejaculated while looking at her beautiful, slim hand with its long, red, polished fingernails as it moved delicately up and down the shaft of his penis. He closed his eyes in ecstasy, overwhelmed by the orgasm. That experience was repeated later on a few times, until she left for college.

The memories remained with him. Again and again he replayed in his mind the events of that summer, always with the same excitement and need for self-gratification. Many times he later attempted to re-create the same atmosphere with another girl (always one who had long, polished fingernails). Sex for him became equated with this one form of sexual activity with no need for intercourse.

Jan dated very few women and married at the age of thirty-four, mainly because his future wife had pursued him. He hoped that her presence might stop him from engaging in his solitary sexual activity, because his fetish made him feel less of a man. He doubted whether he would be able to have intercourse with her but overcame his anxiety, largely because of her patience. At first he felt elated about overcoming his sexual difficulties, but he gradually lost interest in sexual intercourse and returned to his fetishistic activities. His wife became less patient with his sexual failures with her, and with his lack of desire to do something about them. Jan himself blamed the situation on his being overworked. Finally his wife gave him an ultimatum: if he did not seek therapy, she would divorce him.

He went into psychoanalytic therapy for about two years, but his fetishism remained overwhelming. The interpretation offered by his therapist did not make much sense to him. Jan just could not see why he was supposed to be afraid of castration, why he would deny that a woman has a vagina, why the long, red, polished fingernails of a woman represented to him "her penis." He left therapy; without the buffering effect of therapy his wife's hopes for his sexual improvement dimmed. Soon she lost all patience with him. When the pressure at home became unbearable, he finally decided to try a different therapeutic method.

In his second attempt at therapy, Jan finally admitted that his motivation to change was weak. He could not imagine any form of sexual pleasure to replace that which he was getting from his fantasies and masturbation. This attitude appeared to be the key problem in his inability to change. The fetishistic gratification meant more to him than mere masturbatory activity: it represented a concept of sex in which the woman was reduced to her nails, or even denied altogether.

As his sexual behavior became set on fetishistic activity, he had never developed a clear idea of the role of the woman in that context of sexuality. In puberty he understood sexual gratification only in terms of childishly mechanical masturbatory activity, which was then confirmed by the summer experience with the girl. Later, his concept of sex with a woman was somewhat modified: arousal was still triggered by the fantasy of long, polished fingernails but was supposed to be followed by intercourse without any emotional expression. Hence his problems with his wife. His preferred form of sexuality remained basically masturbation by a "fantasy woman" with long, red, polished fingernails.

In order to change he had to develop a sense of the emotional significance of the woman in the intimacy of sexual interaction. The magic of the fetishistic object, the fingernails, had to be transferred to the magic of love, in which body and mind are fused and immersed in the total expression of sexual abandonment and mutual gratification.

EXHIBITIONISM

Magical thinking is also the key to understanding another sexual deviation: exhibitionism or indecent exposure. According to psychoanalysts, exhibitionism is an attempt to deny the fear of castration by displaying the genitals to a girl or woman. The basis tenet of this theory is that the exhibitionist is afraid of normal sexual activity because of the danger of castration. This fear is relieved by his exhibitionist activity, which reassures him against such a threat. It is also asserted that he fantasizes that the woman will herself exhibit a penis. Behaviorists, on the other hand, explain exhibitionism as a simple learned behavior for sexual gratification. There is an element of truth in the behavioristic approach, but the problem is more complex.

Let us take the example of a twenty-year-old male immigrant to the U.S., Will, arrested for the second time because he exhibited himself to several women. The first time he was arrested (a woman complained to the police that he exhibited himself while she was waiting for a subway) he accepted responsibility for the act, received a suspended sentence, and believed that he would stop his exhibitionistic activity. Yet he found himself compelled to repeat it and was caught again. This time he was sent for psychiatric treatment.

He had started this behavior at around the age of fifteen under peculiar circumstances. One day, while basking in the sun on a beach, he became sexually aroused, and as nobody was in the vicinity he started to fondle himself. Then, to his embarrassment, he noticed that a young woman was watching him from behind some rocks. She appeared to be looking at him in surprise and shock. He ejaculated instantly, experiencing pleasure more intense than he had in the past, when masturbating alone. He recalled that the expression on her face, that of surprise and shock, excited him tremendously. He felt that he was a real man to be able to create in her that state of mind.

The next year Will's family emigrated to the United States. He had difficulty with the language, difficulty in school, difficulty making friends. He became more shy and inhibited than before, more withdrawn in his own activities. He was unable to meet American girls because of his difficulty with English, and he did not know any girls his age who spoke his language. He satisfied his sexual needs by masturbation, for the most part, and sometimes he went to cheap brothels. Yet whenever he felt depressed, he had an urge to expose himself, because this had made him feel strong, like a real man who could obtain recognition from a woman. He believed that women were excited by the sight of his erect penis and that only false modesty made them appear disgusted. In fact, he thought that the more surprised or shocked the woman appeared to be, the more she enjoyed seeing his penis. Simultaneously, he considered the exposure of his penis an act of courage and defiance: he was daring to make "direct contact" with the girl, disregarding the socially acceptable approaches of emotional interaction. He had difficulty understanding all the commotion made about exposure when he knew from talking to other boys and from his previous experiences that "girls enjoy looking at the penises of boys."

In further discussions Will admitted that when masturbating alone he enjoyed looking at his penis in erection because it made him feel manly. Sometimes he looked in the mirror with a sense of satisfaction at his display of manhood. He was proud of his genitals, which he thought impressive in size. He had heard from other boys that women like men to have large genitals, and he believed that their display produced a favorable impression.

Statements of this type tend to be interpreted by most therapists as rationalizations of insecurity. The man who exhibits his genitals to a woman is attempting to produce a response that will reassure him of his manhood. Though this is partly true, there has always been a tendency for males to attract attention to their genitals as a sign of their virility and strength. In ancient Pompeii, penises were displayed as statues on frontispieces of homes. In the Middle Ages men used to wear codpieces in order to catch the eyes of women. Men's breeches were embroidered for the same reason that in our day tight jeans are made in such a manner as to clearly display the contours of the male sex organs.

Though women sometimes exhibit their bodies, this does not usually have the same offensive connotation in our society, because breasts or thighs represent only secondarily sexual points of attraction. Yet both sexes are in different ways competing for sexual attention by a more or less discreet display of their sexual attributes. In the ethological evolution of courtship and sexual interaction in primates, we find sufficient evidence that sexual display is an initial part of the sexual relationship. In fact, it is known that most boys display their genitals to each other in order to prove their male qualities, and that most men take narcissistic pride in the size of their sex organs.

Thus it is understandable that a young man might project his feelings about his sex organs onto a young woman, assuming that she will have the same reaction to them as he does and hoping that she will appreciate his manhood as he does. The gratification he may receive through masturbation reinforces the pleasure he derives from reaffirming his masculinity. Unfortunately, displaying his masculinity in this way will only bring a sense of inadequacy resulting from social disapproval, but his aim is achieved in any case because he believes that the woman's negative response actually represents approval. He finds it hard to believe that most women are aroused sexually mainly by tactile sensations. He does not realize, either, that women tend to equate the male's exposure of his sex organ with the intention of rape, thus becoming frightened.

Sometimes a "normal" man turns to exhibitionistic behavior when rejected by his girl friend or wife. Magically he tries to regain his self-esteem and sense of masculinity. The penis represents the highly prized key to the woman's attention and the ultimate symbol of his masculinity. Essentially, the exhibitionist carries childhood patterns of sexual behavior into the adult world, where social restrictions do not permit this type of display. This suggests that some exhibitionistic tendencies are an intrinsic part of sexual behavior, that they are deeply rooted in the relationship between the sexes as a survival of primitive sexual communication. Some men, because they have no other symbol of masculinity to expose except their genitals, are unable to accept the socialization of this impulse and remain within the infantile pattern of exhibitionism. In general, in a more sophisticated manner, the display of success, power, big cars, wealth, or excellence in sports is also interpreted as an expression of the need to attract the attention of beautiful women. This indicates that at the heart of all sexualized symbols there is the same instinctual drive.

TRANSVESTISM

The cognitive distortion of sexual identity appears even more clearly in transvestism. This fascinating example of prelogical thinking magically transforms a man into a woman, and vice versa, by the power of wish-fulfilling fantasy. According to classical psychoanalytic theory, the transvestite has overcome his castration anxiety by assuming that some women do have penises and identifying himself with that woman who possesses a penis. A male transvestite may be strictly heterosexual, wearing women's clothes or undergarments to produce sexual arousal followed by masturbation or to have sex with a woman. Other male transvestites dress as women and have sex with men. According to psychoanalysts. the transvestite homosexual identifies himself with his mother by "becoming a woman." Their explanation for the female transvestite is confusing: it is said to be an attempt to give to other women the illusion that she, the transvestite, *is* a male and has a penis.

It is important to note that psychoanalysts agree that in cases of both male and female transvestism there is a game of make-believe. Yet they fail to explain the whole process in its cognitive dynamics. There are two levels of this dynamics: fetishistic stimulation by the clothes of the opposite sex, and that of the belief that then a person can be magically transformed into someone of the opposite sex. To put it simply, the transvestite has a sexual relationship with the clothes of the opposite sex instead of with a person of the opposite sex.

Some transvestites identify totally with the opposite sex, and as such would like to have a sexual relationship with a member of the same sex. In a magical transformation of himself a man becomes a woman, and as such falls in love with a man. This applies as well to a transvestite woman who would like to think of herself as a man.

Finally, for some transvestites the need to identify with the new role becomes so overwhelming that they become obsessed with the need to change their gender through surgery. This need raises important theoretical questions about the cause of transvestism. The desire of an individual who has functioned as a male to change his sexual identity through surgical removal of his sexual organs calls into question the whole Freudian idea that fear of castration was what caused him to try to become a woman in the first place. In fact, the taking of female hormones prior to sexual surgery results in atrophy of the penis itself, which is a form of castration. Therefore, castration anxiety as the unconscious motivation for becoming a transvestite appears to be a simplistic explanation at best.

Behaviorists attribute the development of transvestism to a deviant learned behavior that occurs in a critical period of psychosexual development, fixating the individual on this particular sexual approach. There is undoubtedly a great deal of truth in this interpretation, but it does not explain why the individual, faced with undeniable evidence that he is a male, can deny it simply by dressing as a female.

To understand the male transvestite, we must explore the correlation between his thinking and his psychosexual development at the time this transformation of sexual identity starts to shape up.

The classic description of boys dressed up as girls by their mother when they are very young explains the transvestite orientation only for a small group. These transvestites, beginning at the ages of three or four, were dressed as girls by their mothers or by other women in charge of their rearing who are most often man-haters. Such women may also be marginal psychotics with a consuming need to humiliate and abuse men. The birth of a male child causes a conflict between the maternal instinct and the hatred and contempt they feel for the male sex. This conflict is resolved by raising the child as a girl. In this way the mother can show love, attention, and acceptance. The boy, when he becomes aware of the dissonance between his gender-identity and his sexual/social role, chooses the latter because he feels comfortable with it and receives the reward of acceptance and love from the mother. Most often he thinks of himself as female, he thinks like a woman and later in life he seeks the protection of a male, with whom he is a passive partner. By and large such individuals become homosexual transvestites. However, some of them succeed in reversing this trend if helped by external forces like school and peers. In adulthood, however, such an individual may be able to relate sexually only to a domineering, or even abusive and sadistic, woman, who reminds him in some ways of his mother. The only attempt to dominate this woman may take place in bed, when he relates to her sexually as a man. Yet his need to dress as a woman may persist as part of his past experience in cross-dressing.

In other cases imitation of the female is more subtle. The mother may begin feminizing the boy at two to three years of age through extremely close interaction. The boy wears her clothes and imitates her behavior as the only model of identity available to him. The mother is extremely permissive, accepting his continual companionship and his imitation of her behavior. She permits him to wear her clothes or may actually later on buy him girls' clothes, never encouraging him to dress and behave as a boy. He identifies with his mother, wants to be like her; he entertains the fantasy of being a woman. Generally in these cases the mother wants him to be a girl because of her ambivalent feelings toward men. In this case gender-identity is changed by a long learning process that, because of the emotional significance of the mother-child relationship, has a binding effect and becomes integrated as a style of life that is unaffected by the normal changes that take place in puberty and adulthood. The individual does not see himself as a boy because masculine behavior has been suppressed to please the mother. He does not need to overcome any fear of castration because he does not like his genitals— he would prefer to be a woman. He too may become a transvestite homosexual.

Sometimes the mother or other older female seduces a boy into feminine dressing by walking around the house semiclothed wearing only bra and panties or by leaving her undergarments lying around. The boy who is around puberty and is already very close to his mother is tempted to try on her clothes, which represent a mystery to him. The texture, the smell, the intimacy that the clothes have with his mother make them desirable things to wear. This is the beginning of the process of identifying with the mother that results in his wanting to be a woman. Because of the simultaneous sexual gratification he derives from these garments by reflex triggering of his sexual response accompanied by masturbation, he becomes fetishistically oriented to female undergarments. In adulthood he is able to relate sexually to women, but the desire to dress in female undergarments remains with him.

Sometimes there can be further changes in the male role. If the individual becomes involved with a woman who, because of latent lesbianism, has an extreme need to make a man dependent on her, she may encourage him to dress as a woman. It may have started as a joke after his confession or her discovery that he uses her undergarments to masturbate. She appears understanding, helpful, and excited to see him dress as a woman, and for a while they have intercourse in this manner. But soon their relationship starts to change: she begins to treat him as though he were a woman. This usually leads to a gradual deterioration of their interaction. In fact, most women have difficulty accepting his pseudomasculinity. Men, on the other hand, become progressively ambivalent about a passive sexual role with a woman and tend to look to other men for acceptance of their feminity.

For example, Tom, a thirty-two-year-old investment lawyer, sought therapy because, among other things, he had difficulty performing sexually with women. His sexual activity was largely restricted to masturbatory fantasies associated with having intercourse with a woman while he was partially dressed as a woman. His obvious difficulty was his embarrassment at actually dressing in women's undergarments while relating to a real woman sexually. At the beginning of a relationship he was able to get aroused only if he could wear women's panties before sexual intercourse. Most of the time he was unable to consummate the act because he lost his erection unless he was wearing, seeing, or fondling the panties. He was only able to perform well sexually when actually wearing the panties and bra of a woman.

According to him, his difficulties had started at the age of twelve, when he became excited, for no apparent reason, at the sight of the panties of his sister (who was four years older than himself) thrown carelessly on a chair. He put them on and experienced an erection instantly. Touching his penis through the panties gave him indescribable sensations. Afterward he stole her underwear a few times until he was caught by her. As his sister was very fond of him, she did not scold him but laughed it off. He had always admired his sister for her beauty, intelligence, competence, and social poise. Wearing her panties, and later her bra and stockings or pantyhose, gave him a special feeling of closeness that made him extremely sexually aroused.

Upon deeper reflection he recalled that ever since he could remember he had been intrigued and emotionally aroused by feminine clothes because they smelled so wonderfully of perfume and were so pleasant to touch. In some ways they reminded him of his childhood closeness to his mother, of sitting in her lap or being embraced by her. Gradually, after the experience with his sister's panties and bra, the desire for feminine undergarments, particularly those that had been worn, became overwhelming.

Tom started to date girls by the age of seventeen and was aroused by the fragrance of their perfume or the touch of their panties. At twenty-six he met a woman who felt emancipated enough to accept his need to dress in women's undergarments while having sexual intercourse. Soon he started to enjoy wearing her undergarments daily, underneath his suit. The relationship between them was extremely pleasant, particularly because of their mutual compliance with each other's needs. She herself preferred mutual masturbatory activity combined with cunnilingus to actual sexual intercourse. With her support, advice, and encouragement, his need to present himself as a woman grew stronger, resulting in his wearing feminine jeans, blouses, and undergarments around the house. It culminated when she suggested, while making love, that they each use a dildo for anal intercourse. The new level of interaction gave both of them a great sense of intimacy, until she started to get bored and refused to participate in these types of games. Soon she became dissatisfied to the point of calling him a "faggot," began to be unfaithful, and finally left him. The whole affair lasted for over three years and left an indelible mark on his future sexual expression.

Though Tom was professionally successful and as such able to find new women, none of them except paid prostitutes was ready to go through this travesty of sex with him. At the same time, his need to reconstruct the experience with his previous lover became obsessional. He even started to buy from prostitutes soiled panties and bras, which he would carefully perfume and wear around his apartment while masturbating to exhaustion. Yet at the same time, in his daily interaction with people in his business life, he appeared normally masculine, direct, and competent.

At the time he came for therapy he was courting a woman whose self-esteem had been damaged by a previous marriage, but who was showing real interest in him. Yet Tom was extremely embarrassed and afraid to attempt to start a sexual interaction with her without the use of at least disguised feminine undergarments. His anxiety at the thought of losing her company, however, was even greater. Interestingly enough, though he wanted her as a woman, he would fantasize about himself sexually as a man disguised as a woman. Under these conditions he felt capable of enjoying her sexually. For Tom the wearing of female undergarments was part of experiencing his sexuality, part of the idea of sexual interaction with women that he had become conditioned to from his earliest experiences of sexual excitement.

However, Tom was never actually confused about his own gender-identity. It has traditionally been thought that there is a clear distinction in perception of gender-identity between men who were cross-dressed at a very early age and those who began later on. It has been accepted that the late cross-dressers are more damaged in their sense of masculinity because of an already established social organization at the core of their male identity; in children who are cross-dressed in their early years gender-identity has not yet been established. Though correct in general terms, this theoretical formulation does not necessarily apply when cross-dressing started late in adolescence but was always seen in pure fetishistic terms, without true identification with the opposite sex.

This distinction demonstrates that the individual is affected in the formulation of his sexual identity according to the level of development of his cognitive processes. If a very young boy wears feminine clothing, then he may at the time become totally identified with the feminine model and may consider himself a woman. But if later he sees the dissonance between feminine clothing and his anatomical sexual identity in comparison with other males, he will most likely attempt to reconcile this conflict according to his level of sexual understanding and perception. For a child the conflict can be solved magically by juxtaposing his thinking about male and female characteristics, leading him to believe he is a special type of person: a phallic woman. Later this approach becomes untenable because of a different level of organizational thinking that has less tolerance for magical associations and dualities that have not already been built into the individual's thinking. In adulthood, an individual must attempt to resolve the conflict to some degree by accepting his feminine needs: either he becomes a transvestite homosexual or he decides to undergo sexual surgery in order to change his gender-identity totally. Tom, however, since he had started to cross-dress later and needed feminine identification only for arousal had maintained the core of his masculine identity, in therapy he worked toward developing a mature approach to his male sexuality.

In other cases of transvestism the sexual role can become more confused as illustrated by this man. Ken, a man in his late twenties, sought therapy because of the conflict created by the antagonistic needs of married life and transvestism. Though his wife accepted and cooperated in his cross-dressing, gradually he came to feel drawn to relationships with men, and this was threatening his marriage.

Artistically oriented and somewhat effeminate, Ken had dressed as a girl for as long as he could remember. His mother, a gentle, soft, seductive woman, laughed it off, if not approved, when he started to wear her shoes, panties, or blouses. She felt that he was cute and was just showing his love for her. Up to the age of six he could easily have passed for a girl. In fact, he played with girls, with whom he felt more comfortable than he did with boys; he found them too rough and unruly. Though by now he was aware of being a boy dressed up as a girl, he enjoyed it. When he went to kindergarten he almost had a tantrum because he had to cut his hair short and dress as a boy. He went to school dressed as a boy only after his mother reassured him that at home he could still dress as a girl. Gradually his mother stopped buying him dresses, but he continued to wear some of her clothing.

Afraid of being ridiculed by other boys, who were calling him "sissy," he started to play sports with them and got tougher, learning to fight and swear. However, his fondness for dresses did not totally disappear—he still fantasized about dressing as a woman at times. Around ten years of age he started to steal feminine lingerie from department stores and to wear it. At one time while he played doctor with a girl living nearby, he put on her panties. He experienced a spontaneous erection and masturbated while the girl watched him. By the age of thirteen he began buying feminine clothes with the money he made from odd jobs. He remembered the thrill he had experienced: to look at himself dressed as a woman was exciting enough to bring on erection and orgasm. From then on he dressed as a boy when he went out in public and as a girl when he was alone in his room and nobody could see him. Though his mother knew about this she ignored his cross-dressing as an eccentricity and a sign of his closeness to her. Otherwise, he was a studious student, sports oriented, friendly with boys but not yet interested in dating.

At eighteen, while working at a summer job, he met an older woman who started a sexual relationship with him. Sex with a woman he found pleasant but less exciting than when he was masturbating dressed as a woman. However, he enjoyed the sense of manhood he derived from being wanted by and having sex with a woman. At the same time the drive for the sexual stimulation derived from dressing as a woman became stronger. During the affair with this woman he attempted to wear her clothes a few times, but her disapproval made him stop. When he was alone, however, he still dressed as a woman and in fact adopted some of her style. Finally Ken started to go out at night dressed as a woman, and to his pleasant surprise men accosted him and asked him for dates. His excitement was so intense after the first such experience that he went home and masturbated in a state of euphoria. After a few sorties like this he accepted a man's invitation to have a drink together, though the man, he knew, realized that he was not a woman. Ken was very excited by their sexually charged interaction in the bar and went home with the man, who performed fellatio on him. According to him, after this homosexual experience he became so upset that he decided to relate strictly to women in the future Yet the need to be admired and wanted by men did not disappear. From time to time he would still flirt with men while dressed as a woman.

At the age of twenty-three Ken met a woman four years older than himself who took a keen interest in him and whom he married. Like his mother, she was tender, sweet, and tolerant of his cross-dressing. As an expression of her love for him, she started to help him dress as a woman with more sophistication and elegance. In fact, she enjoyed having sexual intercourse with him after seeing him in feminine clothes. According to him, both of them sometimes took walks dressed as women, laughing when men tried to date them. They came home excited and had sex together. Yet after a while he started to enjoy going out in female clothes alone and once more dated men in this way. He was fascinated to see how many heterosexual men were ready to have sex with him knowing that he was a man.

This bisexual transvestite life lasted for a few years, until he met a man who fell in love with him and wanted him to divorce his wife and live with him. Torn between his wife and his lover, between heterosexual and homosexual transvestism, he became anxious, depressed, unable to decide on the course of his life. His wife became very depressed and threatened suicide, while his lover enticed him with the promise of total acceptance of his pseudofeminine transvestite role. At this point Ken came for a psychiatric consultation in order to find a solution to his emotional and sexual conflict.

What is interesting is that he had never questioned his ambiguous sexual role with either women or men. Though at the beginning he might have thought of his transvestite activity as a fetishistic exercise that might heighten his sexual pleasure with a woman, gradually he became more and more identified with his pseudofeminine role, to the point of being responsive to the solicitations of men. His gradual identification with the woman's role by wearing women's lingerie or clothes was achieved on a magical level by a concomitant denial of his masculinity.

Ken's facility in switching from the masculine to the feminine role was still a part of his childlike ability to incorporate into the world of reality his own world of make-believe. When the magical transformation of his sexual identity by the mere wearing of women's clothes was accepted by men, the make-believe was reinforced and he felt at that moment that he was a woman. The power of his fantasy progressively took hold of his sexual identity, convincing him at times to be what he had in some ways desired but had questioned before. On a logical level he still had doubts about the rationality of his new role. He was not yet ready to abdicate his male role and accept a completely female role by living with a man. At this point his relationship with his wife remained his only link to his masculine role; without it he felt even more confused and vulnerable to losing his identity totally without truly gaining a new one.

It is true that at this time he occasionally fantasized about surgically changing his sex, but in opposing this idea he also acknowledged his need to maintain his penis as an organ of pleasure. The solution to his sexual conflict was based on overcoming his sense of sexual inferiority, related to his inability to function sexually without female clothing, which had made him almost deny his masculinity to the point of identifying with a woman in relationships with men. His acceptance of his masculinity would also free him from his magical thinking, the only way that he knew to cope with his situation.

MASOCHISM AND SADOMASOCHISM

Another example of sexually deviant behavior whose roots can be clearly identified with the child's thinking development is that of sadomasochism. Here, sexual excitement and pleasure are derived either from inflicting or receiving pain. In some persons both types of activity lead to sexual pleasure.

Most explanations of sadomasochism rely on circumstantial evidence and interpretation based on analogy. For instance, the classical psychoanalytic hypothesis is related to a defense against castration anxiety through the individual's becoming the attacker himself, thereby rendering the alleged castrator powerless. This hypothesis, however, has very little clinical value. It offers little insight into, for instance, why someone would find it necessary to become the castrator and not the castrated one, when his victim in most cases is a woman, who is already "castrated." And how does this theory explain why some sadists can be masochists as well? The psychoanalytic theory of masochism fares little better, although it is based on the empirical observation that the masochist relates sex to the notion of suffering, of paying a price for pleasure.

Yet, independent of these assumptions, a few facts have emerged from the observation of sadomasochistic behavior. Sadistic and masochistic behavior seem to be two sides of the same coin. In both, the sexual act is associated with pain. In both, each person strives for control over the other person—one by administering the sexual treatment, the other by accepting it on his own terms. No sadist can enjoy the situation fully unless the masochist enjoys submitting to his sadism.

This distortion in sexual interaction is part of a concept of sexual activity that some individuals develop at a period in their maturation when their knowledge of sex is confused, fragmented, and at least partially fabricated by the imagination. A young child or an adolescent may be exposed to sadomasochistic sexual scenes that awaken a sexual response and cause him either to become conditioned to the stimulation or to fantasize about sex in these terms. Such responses are reinforced by fantasized associations based on what he, as a child, has heard or assumed about sex. Since in his experience human closeness and intimacy takes place only in the direct expression of physical aggression, of games, and the sexual act has the connotation of rough play, he comes to associate the sexual drive with aggression and roughness.

The hypothesis that masochism represents symbolic punishment for enjoying sex is not sufficient to explain the extension of the threshold of pain to pleasure. Symbolic punishment might alleviate the guilt but would not be changed into sexual pleasure. But most sadomasochistic sexual behavior in fact begins with an experience in childhood or puberty that is interpreted by the child as sexual activity, even though its context may be nonsexual. Physical punishment administered by someone to whom the child has a strong emotional attachment may lead indirectly to sexual arousal and the beginning of the development of masochistic sexual fantasies. In other cases ambivalent feelings of love toward an unreachable figure may lead to the formulation of a sadistic fantasy when the frustration accumulated toward that person is otherwise inexpressible. These fantasies are channeled into sexual expression when they are associated with the coincidental sexual arousal experienced at the thought of the unreachable love object.

After the association between the sadistic fantasy and sexual arousal is made, it is reinforced by the simple process of deriving pleasure from sexual gratification. Over the years the fantasy is amplified and modified according to the new information and experiences that the individual accumulates.

Yet the sexual aspect of sadomasochism is only one facet of the problem. In general, sadomasochism develops only in a particular type of personality that approaches human interaction with either an abnormally passive attitude or an abnormally aggressive one or one that shifts radically from one extreme to the other.

Sadomasochistic personality traits may appear in an individual's social or emotional relationship with others without ever being given sexual expression; sexual sadomasochism itself, however, is always accompanied by other sadomasochistic personality traits. The sexually dominant or submissive mate is only one aspect of the expression of the sadomasochistic drive, which in most cases surfaces in daily social intercourse as well.

A sadistic or masochistic view of the world and of human interaction, whether or not it encompasses the sexual relationship, is developed gradually during childhood based on interaction with family, peers in school, and other significant figures. For instance, the individual with masochistic personality traits has a tendency to place himself in a position of being victimized, abused, mistreated. At the same time, he has a need to complain and to torture himself with self-deprecatory thoughts about past behavior for which he thinks he should be or should have been punished. Furthermore, he provokes people close to him into conflict situations that often lead to rejection, verbal abuse, or physical punishment.

This type of behavior begins when the child first attempts to assert himself. Because of his need for attention, he may annoy others, who retaliate by punishing him. Yet at the same time this attention fulfills his need to see that they care for him. Because the provocation is directed toward those who frustrate him in his need for their love, the child may learn to derive gratification from a form of interaction in which attention, now seen as love, is obtained by this devious method. In his egocentricity the child seeks continual gratification of his need and when refused will demand it by crying and screaming. If the response is punishment because he was "bad," he may still receive pleasure from gaining attention. It is thus to be expected that under similar circumstances he will repeat this behavior. At his level of prelogical thinking, the two different acts are easily interrelated without the need for logic. However, the sexually masochistic connection develops only if the pain is felt as pleasurable within the context of sexual or sexually perceived activity.

For physical abuse to become sexual pleasure it has to become psychologically and physiologically integrated into an individual's sexuality. This is possible only at a particular level of organization of thinking. Masochism, whether in males or females, is based on reverting to a prelogical level of interpretation of causes and effects. In fantasy, or during the administration of corporal punishment, the simultaneous experience of pain and sexual arousal, due to other erotic elements of arousal, though independent of each other, may become associated by the child with the unfolding of sexual pleasure. Although it is true that intense pleasure can become pain, and vice versa, this connection must take place within the context of sexual arousal produced by other factors. The pain, the submission, the whipping, the bondage all become part of the concept of sex in such an individual, who further develops some preference for one or another type of activity by gradually learning new forms of masochistic interaction that add pleasure to the initial ones.

Ted, twenty-nine years old, single, and an investment banker, sought therapy because of sexual dysfunction. He had had difficulty maintaining an erection with a woman at various times, but lately the problem had become almost constant. At first he could sometimes alleviate the condition with the use of marijuana, but often it was necessary to combine marijuana with sadomasochistic fantasies. But real sexual excitement occurred only in situations in which he could be involved in actual sadomasochistic scenes. Over the years the need for sadomasochistic sex had become intense, interfering with his ability to have sex otherwise.

Under narcosynthesis (truth serum) he recalled that at the age of six he had started a fight with another boy, who hit him in the groin. He started to scream because of the sharp pain; his mother came to his rescue and took him home, while he continued to cry. At home he was undressed by his mother, and as he was bleeding from a cut he was placed on a table with his pants down. His mother bandaged his thigh and examined his genitals, asking whether they hurt. She left the room to answer the telephone, and he remained naked on the table. During this time he felt a pleasurable sensation in his genitals, and after she left he started to fondle them while feeling sorry for himself. He vaguely remembered sustaining an erection.

This experience gradually changed into a fantasy in which he imagined he was tied on a table and a woman was playing with his genitals. Later he became interested in sadomasochistic books, which connected with his fantasy and gave him a great deal of additional sexual gratification. He continued to use this type of sexual fantasy as an outlet for sexual expression until the age of eighteen, when he had his first opportunity to have intercourse with a woman. Then he realized that he was unable to perform unless he invoked the masochistic fantasy and created some situation in which he could assimilate sex symbolically into his masochistic needs. His method, however, gradually became unsuccessful, and his girl friend left him. Because he was intelligent, well educated, and handsome, he was able to interest other women, but most of the time he was unable to perform sexually. He became withdrawn, shunning parties and preferring to stay at home to smoke marijuana and masturbate alone with his fantasies. On several occasions he hired a sadomasochistic prostitute who was supposed to follow his prearranged sexual routine; she taught him a few new methods of gratification. By now he was deeply involved in sadomasochism all the while becoming more and more ashamed of himself.

Finally he met a divorced woman who was herself sadomasochistic. They started a relationship that was very comfortable sexually, but he continued to feel extremely guilty and uneasy about himself. He had come to think of himself as a freak, and he hated it. But his problems were more than sexual: his interaction with others was unbalanced too. Most people saw him as unreliable, immature, moody, and irresponsible. He always apologized for his lack of social responsibility toward others (he was particularly bad about keeping appointments or meeting other obligations), but he generally felt misunderstood and mistreated. Although he constantly promised to change, his lack of responsibility was highly self-destructive.

Ted had been considered an extremely bright child. He was graduated with honors from high school, accepted with a scholarship to one of the best Ivy League colleges, and received a law degree from a prominent law school. But over the years his academic performance had declined. During his school years he was plagued by his sexual fantasies, by his inability to cope with the pressures of social life, and by a sense that he was being abused by others. During those years he underwent five years of psychoanalysis which partially helped him to accept his difficulties but not to solve them. At the time he returned to therapy he felt alienated and rejected but wanted to reverse this negative pattern.

Ted's sexual sadomasochism can be clearly traced to the association he had made between injury and sexual arousal, but his sadomasochistic personality traits were more complicated. His relationship with his father shed some light on that matter. Ted described his father as discontented, always angry, inconsistently involved in family matters and even then quarrelsome and petty. He disliked his father very much, yet was afraid of him because of his father's outbursts of rage. The only way for him to relate to his father was to be very compliant; he could not answer back or question his father's decisions unless he was looking for trouble. He had plenty of that anyway, because his father frequently punished him severely for trifles. He fared better with his mother, but she also put pressure on him to behave in a particular manner if he wanted to be accepted and loved. Basically, their expressions of love were conditional, dependent on his submission, obedience, and execution of their wishes. Ted's sadomasochistic pattern of interaction had become established in his family, in which his need for love was equal to his parents' demands for submission.

He came to perceive the expression of love for him by others in terms of their controlling him, demanding that he meet their needs. His sexual sadomasochism was a simple extension of his relationship with his parents coupled with his mother's inadvertent sexual stimulation of him and his construing of that event as an expression of love. The pain became an extra element associated with the fantasy of being tied to the table and was integrated into the concept of sexual activity by association with sexual arousal. He was unable to perform sexually otherwise because his sexual arousal system had been activated and then reinforced by pain stimuli, and he became unresponsive to any other type of sexual stimulation.

Sadomasochism in women generally follows the same lines of psychological development. In addition, however, biological and cultural factors reinforce it. In fact, female masochism alone is extremely common. The sexual act in itself presupposes the submission of the woman to the man, placing the woman in a symbolically defenseless position. A woman's physical weakness relative to a man often strengthens her sense of dependency. This submissive position is further maintained culturally by her role within the family. For some women sexual masochism is merely an extension of a psychological masochism that is already a part of their personality. In these cases this masochistic tendency comes to be triggered sexually, and normal sexual sensations become confused with it. Women who want to be tied up, beaten, or otherwise ill-treated by their lovers have come to associate this behavior with the expression of sexual power and passion on the part of the man. It is an exaggeration of their desire to be taken and possessed by the man. To persuade themselves that they are loved, they goad their lovers or husbands to the point of making them angry. The experience of pain is integrated as pleasure, becoming part of sexual arousal and stimulation; her sexual excitement increases to such a pitch that the distinction between pain and pleasure disappears. This is often a symbolic repetition of interaction with childhood's authority figure.

The sadomasochist, male or female, who is oriented mainly toward sadism presents basically the same problem in reverse—he wants to control the sexual relationship by submitting his partner to pain and humiliation. He derives pleasure from obtaining the final proof that he is wanted and loved: the other person's complete acceptance of his power. The need to control and dominate is present in most people as part of their biological heritage. The expression of this drive through physical cruelty is also part of a primitive behavioral mechanism that explains the instinctual implementation of Darwinism and the hierarchical order of the group. Children are often very cruel in their attempts to impose control on each other, and only through socialization do they learn to suppress this powerful drive. Some never learn to suppress the need for control through cruelty, and later in life they manifest sociopathic tendencies or become outright psychopaths. Their behavior is usually related to their hatred for an environment they perceive as hostile.

But for the sadist the purpose of ritualized cruelty toward a sexual partner is symbolically to subdue him in order to ensure control and total ascendency in the interaction. The sadist actually achieves sexual arousal by administering pain to his partner. Thus the sexual interaction is reduced to a symbolic struggle, a game, between the protagonists in which the sadist is the victor. The masochist provokes the sadist, challenging his authority in the sexual interaction. The sadist responds by forcing the challenger to submit. In order to simulate the victory of domination, the partner has to be perceived, at least in terms of the sexual situation, as an adversary, a hostile, unwilling party. In the act of sadism the sadist expresses his anger toward his sexual partner. The assertion of the sadist's power requires that he break the will of his partner, even if symbolically. For the sadist this is the affirmation of his sexuality. In general, sadism is encountered more in men than in women. While this could be partly related to the man's tendency for dominance and control in sexual interaction, the sadistic behavior still remains deviant. For women sadistic behavior is basically related to the expression of their hate for men channeled into sexual interaction.

Psychologically, sadomasochism in both sexes is a game of self-assertion: by the sadist for control and the masochist, by imposing his terms of submission—illusory helplessness. The pain is the means of communicating this mutual need in the sexual interaction. In a wider sense, sadomasochism in a minor form is found in all love relationships, serving as a means of testing the strength of love and desire between lovers.

The sadist, like the masochist, distorts the meaning of sexual interaction. Both of them, either as executor or recipient of punishment, may see sexual interaction as forbidden, and for their participation in it they feel they must pay a price. In this travesty of sex each partner attempts symbolically to place the blame for his participation on the other. This symbolization often becomes highly structured and compulsively organized in order to bring the necessary emotional relief and expiate for the sexual gratification obtained in the forbidden act.

This symbolic relationship can also be seen as an attempt to reenact the adult-child relationship—protector-dominant versus protected-submissive—exactly as sexual interaction may have taken place in the first imagined or experienced sexual arousal of an individual during childhood or adolescence.

The sexual game becomes a reenactment of this childhood fantasy, magically relived. For the sadist or masochist this sexual interaction is authentic sex. The person has forgotten that it was part of childhood fantasy. After its consummation the magic is gone, and both partners return to their adult roles, in which the dominant-submissive interaction loses its primary meaning.

In isolated cases sexual sadism is associated with a psychopathic personality or with paranoia. Sexual "games" with such individuals may be very dangerous for the partner. The violence of the sexual interaction, combined with the hatred of and need to destroy the victim, may lead beyond symbolic reality to actual injury or murder.

HOMOSEXUALITY

Homosexuality—its causes, psychodynamics, and social acceptance—is one of the most debated types of sexual behavior. Explanations of this complex variation in sexual identity range from constitutional (biological) factors to pure conditioning in childhood or adolescence. The classic psychoanalytic scenario for male homosexuality presupposes identification of the boy with the strong mother and rejection of the weak father, resulting in a negative attitude toward the opposite sex. The neo-Freudians expanded the dynamic framework by adding the dimension of a specific personality structure leading to difficulty in adapting to heterosexual interaction. However, these hypotheses about male homosexuality's mechanism of development are unable to pinpoint the determining social elements as specific causes of it.

In fact, the same factors traditionally considered responsible for psychosexual development leading to homosexuality could also lead to transvestism or even heterosexuality. Another difficulty with psychoanalytic assumptions is that they attempt to explain both male homosexuality and lesbianism by unconscious mechanisms, which cannot be proven or disproven by the patient. For instance, castration anxiety, the basic tenet of the psychoanalytic explanation of homosexuality, is not present in women; in their case it is replaced with fear of the penis's penetration. Yet on a clinical level there is no evidence to support either of these assumptions.

When applied to the therapeutic process, these assumptions have proved unrewarding. Freud himself admitted to pessimism regarding the results of therapy for homosexuals.

The behavioral learning theory, on the other hand, is more successful in the actual treatment of specific types of homosexuality, but it fails to explain its development. For instance, according to the Kinsey Report, about 40 percent of the males questioned and 19 percent of the females had had overt homosexual encounters that did not lead to permanently homosexual behavior. It is more likely that the learning experience at the heart of the behaviorist approach plays a role only when there is a lack of appropriate sexual identity to begin with.

Recent studies emphasize that homosexuality is caused by still undetermined biological factors. These studies acknowledge that it has not yet been found that any particular set of family patterns is responsible for the development of homosexuality. What is identifiable is only a pattern of feelings and orientations in the individual's childhood independent of any particular set of familial or social experiences. In other words, the lack of a consistent developmental model has led some theorists to conclude that in the male homosexual the psychological sexual identification that starts with a gradual awareness of his sexual attraction to the same sex is caused by unknown biological factors. But this remains a highly debatable position in itself when generalized to all forms of homosexual behavior.

The child's admiration or emulation of an older male, combined with a need for closeness and acceptance by him, does not necessarily suggest biological programming in a homosexual direction. In fact, these are normal feelings present in most boys and with no homosexual connotations, unless they are followed by his realization of erotic preference for the same sex. This awareness for homosexual preference, as expressed in fantasies or carried out under induced or provoked circumstances, takes place during or after puberty and happens regardless of any previous homosexual experiences. Yet even in adolescence homosexual behavior and sexual preference vary according to the individual's perception of his needs as they develop in his search for confirmation of his masculinity. In some cases the feelings may start with an accidental involvement in homosexual behavior that leads the individual to the realization of the potential for erotic gratification with the same sex, though a true homosexual identity may never emerge. While homosexual feelings may remain, they may be expressed either in sporadic homosexual encounters or only in fantasy. On the other hand, the declared male homosexual has a continuous need to reaffirm his masculinity, obsessively attempting magically to incorporate the maleness of others into his own male identity. The homosexual is continuously fascinated by the attributes of masculinity, which he feels he lacks.

Two elements are predominant in the behavior of the homosexual: lack of acceptance of his sexual identity and sexual rejection of the opposite sex. During maturation in his search for confirmation of his male identity he develops a pattern of sexual interaction that gives him at least temporary reassurance of his manhood through the acceptance of other males. The exclusion of the opposite sex to various degrees as a means of reinforcing his masculine identity leads to the development of a particular type of homosexuality: oriented either toward dominance and the assertion of pseudomasculinity or oriented toward femininity in interaction with a male partner.

Complex factors contribute to the development of the initial feeling of male sexual inferiority, from particular family patterns to interaction with peers. A boy may develop sexual doubts if his father does not offer a positive male model and his mother is seductive and overprotective. In addition, his image of himself as a boy as compared to other boys may be negative. All of these factors contribute to the disorganization of his sense of sexual identity. The seductive, overprotective attitude of the mother eroticizes the normally binding relationship between child and mother while inhibiting the normal development of the child's sexual expression. The result may be the desexualization of his relationships with all women. At the same time, if the detached, weak, or autocratic father does not provide the necessary support and model for the formulation of a sense of masculinity, the boy becomes further confused in his efforts to become more assertive and independent with other boys. Such a boy may attach himself to an older boy or a man who will function as his model. This man becomes his masculine ideal, endowed with all the attributes he should like to possess.

Yet another set of elements must be present for homosexual behavior to occur: both an erotic attitude on the part of the model and the boy's own deep sense of male inadequacy in his relationships with peers.

Peers play an extremely important role in the evaluation and confirmation of the child's self-concept. Their continuous rejection of him as an equal in sports or other interactions may have lasting effects, convincing him that he is weak and unmanly. He will look for the protection of those who are stronger than he, preferably in a socially acceptable form. He may want to be the friend of a powerful athlete, of a leader in his school, of someone who gives him a sense of security and whom he admires. Sexual interaction is often a question of appropriate circumstances if it is demanded by the person who so well fulfills his other needs.

All of these conditions may be present and yet not lead to homosexual behavior unless the adolescent, in his struggle to compensate for his sense of sexual or male inferiority, believes that the sexual interaction with another will prove his masculinity, as though the other's masculinity can rub off on him. This explains why the more "male," athletic, handsome, or sexually well-endowed this "other" may be, the more desirable he is.

A case will demonstrate this point. Ron, a young, college-educated designer, sought psychiatric help because he felt unhappy, lonely, and socially isolated. Although he was functioning very well in his business, his social and emotional life was in turmoil. He admitted that he was infatuated with a man who did not reciprocate his feelings. He felt uncomfortable with his strong emotions toward this man, who appeared to be aware of them but did not encourage them other than by flirting with him. Ron thought of the man as handsome, good-natured, and sexually attractive. He had two conflicts: he was unwilling to admit to his friend that he was interested in him sexually, and he was unhappy with the idea of living as a homosexual, for he very much wanted a family. This was not his first infatuation with a man. In adolescence he had had an infatuation for a young man who rejected him. He became acutely depressed and required psychiatric attention for a time. Yet his pattern of life did not change much. The fact that he was unable to change increased his sense of loneliness and his dissatisfaction with himself.

A short inquiry into the childhood of Ron revealed that he was the youngest child of an upper-middle-class family. As the youngest child, separated by many years from the next sibling, he received a great deal of attention from his mother, whom he described as soft, sweet, tolerant, and protective. Though she was not overtly seductive, he remembered cuddling in her lap and being caressed affectionately. In fact, she was protecting him from the wrath of his father, who was brutal, violent, inconsiderate, argumentative, and usually detached from family matters—at best "a moody, sometimes benevolent tyrant." Ron grew up shy, with very few friends, feeling less manly than other boys. Physically he felt unattractive, unathletic, and undesirable to others. Around the age of fifteen he developed a strong admiration for another young man around the same age as himself who appeared to him to be handsome and successful with boys and girls. He wanted to emulate him, to be close to him. He felt safe and happy in his presence. Many times, while masturbating, he fantasized about being with the other boy. In retrospect he recognized that these sexual fantasies represented total acceptance and closeness. His father made him feel worthless, and his only other close source of male identification, an older brother, was detached and uninvolved with him. He was jealous of his brother because he thought that he was handsome and successful with his peers.

With the advent of puberty his image of himself as a male became even poorer because of his shyness and what he thought to be his social awkwardness. He was uninterested in girls because he thought of himself as unattractive and undesirable. He felt inferior to other boys and yearned for their acceptance and friendship. Yet members of his family assured him that there was nothing wrong with him physically. He was a normally developed, average-looking young man. However, Ron thought of himself differently and felt unmasculine. He was unable to define it, yet his sense of masculinity depended only on the acceptance of other boys. No matter how much reassurance he received from his mother or other adults, only recognition from significant peers or men of special physical attributes were able to satisfy his consuming need for confirmation of his masculinity. For him sexual interaction meant being loved, hugged, and fondled—no direct sexual interaction was really necessary.

The replacement of his own nonacceptance with the need for sexual recognition by his peers presupposes that Ron maintain the type of thinking already mentioned—precausal, prelogical, and magical. The substitution would not have any meaning in rational terms: his male insecurity could not be replaced by a friend's sexual acceptance. But this acceptance was sought just the same as proof of his masculinity.

Peer acceptance, an important aspect of adolescent socialization, was also used by him to achieve sexual identity counter to its major aim of social adjustment. The young man with whom he became infatuated as a teen-ager gave him full acceptance except on the sexual level. Ron's concept of acceptance by another man with whom he wanted to identify was completed only in the sexual embrace. For him, sexual intimacy represented only an aspect of the total and unconditional acceptance he sought. It cemented the interaction and produced sexual gratification, which compensated for the absence of a relationship with a woman. The expression of his sexual instinct toward the opposite sex therefore remained latent because of suppressed interest and fear of failure.

After being rejected by the first young man, Ron became acutely depressed. He felt hapless and despondent. He received some psychiatric help, with the result that he accepted his homosexuality, at least temporarily. A few years later he had his first sexual experience with a man who he considered handsome. He felt good in the interaction; he was excited about the idea of being wanted and loved by a man of great physical attractiveness to whom he felt equal in the lovemaking process. But afterward a feeling of depression overcame him, his sense of loneliness became all-encompassing, and his life seemed to be suspended between long periods of overwhelming isolation and sporadic calls from his lover. The wait became more and more oppressive, until he lost patience. He went out again for another encounter. When he was unable to attract someone who meant something to him, he felt completely rejected and became extremely frustrated.

At one time he attempted to have a sexual relationship with a woman but was unsuccessful. He became even more upset, because the experience made him realize the extent of his anxiety regarding intimacy with a woman, anxiety caused by his fear of nonperformance. So he continued to have relationships with men, infrequently but always with the same feeling of dissatisfaction, until he fell in love with his new friend. Merely talking on the telephone to him aroused him sexually to the point of masturbating. They spent a great deal of time together, taking trips, dining. There were flirting remarks and sexual innuendos passed between them, light touches of the hands or knees, brushed arms, and glimpses of each other's bodies when they shared a room during vacations taken together. Yet neither was ready to admit any emotional involvement greater than close friendship. Ron would have pushed the relationship to the sexual plane if he had not feared rejection and social exposure.

It was obvious that he was unable to accept his masculinity, unless reinforced through the emotional acceptance of other males, males who met his criteria of manhood. Women were not considered able to offer him this reassurance because his fear of not being aroused in a sexual encounter made intimacy impossible. For him, women were strange, untouchable creatures. He felt caught between men, who in closer interaction made him feel masculine but at the same time reinforced his homosexual dependency (a situation with which he still felt basically ill at ease), and women, who instead of supporting his masculinity further diminished it by heightening his own sexual anxieties.

The stress caused by this dilemma forced him to try to explore, through therapy, all his options before identifying himself as homosexual. But the option of becoming heterosexual was clouded by his lack of understanding of women and of their emotional and sexual needs. In the process of his new therapy, by discarding his magical thinking, he learned to relate to women in close interaction; only then was he able to take another look at his sexual and emotional needs. Then he saw that he could express those needs without the magical possession of the maleness of others through homosexual encounters.

He realized that he had become conditioned to male attachment since early adolescence for the affirmation and reinforcement of his masculinity, and as such he shunned the company of girls. The exaltation of his own sex made him even more ready to denigrate the role of women as a source for the assertion of his manhood. Though in general this is only a phase of the adolescent's thinking regarding the affirmation of his masculinity, Ron did not resolve his male identity problem. Lack of a strong male self-image, a deficiency carried over from his developmental years, had resulted in his attempting to continue the search for his adolescent masculine ideal in adulthood.

In general, this seems to be the reason that the emergence of homosexuality is so closely linked to adolescence. This is the time when the sexual roles of the male and female become clearly defined in terms of both physical and personality characteristics. Male identification may lead a boy who has difficulty with his self-image to attempt to possess the characteristics of masculinity that fit his ideal. Physical beauty, strength, and a large sex organ become the most desirable qualities. He fears that he lacks these attributes and thus attempts to obtain them from another by a magical process of assimilation, thinking, "He wants me, and he is a real man; therefore I must be a real man." In possessing him, I become like him. In other words, the sense of manhood is transferred magically from one person to another. This is a typical mode of pseudological assimilation, a part of the preoperational thinking of the child. In the homosexual this childish thinking persists as an isolated island in his adult thought because his insecurity about his masculinity has been carried over from childhood or adolescence and never resolved. The instant gratification obtained by possessing the manhood of the other gives way to his earlier insecurity as soon as the sexual act ends. He attempts to regain the temporary sense of masculinity by compulsively searching for a new partner. This may explain the proclivity of homosexuals toward promiscuity.

A related question is the exaggerated fascination of the homosexual with a large penis. Most young men, regardless of whether they have homosexual tendencies, are interested in the comparative sizes of their penises as a sign of manliness. Since time immemorial penis size has been equated with sexual prowess and with fertility, and the symbolic phallus even cast in statues and sculptures became an object of adoration and worship by women. In the primitive mind a clear connection existed between the strength of a man, the size of his penis, and his masculinity.

The value of a large sex organ as a visual sexual stimulant is proved by the whole gamut of soft- and hard-core pornographic magazines that emphasize, for both sexes, this aspect of sexuality. Some sexologists attempt to play down the size of the sex organ in sexual interaction, but most people continue to believe that a large (but not freakishly large) penis is necessary to satisfy a woman fully.

Though most men, after receiving the acceptance of a woman, settle their doubts about penis size in favor of its ability to function, some do not. Their doubts, reflected in their sexual insecurity, affect their performance with women. Others attempt to solve their problems more drastically. Instead of relating to women, some deeply insecure men continue to search for the acceptance of their penises from other men, exactly as they did in their youth. The need to see, to touch, to possess a large penis is transformed from an aspect of self-discovery into an obsession. They compare in order to get reassurance and eventually feel that the other penis belongs to them. This magical incorporation of the other's penis is analogous to the primitive practice of eating the heart of a defeated warrior in order to gain his strength. An example may be illuminating.

Don, a young writer, had gradually become depressed, isolated, and unhappy with his style of life. He mainly questioned the meaning of his sexual life, which was directed toward gratification of his needs by masturbating and fellating other sexually well-endowed men. Most of his free time was obsessively dedicated to the search for and possession of the large penises of other men, particularly heterosexuals. In the lavatories of restaurants, subway stations, and bus stations he continually approached other men in the attempt to make sexual contact with them. The display of a large penis in a lavatory would induce in him spontaneous erection combined with a powerful desire to consummate the sexual act. At the same time he profoundly disliked his own penis, which he thought was rather small and ugly. He could not change his penis, but at least he could compensate by seeing and touching another one, a "real" one.

Over the years he became a connoisseur of different shapes of penises, which he classified according to various aesthetic criteria. In his search for the right penis, he looked at men's sex organs whenever he had an opportunity. Some evenings he succeeded in having sex with five or six men—most of the time he did not even know who they were. The whole interaction was related to the penis, which he admired and wanted. The pleasure of handling the other man's penis was ineffable, though of too short duration to really fulfill him. It left him frustrated and desirous of renewing the experience with the same man or someone else as soon as possible.

During sexual interaction with another man he almost always denied the existence of his own penis unless the other man was interested in it. The other's interest was accepted apologetically and anxiously. He was afraid that his partner, by noticing the size of his penis, might reject him. If he was accepted sexually, he enjoyed the interaction even more. Over the years his drive to possess the maleness of others became unfulfilling and frustrating. The large penis of someone else became a fetish, the possession of it an addiction. He became weary of the difficulties associated with obtaining the object of his gratification, tired of the time wasted waiting to meet a potential partner, demoralized by the inevitable rejections and insults. The loneliness of his life started to weigh heavily on him. The obvious alternative would have been to find a partner with a large penis and live with him, but in fact he was unable to accept his homosexuality outside of the short encounters. He found the prospect of sharing his life with another man disturbing and uncomfortable.

To free himself from this obsession he sought variety, a way either to curb his continual search even attempting to replace "cruising" with watching porno movies or to accept his homosexuality in a more sedate and conventional form. This tormenting situation brought him into therapy. In order to find the answer to his sexual difficulty the therapist had to explore the development of sexuality that led him to his present condition.

Don's psychosexual history appeared simple. At the age of seven he had been introduced to sex by a cousin who was four years older and whom he admired very much. He was impressed by the size of his cousin's penis. This cousin had taught him to masturbate. Shy, inhibited, a daydreamer, he found out that through sex he could make friends with older boys. Unfortunately, whenever he compared himself to other boys he felt that he had a smaller penis than most of them. Although he was reassured by his cousin and his mother that he would be all right, he continued to feel smaller sexually than other boys. During puberty his real trauma began: he felt that he was not developing as fast sexually as other boys. In bathrooms or showers he frequently looked at the penises of his peers, which he found bigger than his. He became fixated on penis size. His penis finally grew, reaching normal size, but by that time he felt sexually inadequate and had developed a sense of admiration for the penises of others. He wanted to see how big they were in erection. He was aroused and had the desire to hold a penis whenever he could. This need was expressed in homosexual encounters. He was not interested in knowing his partners' names or the details of their lives. If they were average-looking, with no obvious physical defects, adequately dressed, low or middle class, and well-endowed sexually, they were automatically candidates.

In his obsession he tried by various means to increase the size of his own penis, from metal rings to a vacuum aspirator into which he introduced his penis in the hope of dilating it. To boost his sense of masculinity, when he went out cruising he wore tight pants and enlarged his penis by wrapping it in gauze or putting it into a hollow dildo. For a moment the fantasy would become real, which made him feel good. Yet the magic was short-lived, and later he felt even more inferior and unmanly. He did not consider that his penis might have been found acceptable to a woman of normal sexual orientation, or that masculinity is not necessarily related to the size of the penis.

Don's concept of maleness was highly distorted by his infantile thinking. His obsession with magically possessing and incorporating the penis of another man could not be treated without a maturation of his basic concepts of masculinity and femininity and their role in sexual interaction. He was fixated at a preadolescent level of understanding his masculinity, and his sense of sexual inadequacy became the basis for the organization of his social and sexual life.

One of the best descriptions of this preoccupation with the penis is offered by the French writer Jean Genêt, who, in a somewhat romanticized autobiography, *A Thief's Journal*, describes his obsessional involvement with the possession of "the magical penis", the final source of masculinity. The totality of male qualities, such as brilliance and power, was dependent on "the penis and that which will complete it . . . the whole apparatus which is so beautiful. . . ." Genêt expresses his thoughts and dreams about the possession of the magical penis: "I invented the biggest and loveliest penis in the world, I endowed it with qualities; heavy, strong, and nervous. Beneath my fingers I felt it sculpted in oak, its full veins, its palpitations, its heat, its pulsations."

It is generally agreed among homosexuals that the penis is as important a source of sexual fascination as the beauty of the body. They desire the penis of another man and the acceptance or admiration of their own as the supreme tribute to their masculinity. The degree of preoccupation with the penis varies greatly among homosexuals. It is affected for the most part by the masculine image that they want to capture from others. The desire to possess a large penis, a masculine-looking body, or the total emotional acceptance of another male all represent the same need: to compensate for an inadequate sense of masculinity in oneself.

The choice of a homosexual partner is directly related to the degree of masculine deficiency experienced by the individual. Preferences may range from the athletic, muscular type to the effeminate, soft, delicate type, with a premium placed on sexual acceptance by a heterosexual. The muscular man, symbolized by the "hard hat" truck-driver type, is thought to magically offer the missing male strength and power that the individual covets. The effeminate, delicate man represents the closest link to women. The effeminate man prefers the strong muscular type, compensating for what he believes he lacks. In any homosexual encounter at least one of this triad of desired masculine traits must be present: handsomeness, a rugged muscular physique, and a large penis. These attributes are ideal if present in a heterosexual man; the possession of them in the sexual act is for the homosexual the realization of a dream.

In men it is easy to identify the physical attributes of masculinity toward which the homosexual dedicates his emotional life. But the development of female homosexuality involves qualities of femininity that are less clearly defined. Femininity is defined less by the size of the breasts or by any other physical quality than by less tangible personality traits, a particular way of moving, or a certain approach to human interaction, all associated with a degree of physical attractiveness. The complex definition of femininity is based partly on the social context of society's expectations of the female and partly on intrinsic qualities related to her psychobiological functions. In general, these characteristics are described in broad terms as tenderness, sensitivity, softness, sensuality, emotional warmth, and need for closeness. Yet some women do not fully develop these qualities or even feel their lack.

The explanation appears to lie in a disturbance in gender-identity caused by lack of a proper feminine model in the developmental years. Certainly the best feminine model, in our society, is a loving, contented mother. But sometimes the mother is not the proper model; she may be cool, unavailable, moody, or inconsistent. In other instances she may not have the qualities that the daughter aspires to possess. In any case, the daughter has difficulty finding in the mother the ideal image that she seeks. Another woman may fill the emotional vacuum, being idealized by the girl as possessing the characteristics she wishes to emulate. Her feelings for this woman may range from admiration to adoration, combined with a need for acceptance, closeness, and identification. This adolescent process of identification normally helps a girl to realize her sexual identity and to gain the sense that she is a desirable woman. But some girls, even before puberty, have serious difficulty accepting the feminine social role, and with the advent of puberty and adolescence they feel even more estranged from that role. They question their femininity, their ability to attract men, and search for acceptance by their own sex to prove their femininity.

In general, they are insecure sexually as women and feel more comfortable relating to their own sex. This pattern continues into adulthood because these women are never able to develop a means of fully accepting their femininity. This is why most lesbian couples are mutually dependent. In some cases the need for expression of affection, acceptance, and love takes precedence over sexual fulfillment. The loved woman is magically endowed with the feminine qualities that the lover wants to possess herself; through their relationship, she feels, she will come to share them.

Pat, a divorced college graduate, sought therapy because of her feelings of depression and anxiety after the termination of her relationship with her female lover. Pat had been married at the age of twenty-three, for one and a half years, but was unable to function in the marriage because her husband was irresponsible, cold, and uninterested in her. They fought constantly until she decided to ask him for a divorce. A year later she met an older woman with whom she became friendly. This woman, thirty-three years old, showed her understanding and compassion, and provided the companionship she sought. Soon her friend revealed that she had had lesbian experiences, which excited and mystified Pat. She became interested in experiencing this intimacy, which at the beginning consisted of merely kissing and closely embracing. She felt extremely comfortable in this interaction because it fulfilled her need for the affection she had always craved. After a period of time her friend proceeded to a closer sexual intimacy as a natural consequence of their closeness, to which Pat did not express any opposition. They started living together and became lovers. Their relationship lasted about three years and was terminated because of the unfaithfulness of her lover, who enjoyed seducing other women. After they split up, Pat became depressed, withdrawn, and bitter. What she resented mostly was her former lover's promises of "undying love." She fondly remembered the closeness, the hugging, the time spent in each other's arms, and she was in fact unable to explain why she missed the touching and the embraces so much, instead of the sexual gratification.

After a year of mourning her last lover, she started to date again. She went to gay bars and easily met potential lovers. She started affairs with some of them, but she felt unsatisfied because the intimate interaction that she needed was missing, that is, affectionate closeness expressed in fondling and embracing followed by mutual masturbation. By chance she met a somewhat older professional woman, attractive, independent, but undecided about committing herself to lesbian life. Pat believed that she would succeed in overcoming the reservations of her new lover. The effect of the relationship on Pat was salutary. Suddenly she felt happy, full of life, and looked forward to each meeting with her lover. But after a brief period of intense interaction her lover started to cool off, wanting to keep her sexual options open. Pat became frightened about losing her lover, the only source of emotional support. She became despondent and suicidal.

Her need for closeness with the other woman was overwhelming. She began to realize that her dependence had something to do with the uncontrollable state of anxiety she had developed. She noticed that whenever they were in each other's arms she sank into a state of calmness and serenity, which made her feel like a baby at her mother's breast. Her lover persistently refused to commit herself to the relationship, and Pat became more and more anxious and socially nonfunctional. The mild tranquilizers she was taking provided only short-term relief for her continual mental suffering. She sought therapy because she wanted to be free of this overwhelming dependence on her lover or any other woman. She enjoyed their companionship and lovemaking but resented terribly the enslaving need for acceptance and closeness.

The patterns she had developed since early childhood help in understanding her predicament. She had been brought up by a nanny who was efficient, good, but matter-of-fact in personal interaction. Most of the time her mother was either not feeling well or was too busy, and she showed little interest in playing with her or giving her emotional support. Pat remembered how much she had enjoyed it when one of her aunts was affectionate to her. Later, she became somewhat closer to her father, who was more affectionate, but they rarely spent time together because he was very much involved in his business. She grew up reserved, detached, efficient, but somewhat sad, without knowing what was missing. She became closer intellectually to her mother, but she realized that her mother could never freely express her emotions.

However, there remained a missing link in understanding her insatiable need for affection and acceptance from a woman. She was unable to provide a connection herself, but after she had discussed the matter with her parents an interesting fact emerged: Her mother had been extremely close to her in the first ten months of her life. Then her mother suddenly became ill, and they were separated for a few months. Pat did not remember this, yet apparently the change had been registered reflexively, hence her need for close emotional contact. She had been deprived of maternal contact at a critical period of emotional development, and the need for it was rekindled later in life, when her desire for emotional closeness to a woman became overwhelming. The other woman was magically transformed by her into a caring, loving mother. Because this need had not been satisfied, she had been unable to develop her emotional relationships further. But outside of sexual interaction she and her lover became two adult women who saw each other within the framework of an exchange of mature needs. Neither one was able in their daily interaction to play either the role of a child or that of a mother. As a result, their interaction was marred by frustration and resentment and strained by unfulfilled emotional expectations.

But it would be unrealistic to assume that Pat had become a lesbian for only this reason. Other powerful needs contributed to her change in sexual role. Her mother had been unable to provide the desired female identity model. The girl's image of femininity became dissociated and was truncated by her unfulfilled need for affection. This, reinforced by her disappointing marriage, explains why she was unable to feel fulfilled emotionally by a man, while she could otherwise accept her feminine social role.

In general, regardless of whether a relationship between two women is a pseudo–mother-daughter interaction or the more common pseudo–masculine-feminine interaction, the artificiality of the situation very often confuses and upsets the partners. The sexual gratification and companionship provided by the relationship do not necessarily cancel out the competition of personalities or fully replace an interaction with a man. It requires a continual effort on both their parts to maintain the illusion of fulfillment.

In some cases the young girl, because of a strong identification with a powerful, seductive father, rejects her femininity and takes on a masculine role. Usually the mother appears to her to be weak, faceless, and detached, while the father is seen as strong, interesting, and charming, the only person who offers her a close relationship in the family interaction. She imitates her father, who encourages her to become a tomboy, a fact that makes identification later on with the female role more difficult. As an adult she continues to cultivate manners, attitudes, language, and clothes that suggest a masculine orientation and needs. She denies femininity in her behavior, detesting the pursuit of feminine activities and interests. Sexually, she likes to possess a woman; it represents the supreme confirmation of her identification with men. Yet, because she cannot deny possessing a woman's body, she must rely on the same magical thinking that she originally used to identify with boys and later men. On the level of logical thinking she knows that she is a woman, although she dislikes her social role and sexual gender-identity. She has oriented her social role toward masculinity, but gratification is combined with frustration at the limitations of this role. Gradually she has the need to relate to a woman sexually, then logic is overshadowed by the fantasy of being a man and possessing the means to sexually gratify another woman. In the sexual interaction she attempts to use her body as a man's; at that moment, in a magical denial of reality, she sees herself as a man, or, more exactly, her perception of being a man. The penis is replaced by her finger, tongue, or even breast, giving her the illusion of playing the sexual role of a man. Her gratification is primarily psychological and secondarily sexual. Indeed, in the sexual interaction she functions in a state of self-suggestion, which permits her to undergo an emotional transformation. Its roots are in her magical thinking. An example may help illustrate the state of mind of the pseudomale lesbian.

Michelle, a thirty-two-year-old unmarried social worker, masculine in dress and manner, sought therapy because of difficulties at work and turmoil in her emotional life. At work she had conflicts with co-workers because of her extreme assertiveness, unyielding position regarding office matters, and inability to accept male authority. She was bright, a hard worker, and very well qualified for her position, but her personality forced her to change jobs often, being unable to find a place for herself.

Her private life was no better. She had been living with another professional woman for the last two years, and her lover was at the point of breaking off the relationship. Michele had had a few affairs with women, but all of them had been terminated, mainly because of her unfaithfulness. She was always looking for a beautiful woman who would fall in love with her, symbolizing to her the full acceptance of her power over other women and her indisputable ability to compete with men in the quest for the possession of beautiful women. Her feelings toward men were ambivalent; she admired and identified with strong, successful ones and despised the others, whom she considered inferior to her.

In order to understand her concept of masculinity and femininity, it is helpful to look back into her childhood. She was the oldest daughter of a businessman who always treated her like a boy. Though he never told her that she should behave like a boy, he did things with her that he would have done had she been a boy. By playing ball, bicycling, or riding horseback, she could please her father, who was happy doing these things with her. He often told her that she could do things just like a boy because there was no difference between boys and girls with regard to sports or other activities. In school she sought the company of boys, with whom she felt comfortable and liked to compete. She treated them as friends, without any other emotional interest in them. Other girls were envious of her success with boys, but she believed that girls were silly in the way they tried to attract the attention of boys.

Her relationship with her mother was friendly, but she felt that her mother was too passive, too involved in the household, trying too much to please her father. She also felt that her mother was not very intelligent. In adolescence she began to look down on her mother as "just a nice housewife from suburbia," while her father was interesting, exciting, and charming. At the same time, she was flattered by the sense that younger girls admired her because of her abilities and wanted her companionship. At summer camp, when she was seventeen, a younger girl "fell in love" with her. Their relationship, which consisted of kissing and embracing, made her feel very good and important. The relationship ended in the fall when the other girl became frightened of her feelings. Michele, however, met another girl who initiated her into lesbian intimacy. She enjoyed the relationship, particularly because the other girl admired her and accepted her control.

At college she had sporadic relationships with women in which she always took the male role. Only once did she have a short affair with a man. She described their relationship as pleasant but emotionally and sexually unrewarding. She felt uncomfortable, cold, and detached. After a while they started to fight because of irreconcilable differences of personality and opinion. He left her for another woman whom he found more attractive and feminine. According to Michele, the only benefit she derived from this relationship was that she learned the male approach to sexual interaction. Afterward, all of her affairs were with women, with whom she felt comfortable and loved.

She was aggressive, demanding, and for a time emotionally protective of each of her partners; yet ultimately the relationship became boring and she looked for another partner. She was generally unhappy. The affairs always had an air of unreality and artificiality. In the heat of an argument with a lover she would try to impose a kind of male authority, and she was always criticized for that. She suspected that her last lover had rejected her for a man. Sometimes she considered becoming a man, but she was afraid that she would lose her genital pleasure if she underwent a sex-change operation.

In the course of therapy she came to understand that her needs were induced by the unfulfilling sexual role she was playing. Her concept of her social role and sexual identity had been conditioned by family dynamics during childhood, creating a type of attitude and thinking that distorted the meaning of her sexual relationships.

Within the range of lesbian interaction, at the opposite end of the spectrum, there is another type of woman who retains all the characteristics of feminine behavior and identity but wants an emotional and sexual partner of the same sex. This woman does not identify with men; she wants to be dominated and possessed by another woman who will reassure her of her femininity because she dislikes men. The thought of being touched by a man makes her cringe. In a relationship with a man she feels abused, even raped; with a woman the synchronization of feelings, actions, and thoughts makes her respond to the point of orgasm. These negative feelings are the result of her relationship with her father or with some other significant male figure who mistreated her. She became resentful of men, rejecting them on any level of sexual interaction. Some clinicians have assumed that the lesbian who has a need to be taken care of affectionately by another woman wants to reenact the mother-daughter relationship, which may in reality have been distorted in some way. In fact, she is unable to perceive men as loving, affectionate partners. She is conditioned to respond negatively to them. It is true that in some cases an emotional closeness between mother and daughter from which male interaction has been excluded precludes the possibility of the young girl developing a model for relating to men. In these cases there is, in addition, a detached or an abusive father who inhibits the girl in developing any future attachment to men.

Regardless of which factors have caused an individual to become a lesbian, her attraction to a woman is based on the use of magical thinking to transform the partner into a man without a penis or to become a man herself. She wants a partner who possesses feminine traits such as supportiveness, tenderness, and warmth, combined with those of a weak man. One type of lesbian wants to interact with another woman who will evoke the relationship that she had or missed having with her mother, while the other type identifies with a man, playing a pseudomale role and denying her femininity in order to enjoy it in the woman she possesses. In either case both partners play a fantasy role supported by the magical thinking maintained unchanged since childhood.

It is interesting that while male homosexuality is considered by some to be caused by genetic/biological factors, this hypothesis was not extended to lesbianism. Sexual anatomy and the receptive role of women in sex make it possible for most lesbians to interact with men if they wish to, which is not the case for male homosexuals, who, if untreated, are unable to perform sexually with women.

Regardless of whether homosexuality has or has not a constitutional basis, the dynamics of magical thinking is still responsible for the way the homosexual perceives himself or herself in relation to the opposite sex. Recourse to magic makes it possible for them to see themselves differently than gender would indicate. The homosexual, like the heterosexual, can develop a wide range of other sexual polymorphic behavior, from fetishism to transvestism to sadomasochism, in addition to distortion of gender-identity. It is finally a question of the degree to which an individual appeals to magic to replace reality in sexual interaction.

9

A NEW APPROACH
TO THERAPY

Maturational
Thought-Process Therapy

Each theory becomes a Procrustean bed on which the
empirical facts are stretched to fit a preconceived pattern.
—ERNST CASSIRER, *An Essay on Man*

THE OLD THERAPEUTIC PROCESS

It seems that most neurotic people operate on two cognitive levels in negotiating their environments: the adult, logical level, and the prelogical level of
childhood, which reveals itself in maladaptive coping responses to certain
stressful events. Although the neurotic may appear reasonable when he is
operating on the logical level and may even be aware of the "irrational"
nature of the neurotic aspects of his behavior, this logic alone cannot help
him control his neurotic responses, because these responses are the result of a
long-established, distorted manner of perceiving and responding to certain
types of situations. The neurotic in fact operates with alternate states of
consciousness according to the conditions with which he is faced. In specific
types of situations that have become emotionally charged for him because of
past experiences, he suspends logical evaluation and replaces it with automatic neurotic responses based on his consistent perception of such situations
as threatening. Thus the neurotic behavior is based on faulty perception of

both environment and self, which is triggered by the combination of his faulty appraisal of a situation and the attempt to solve it by irrational beliefs and magical means.

Though an individual comes to a therapist to alleviate his emotional suffering (such as anxiety, depression, and so forth), to be effective the therapeutic process *must* deal with these underlying psychological conflicts, the conflicts of distorted perceptions and judgments that result in the patient's faulty emotional response. Regardless of theoretical claims about the origins of the neurotic conflict, any therapy, in order to reach the patient and succeed in modifying his maladaptive behavior, must ultimately address the patient's conceptual and thought distortions.

Any interpretation given to a patient by the therapist (in the context of psychoanalytic theory or behavioristic models) is essentially an attempt to formulate the patient's distorted appraisal and response to events into a set of explanations or procedures that should correct that distortion. Although therapists differ in theoretical explanations and strategies employed, they have something in common: the interaction with the patient that permits the therapist to persuade him that they will work.

In order to appreciate the importance of this interaction in the dynamics of therapy, we must examine the factors recognized by researchers as basic to the success of the therapeutic process. In fact, the most important of these factors appears to be related to the positive nature of the personal interaction between the therapist and the patient. It is the factor responsible for the patient's hope of a cure that is strongly based on the therapist's claims about his professional experience and previous successes. In this interaction the therapist claims that he possesses a body of knowledge that can explain the nature of the patient's mental conflict and provide effective ways of dealing with it. Thus the therapist asks the patient to believe in him and his methods. In exchange, the patient entrusts his emotional difficulties to the therapist and commits himself to the therapeutic procedure. To a great extent the specific nature of the therapeutic procedure may be less important than the quality of the relationship between therapist and patient (this can be inferred from the fact that neuroses can be treated, at least temporarily, with the same success by therapists whose theoretical backgrounds are at odds with one another).

The therapist and patient support each other in their interaction by a reciprocal set of beliefs that sanction the validity of their relationship. The patient, in his need to believe that this therapist will be able to help him, must have faith in the therapist's qualities as a healer; while the therapist believes that his knowledge and expertise indeed give him the power to solve the emotional conflicts of others. If, in this reciprocal relationship, either therapist or patient retreats from his position, the therapeutic process collapses.

A revealing example of the dynamics of the therapeutic interaction, based on mutual acceptance of the magical power of the process, is given by Franz Boas in the story of a Canadian shaman who became famous for his talent in treating various physical and emotional afflictions by simple exorcism. This shaman, during his period of training, had believed very little in the methods of his teacher, and had followed the teacher's success in the treatment of sick people with skepticism; but when he mastered his teacher's methods and had his first success with a patient, he started to believe in them. He modified his methods to suit his own needs and became extremely successful. Patients were drawn to him because of his spectacular methods of exorcism, and he gained the confidence of the community. This confidence ensured his success and strengthened his belief in the reliability of his methods. The older shaman gradually lost his clientele to his pupil, as well as the support of the community, and he went mad.

But we need not refer to primitive societies to demonstrate the role played by the power of belief in the interaction between therapist and patient. Mesmer's success in the eighteenth century in treating various illnesses that might now be diagnosed as hysteria shows that people in civilized societies are also susceptible to the power of magical thinking, especially when faced with the immediate need for relief from suffering. Mesmer's proclamation of "animal magnetism" as the basic principle of a new therapy made him, for a short time, a famous therapist in Vienna and Paris. But when the French Academy withdrew its sanction of his therapy, his success faded almost immediately. Nevertheless, he was the precursor of modern psychotherapy through his discovery of the use of hypnosis and suggestion in therapy, even though he misinterpreted its meaning. What he called *animal magnetism* is still a key part of the therapist-patient interaction. It is known today as suggestion on the part of the therapist and suggestibility on the part of the patient.

Modern psychotherapy traces its origin to the techniques of suggestion and hypnosis as developed by the French school of the nineteenth century. What Freud did was to replace hypnotic suggestion with a sophisticated interpretative form of suggestion that was supposed to lift the repression of the emotionally charged memories. It involved a continual process of reincantation of the individual's childhood experiences punctuated by periodic interpretations by Freud himself.

This process was enhanced by a mystical ambiance and a ritualized interaction between therapist and patient. The dim lighting, the secluded atmosphere, the image of the patient reclining on a couch while the analyst sits by, detached and impassive, are all parts of the mystique of the therapeutic process; all serve to heighten the confessional atmosphere, the illusion of a sanctuary in which time is suspended and the patient's life is reconstructed and relived under the guidance of the all-powerful healer. The sessions, three to five times weekly, are designed to encourage the continual intimate interaction between the therapist and patient.

The importance attached to the interaction between therapist and patient in psychoanalysis is demonstrated by the elevation of this relationship to a mystical level in the principle of transference. In the dynamic of *transference*, the therapist plays a double role for the patient: first, the patient transfers to him the unconscious attitudes and emotions of his past, related to other significant figures in his life (the patient's anger toward his father, for instance, may become anger toward the analyst); second, the therapist serves as a corrective emotional model for the development of healthy interpersonal relationships. Though transference is theorized as part of an unconscious dynamic interaction between patient and therapist, in reality it can be explained as an intense relationship that facilitates intimate communication and permits gradual indoctrination of the patient into the theoretical model of the therapist.

The dignified, sacerdotal atmosphere of the therapist's office, to which is lent the prestige of his title as physician-healer, facilitates the therapeutic process, maximizing the patient's belief in the healing power of the therapist. The therapist, protected by a set of unverifiable hypotheses, places himself beyond criticism. Any objection by the patient to the therapist's interpretation of his behavior is considered resistance to therapy; any failure of the patient to improve is considered a sign of such resistance. Furthermore, since the length of the therapy is decided by the therapist, any termination by the patient, regardless of how many years he has been in therapy, can be considered premature, the ultimate sign of the patient's resistance to his own improvement.

This foolproof system of defenses places the therapist in an enviable position of infallibility that until recently enhanced his standing with the community. For the patient, however, this often proves detrimental, as it encourages him to conceive of himself as relatively powerless and of his problems as beyond his own ability to control.

THE CHEMOTHERAPEUTIC AND BEHAVIORIST APPROACHES

With the advent of tranquilizers and antidepressives and of sophisticated methods for evaluating the effectiveness of psychotherapy, acceptance of psychoanalysis started to ebb. At the same time cognitive-behaviorist therapies came into prominence. The latest cognitive-behaviorists believe that the irrational thoughts and behavior of the neurotic are caused by naïve convictions that result in maladaptive behavioral expression. They believe that through deconditioning and persuasion the patient will change his attitudes and modify his maladaptive behavior. In this context, the therapist-patient relationship is important in terms not of transference but of the ability of the therapist to convince the patient that errors of judgment are responsible for his discomfort. It is the goal of the cognitive-behaviorist therapist to refocus the thinking of the patient on the current conditions of his life that require rational reinterpretation as offered by the therapist, so that the patient can develop the ability to control his irrational beliefs. But the patient would not be able to control them on his own without being guided by the therapist.

In behavioral therapy, although the interaction is focused on modification of the symptoms by deconditioning, the mutual beliefs of the therapist-patient interaction still play a crucial role. The behaviorist who, for instance, works to decondition the anxiety responses of a phobic (such as someone who is afraid to cross the street) acts not only as the implementer of a therapy but also as an authoritative supporter who has the power to help the phobic against his irrational fears. This is confirmed by the fact that a phobic who is given a manual about "desensitization," explaining how to proceed step by step in controlling his condition, will not be able to succeed. When the time comes for him to "desensitize" himself to the fear of crossing the street, by crossing the street, he will be too afraid to step off the curb. Only under the supervision and in the office of the behaviorist is he likely to be successful in overcoming his fear. He requires the extra support connected with the power of the healer-therapist, who, the patient believes, possesses the special qualities that enable him to free the patient from his magical thinking.

On closer examination of both therapeutic systems, psychoanalytical or cognitive-behaviorist, we note that both assume that the thinking and behavior of the neurotic person in the areas of his distress are *irrational*. However, the methods by which they attempt to effectuate changes are far apart. The psychoanalytic therapist attempts to induce changes by replacing the repressed eroticized thinking of the patient with a systematized, all-inclusive set of explanatory beliefs about his behavior; the cognitive therapist attempts to correct the patient's faulty thinking by adjusting it to the social reality. Yet the patient faced with either one of these approaches is inclined to relate more to the therapist than to the theoretical system he espouses. The more confidence the patient has in the therapist, the more inclined he will be to accept his point of view. The higher the suggestibility of the patient, the easier it will be for him to assimilate his therapist's teachings.

If various forms of therapy relied only on the interaction between the therapist and patient to bring about the desired changes in the patient's thinking and behavior regardless of the concepts underlying them, then we should have to admit that any psychotherapeutic approach seems as valid as any other. However, this is not strictly the case. The psychological explanations of his behavior that are offered to a patient during the therapeutic process do have an impact on changing his behavior if they are the *right* explanations, regardless of their theoretical framework. In the final analysis, all interpretations discussed during the therapeutic process are indeed incorporated by the patient into his own system of logical thinking, as long as he is somehow able to find them specifically meaningful in terms of his perception of reality. Generalizations and abstractions about the patient's behavior, such as those dictated by the preconceived notions of psychoanalysis, are more likely to be meaningless to the average patient, or to distract him from his real difficulties and ensnare him in a whole new set of mythological beliefs. This is hardly likely to help the patient correct his poor perceptions of situations that cause him anxiety.

In this light the cognitive-behaviorist approach would seem to hold more promise of success, since its practitioners attempt specifically to recondition the patient's responses to misperceived stimuli and to correct his maladaptive attitudes. However, although behaviorist conditioning is often successful in freeing patients from phobic reactions or mild forms of sexual-compulsion patterns, it is much less useful in treating other forms of neurosis, such as paranoia or hysteria. This is because of the behaviorist's narrow focus of treatment, which defines the patient's problem solely in terms of the stimulus-response dynamic related to the specific maladaptive behavior. This approach is well suited to some neurotic conditions, because these patients are usually receptive to conditioning, and because their problems are clearly maintained by conditioning; but such a narrow approach does not permit a true evaluation of the pattern of development of the maladaptive behavior and of the general pattern of thinking that the behavior reflects. The behaviorists or the neo-behaviorist-cognitive therapists deal with isolated symptoms of neurosis, but if the neurotic behavior is a result of the interference of remnants of prelogical, childish thinking that are integrated into adult judgment, then to cure the neurosis we must first correct this defect of thinking; otherwise the same type of behavior will manifest itself in other areas of individual activity.

The attempt to correct the irrational thinking of the neurotic is nothing new. In fact, the Russian school of psychotherapy has strongly espoused the rational approach to the control of neurotic behavior, in addition to selective deconditioning. In the United States rational-cognitive therapy sprang up as an alternative to the ebbing psychoanalysis. But both the Russian and American schools of rational therapy deal only with irrational thinking as related to and displayed in the symptomatic neurotic behavior. The neurotic is made to see the implications of his faulty reasoning and is guided toward change in his behavior and thinking by a process of persuasion or confrontation.

The problem with this approach becomes clear when we consider that the "irrational behavior" of the neurotic is inextricably associated with emotionally laden past experiences. The feelings associated with these memories are likely to overpower any attempt to correct the neurotic behavior by a simple appeal to the logical rules of thinking. The persuasion of the therapist will work only in situations where the power of his convictions as perceived by the patient is strong enough to overcome the anxiety produced by the emotionally charged situation. Most often the patient cannot respond to the persuasive approach because the emotions associated with the development of the neurotic thinking are too strong. In the case of the phobic or compulsive, for instance, the knowledge that his behavior is irrational and detrimental to his own interests is of little help; he knows this very well, yet he is unable to alter his behavior. The discussion of faulty logic and the analysis of erroneous generalizations in his thinking, while important to the patient's growth in awareness, are not in themselves sufficient to solve his difficulties.

MATURATIONAL THOUGHT-PROCESS THERAPY

What is needed, then, is a therapy that will address the illogical thinking while not failing to take into account the emotional residue of past experiences that have led to the patient's faulty perception and reasoning; a therapy that recognizes the influence of childlike thinking and childhood experiences on the thinking of the adult, without bringing to consideration of the childhood influences any preconceived notions (such as the theories of Freud) that might prejudice interpretation of these experiences.

A therapy must take into account that a maladaptive response is the result of an interaction between environmental forces and the learned coping mechanisms of the individual, which themselves are affected mainly by his inability to perceive correctly a given situation. The therapeutic process must modify this incompetent or inadequate thought-process system. The emotional reaction experienced during the event should be viewed as a signal of the patient's discomfort with the situation and an indicator that the situation has been poorly resolved.

In fact, in any new situation the patient's reflexive assessment of the new event is also within the context of his previous experiences and will bring back the same set of emotions experienced in the past, unless the perceptual appraisal of the event is changed. This reflexive response to new situations does not permit the patient to search for alternative means of responding in a more effective and productive way. Although he may realize that his behavior is "irrational," the inadequate responses based on beliefs are so well ingrained that he is afraid to change because he fears that he will experience even worse emotions associated with the initial event.

What is required is an all-encompassing therapy that addresses the patient's individual development and view of the world not as a theoretical paradigm but as a unique case of problematic reasoning. Since such a therapy would focus its attention on the past and present developmental patterns of the patient's perceptual and logical evaluation of reality. I would call it *maturational thought-process therapy*. It is maturational to the extent to which it attempts to discard, through a specific therapeutic process, the old pattern of thinking formulated in childhood, in favor of the new, mature, logical evaluation of reality. Otherwise, if these patterns of thinking are not changed, they distort the individual's perception of reality, interfering with his ability to cope efficiently with significant events of his life. It is a therapy of redefinition, in logical, mature terms, of the meaning given to his behavior, and others', free of beliefs and magical assumptions about reality.

THE TREATMENT OF ANXIETY WITH
MATURATIONAL THOUGHT-PROCESS THERAPY

In general, every individual suffering from neurotic anxiety has a poor style of coping with normally stressful situations. In this case it is important not only to identify the patterns of prelogical thinking responsible for his anxiety reactions but also the meanings he attributes to those events that are the main source of his anxiety. The entire world of the anxiety-ridden individual has to be analyzed, evaluated, and restructured in adult, logical terms. Only when the individual is able to recognize the distortions of his thinking, only when he is able to free himself emotionally from the nonsensical nature of his forebodings, will he be able to give up these fears. When he is able to give up his belief in his projections of negative events, he will be free of his anxiety.

Consider, for instance, the plight of the patient suffering from desertion anxiety, from the fear that his partner will reject him because he is somehow unworthy of love. He is filled with doubts about himself and about his ability to maintain the interest of his partner. He feels insecure, inadequate, inferior. All of these feelings stem from his childhood perception of himself in his relationships to significant others, a perception that has remained unmodified. His distorted perceptions of his interaction with others aggravate his feelings of inadequacy, which in turn reinforce his need for approval and further undermine his ability accurately to assess the attitudes of others toward him. To become free of this circle, he must upgrade the pseudological level of thinking on which his view of himself rests to a logical, adult level of evaluation of himself and others.

The therapy for such a patient should attempt to analyze the meaning of the concepts of love, acceptance, and closeness that he developed in childhood, in order to help him see the origin of his present irrational interpretation of his intimate interactions with others. He must see his concept of love as only a means of obtaining the acceptance of another, to compensate for his lack of self-esteem and insecurity in intimacy, before he can attempt to formulate another concept.

For such an individual, when the love of the partner fades away and the magical protection of love that made him feel secure and adequate disappears, his sense of inadequacy becomes even stronger. The rebuilding of self-esteem will be possible only when the anxiety-ridden person is able to accept an accurate view of himself instead of a false, distorted one. The therapeutic process should make him aware of the qualities he offers. At the same time, he must develop a critical attitude toward his partner in order to weigh more objectively how well each meets the other's real emotional needs. Gradually he must extend this objectivity to all of his interactions. Only when he realizes that in any interaction between two people each offers something of value to the other will he be able to see the true nature of such interactions and to attempt to balance them objectively. He may still face crises and have anxiety when faced with difficult interpersonal situations, but this anxiety will be proportional to the normal anxiety experienced by most people in coping with life.

Similarly, for a phobic patient to overcome the anxiety related to a specific act or object that causes him extreme and irrational fear, he must become free of the whole pattern of his prelogical thinking through maturational restructuring of his thinking. This requires an analysis of his faulty appraisal and response to events, especially of events he perceived as traumatic. After he comes to understand that his judgment is faulty, it is necessary to determine whether the same sort of interpretation has been repeated in similarly perceived circumstances throughout his life. This reconstruction of the patient's neurotic thinking enables him to dissociate anxiety-inducing events and situations from the concomitant emotional response he brings to them. Once he is free from the emotional reactions that interfere with his coping responses, he can learn new logical approaches to appraising and solving events.

In the case of Susan, the phobic young woman described in chapter 4, her fear of subways did not subside until she became more secure in her rational appraisal of events in her life and more confident of her ability to cope with them. Then she became free of forebodings. As her pattern of thinking matured in this area, her attitude toward herself changed and she no longer saw herself as helpless and lost in the face of situations that normally would have been nonthreatening. The examination of her fears of abandonment by her boyfriend, which she associated with memories of abandonment by her father, enabled her to see clearly the difference between the two unrelated situations. The experiences of childhood and those of adulthood were compared in terms of their significance to her present sense of herself and in light of the different types of thinking that she used then and should use now. Her fear of riding subways was also discussed in the context of the association she had made to her childhood fears of abandonment, a lingering anxiety reactivated when she found herself lost in an isolated station. Her dizziness and nausea were appraised as a reaction of the autonomic nervous system, an expression of her anxiety that would have passed as soon as she perceived the situation as no longer threatening. Gradually she came to realize that her fear of fainting in subways was a simple projective image related to her view of herself as a helpless girl. She realized that she had been extrapolating feelings from childhood experiences to adult events, which she perceived in a similar manner. The judgment used in the situation was formulated on a pseudological level of juxtaposing unrelated events, of projecting magical beliefs that terrible things would happen to her if she were not protected by a man—the same type of thinking she had used to conclude that her father would abandon her.

At the same time she was encouraged to take short trips by subway, during which she was to give herself positive suggestions appropriate to her new evaluation of herself. After testing herself on these trips, she went on longer trips, first accompanied by someone who would get off after a while and leave her alone to continue the trip. With this type of support she was able to overcome her anticipatory anxiety, and eventually she became free of any fear of subway riding. Interestingly, a new state of anxiety (though less intense) started when her relationship to a new boyfriend became unstable. However, at that time she experienced only mild anxiety in riding the subway, and she was able to overcome it by reminding herself that there was no relation between traveling by subway and feeling upset about her new boyfriend. During the therapeutic process, other beliefs, fears, and superstitions that were remnants of her childhood magical thinking and had become part of her coping response to situations were discussed. Gradually they were replaced by a more adult and logical view of the world.

In addition, examination of her pattern of thinking and coping mechanisms revealed that whenever she was faced with stressful events she had a tendency to introject a sense of magical expectations. This magical response indicated the extent to which, underneath a veneer of logical evaluation of reality, she was still controlled by the old coping mechanism of childhood that was her response to crises.

The treatment of the obsessive-compulsive patient must similarly attack the problem of controlling or discarding irrational thought. Here the therapist is dealing with an individual who believes in and performs acts of pure magic, such as the ritual acts of Dorothy, the woman cited in chapter 4, whose compulsive behavior patterns included checking and rechecking the knobs of the gas stove or repeatedly verifying the contents of her purse before any important business appointment—acts whose significance defies adult logic. Yet for the compulsive person these acts have great significance. For Dorothy, the checking of the stove protected her against forebodings of imminent catastrophe, and verifying the items in her purse reassured her that she was in control of the transaction she was about to negotiate. When these acts were scrutinized more closely, it was found that they were part of a pattern of behavior she had used as a child. She had to be sure to leave everything in order in her room as she left for school, or else her mother would scold her, which in turn would make her upset and cause her to have a bad day in school. The need to have her home and purse in order when she left for work was an extension of the same pattern of behavior. The repeated checking of stove knobs and electrical outlets stemmed from the fear instilled in childhood that she might make mistakes involving these objects that could have dire consequences for her life.

This educated woman also believed that she possessed the power to protect the lives of others by performing special rituals. This was another facet of her belief that by various manipulations she could influence how things would happen. She believed, for instance, that by keeping the lights in her living room turned on all night and repeatedly thinking positively about a person she wished to protect, she could protect him, wherever he was. This magical belief was traced to experiences of her childhood: when she waited for her father to come home from a long trip, she would keep her light on so that he would come to her room to see why the light was on. This was proof to her of the power of her wishes.

Therapy for Dorothy was directed toward retracing the evolution of these patterns of thinking from their formulation in childhood, within the context of the emotional circumstances responsible for them, to the present time. To understand the mistaken notions of cause and effect based on circumstantial links that had determined her interpretations of these events as a child was crucial if she was to come to understand the reasons behind her compulsive behavior. She had to see that in situations perceived by her as similar to those of her childhood she responded with this ritualized behavior in order to control her anxiety. In other words, her incompetent appraisal of stressful situations and her inadequate responses to them carried over from childhood were the cause of her madadaptive performance. Then she had to begin to learn new skills for evaluating anxiety-producing situations. The magical "foolproof security," which she constructed in childhood but which did not work in adulthood, had to be replaced with a realistic evaluation of the potential risk involved in her activities.

Such a process is difficult for the obsessive-compulsive person. He must learn to see his compulsive actions, as well as the situations that give rise to them, in the context of the laws of logical causality. Yet the renunciation of rituals brings on strong anxiety and depression, unless the process of reorganization of thinking is done gradually and meaningfully for the patient.

For instance, a compulsive person who does not touch specific objects because he is afraid of contamination with germs from other people may be able to overcome his misconceptions if he is gradually deconditioned from them by being convinced of the reality that he does not in fact get sick after contact with the "infected object." However, obsessive-compulsive thinking is rarely restricted to only one area of activity; in general, it is a mode of thinking and approaching reality that affects all of the patient's psychosocial activities. Such an individual has a rigid concept of the world and of himself. His concept of human interaction is centered on his need for a feeling that he is in control of things. Because his system of beliefs and rituals is inefficient for coping with the event, his anxiety continues to increase, resulting in an intensification of his ritualized behavior. The attempt to check the anxiety by increasing the amount of ritualization has gradually gotten out of control.

The therapy must question, test, and replace this all-encompassing sys- .

tem of beliefs. Once the patient realizes, by gradually reducing the number of times each ritual is repeated, that nothing will really happen to him as a result of his failure to repeat it, his anxiety will be reduced and his system of beliefs will start to crumble. If at the same time he works with his therapist to reorganize his thought processes on an adult level of thinking, he may be freed from the interference of magical thinking.

In some cases, however, the patient's anxiety remains despite this gradual reorientation of his thinking. It is then advisable to explore his conceptual interpretation of the world, its superstitions and beliefs, and the symbolic significance that he attaches to things in all phases of his life. This involves a shift in emphasis from the illogic of his compulsive acts to the magical basis of his mode of existence.

In other cases the individual is plagued by obsessive thoughts that may or may not be accompanied by compulsive behavior. These thoughts are the direct manifestations of his irrational interpretations of phenomena, as characterized by extreme fear of potential disasters in certain situations, fear of accidents, fear of causing his own death, or obsession with obscene words or acts. The obsession is the unrealistic, anxiety-producing idea that the individual tries to offset either by the performance of the compulsive act or by an activity or another positive thought. The obsession and the compulsion are bound together by the emotional link of anxiety. In this case the obsessive thoughts represent only one aspect of more general unexpressed systematized beliefs and superstitions that are incorporated into his routine activities.

For instance, a patient was obsessed, while walking, with counting young women dressed in sports clothes. This was found to be related to a pleasant association with a young woman dressed in sports clothes whom he had met by chance on the street and with whom he had a transient, enjoyable affair. She had left him abruptly, and he did not know her address. Whenever he thought about her, a strong desire to search for her or for other women dressed in sports clothes made him scan the street. He counted them up to seven—because seven was his lucky number. If he did not recognize her or notice any other attractive woman among the seven, then he lost his hope of seeing her or meeting a replacement. A few minutes later he would start the ritual all over again. After a series of attempts he would become depressed, and the obsession would lessen, replaced by a feeling of helplessness. Only when he realized that his counting up to seven was part of the magical thinking by which he was attempting to find her, only when he accepted the probability that he would never see her again, was he able to reduce his desire to look for her. His obsession truly disappeared when he met another woman, who diverted his attention from his old love.

Other obsessions appear even more bizarre, like that of an educated young Catholic woman who was obsessed with four-letter words for penis or sexual intercourse. Her sexual obsession extended to the association of any cylinder-shaped object on the street, or in a store or house, with a penis and intercourse, which upset her even more. Her conflict was between her religious beliefs that were denying her sexual freedom and the changed social values that made her aware of her sexual needs, resulting in great frustration. She felt that her upbringing and religious moral censorship had cheated her of freely enjoying her newly gained understanding of her sexuality. Her obsessions were eliminated when she focused on her changing sexual attitudes, more freely pursuing her love affairs. It is interesting to see how she utilized magic in her desire to solve her sexual conflict. For her, utterance of the "dirty words" was an act of sexual freedom, yet her moral values made her feel ashamed and guilty, thereby increasing her conflict. As a result, she started to think that she did not have control over her thoughts because they were expressed against her will, while in reality she was uncomfortable about facing and solving her sexual conflict.

In general most obsessive thoughts represent mental pictures of acts or situations that would be repulsive or undesirable to the patient if they were actually to happen. He is afraid that he will lose control over the thought and perform the act or will get involved in that distressing situation. The individual truly believes that the thought can be executed or expressed without his will, exactly as children in their prelogical level confuse the thought with the act.

The therapy must attack the patient's unjustified beliefs or fears, as well as his belief that he has no control of the execution of his thoughts. When both these beliefs are destroyed, he will be able to give up his behavior and conquer his anxiety. When he is able to recognize and correct the entire complex of his magically oriented, childish thinking, he will be able to develop new and more viable ways of coping with life.

The world of an anxiety-ridden person is filled with real or imaginary worries. As we have seen, the unfolding of any significant event in a particular area of his concern, be it his health or his relationship with a loved one, is fraught with danger because he is not sure of the outcome. Signs, clues, and statements that are at best questionable are interpreted by the anxious person as possible evidence that something unpleasant will happen to him. If he is preoccupied with his health, shortness of breath becomes a sign of impending death, a pain in the chest forecasts a heart attack, a swollen gland is a malignant tumor, and a cold is the beginning of pneumonia. Because he sees himself as weak, always threatened by illness, to which he may succumb, a great deal of his time and effort is devoted to monitoring any irregularity that, if not immediately attended to, may result in a catastrophe.

What must be made clear to the patient is his confusion about the role of the thought process in the arousal of anxiety. The anxiety appears to him to be triggered automatically, without apparent relation to any evaluation of the event. In other words, the anxiety seems to him to be set off without any demonstrable reason. In reality, what he does not realize is that the evaluation is reflexive, based on the stored affective memory, specific to the event that is automatically recalled in any similar or similarly perceived situation. However, this evaluation is based on prelogical memories. As a result, his response is automatically "irrational," as it stems from the magical, not the rational. This is why the therapeutic process must focus on the distortions of reality caused by these primary thought processes in order to help the individual replace his "irrational" approach with an evaluation based on logic. When this is repeatedly done successfully, mature thinking becomes the individual's routine approach to reality.

TREATMENT OF DEPRESSION

The individual who becomes excessively depressed for a long period of time, when faced with a significant loss or failure, betrays the fact that he has never understood or accepted the true nature of human life and the uncertainty of human fortune. It is likely that since childhood he has shown at various times a lack of resiliency in adversity, a low tolerance for frustration, and poor adaptability to difficult situations. Therapy for such a person must critically reevaluate the development of his thinking through his formative years in order to discover how that development might have led to his depressive tendencies.

As was mentioned in chapter 5, some unpleasant childhood experiences, such as separation from the mother at a critical period, death of a parent, or family interactions leading to a learned sense of helplessness may predispose an individual to depression—particularly when these early experiences are reinforced by further frustrations in life. An individual thus predisposed has a tendency to see himself as powerless in the face of adverse events, or helpless and lost when faced with unrecoverable losses. This tendency can be corrected only after a critical reevaluation of his real adult capabilities, his true powers of coping with distressing situations. The therapeutic process must help him overcome his negative view of himself. The feeling that nothing will work out for him or that the future holds nothing for him must be replaced by a realistic appraisal of his achievements and expectations, in an attempt to give more meaning and direction to his present and future activities.

Some individuals become depressed because of the emotional conflict arising from overly strict adherence to a set of social or moral values. In their childhood they learned a set of moral and social values that, since that time, have become guidelines for the conduct of their lives. When their life experiences contradict their fundamental social values, they feel that they have suffered a loss and become depressed. The depression is caused by their inability to accept the unreliability of the human code of social and moral values, or to admit the frailty of human relationships. They feel that they have been rejected by others. Obviously their view of human interaction is distorted. Therapy must help them reappraise these views in the light of the inconsistency of human nature.

It is common for people to become depressed after some significant loss such as failure in business, or the loss of a loved one, but when the event takes on catastrophic proportions, when the depression lasts an inordinately long time, then it is neurotic and therapy is necessary. The depressed individual feels that life has lost all value and can derive gratification from nothing. The therapist must question the patient's attitude toward life and reevaluate the significance with which he has endowed the lost object or person. Analysis of the lost activity or person often reveals that it had enough *un*desirable aspects to cause the therapist to question the patient's extreme grief at its loss. For instance, the loss of a lover may be viewed as the loss of a source of pure joy, when in reality the patient's relationship with the lover was not that pleasant. Ed, whose rejection by his wife was discussed in chapter 5, was unable to find fault with her at first, but after some soul-searching he admitted that she had had personality problems that had made her difficult to live with. The more he thought about certain aspects of her personality and her behavior toward him, the easier it was for him to mobilize his anger against the object whose loss was the source of his depression. When this is possible, it has a salutary effect on the depressed individual's self-esteem, and helps him seek direction for a reorganization of his life.

Another emotional conflict that the therapist must help the depressed patient solve is that of guilt. The depressed individual often feels guilty with regard to his alleged failures in the relationship with a lost or dead loved one; he accuses himself of having treated that person unjustly almost as though he has committed a sin. In his judgment, based on the assumption that there is a causal connection between punishment and sin, he believes that he is responsible for his own tragedy. He believes that his present condition is, in a sense, the fulfillment of a destiny. Though he lacks evidence, he reacts as if he were purposefully destined for punishment by divine forces. This type of guilt is the result of his misinterpretation of his own moral beliefs, familially or culturally developed, which make him think that his acts are arbitrarily classified as sinful, hence deserving of punishment. While on the one hand he holds himself responsible for his unfair treatment of the lost love object, on the other hand he blames his loss on an inplacable destiny that has singled him out for suffering. Thus he feels unworthy, self-accusatory, or even suicidal.

His pseudologic, along with its negative emotional baggage, must be carefully reviewed with the patient, in the light of his particular moral beliefs about his unmet responsibilities toward the lost party. He must be able to see his failures as the result of error and human fallibility rather than of his innate wickedness or worthlessness. The facility with which he can overcome his feelings of guilt will be determined by his ability to view the distressing situation as part of the continuum of favorable and unfavorable events that constitutes his life, as an unpleasant learning experience that can teach him how better to mobilize his resources toward future crises and future successes.

Applying the same logical approach to the suicidal thoughts of the depressed patient, it becomes clear that suicidal thinking is an indulgence in self-pity combined with loss of ability to project a positive future. Sometimes it is also an attempt to gain the pity of others. Suicide can thus be viewed as an act of total self-rejection, or as an irrational attempt to punish others or totally sever relationships. If the individual survives, he may come to see this act as a meaningless, impulsive gesture.

Since, for the suicidal person, life has lost its value, the therapeutic process should reevaluate the judgment that led him to that conclusion and restore his sense of worth by anchoring that sense to whatever aspect of life still appears to arouse interest in him. The balance of his motivation should be restored by helping him see life in a different perspective, one in which his suffering and problems are temporal, relative, and unworthy of the sacrifice of his life. Most suicidal patients are ready to grasp at any solution that offers them the option of continuing living. Many suicide attempts represent a "cry for help"; the individual does not really want to die but is unable to cope with his emotional pain. The therapist must help him to restructure his thinking and meaning of life so that he can see more readily the reasons to continue living.

If the depressed or potentially suicidal patient shows a lack of resiliency to setbacks, inability to cope with the vicissitudes and tribulations of human fortune, and poor adaptability to unfriendly circumstances, then the therapeutic process must help him change his view of the world and of himself. He must learn to accept the unreliability and unpredictability of human nature and fortune and to rely more on his own resources in achieving his goals.

THE RELATIONSHIP AND TREATMENT OF CHRONIC ANXIETY AND DEPRESSION

I have been referring to anxiety and depression as two separate emotional responses. However, although each one of these emotional reactions may occur separately, they are usually experienced together. For instance, anxious people, when they function poorly as a result of their fears, become depressed; and depressed individuals suffer from anxiety when they ruminate about the succession of events leading to their failure or loss. The individual's feeling that he is unable to prevent a loss causes him anxiety, which is replaced by depression when he feels powerless to recover from the loss. Anxiety and depression represent alternative emotional reactions resulting from incompetent coping responses to conflicts perceived either as threatening to the individual's sense of well-being or destructive to the value of his life.

It is important to note that the focal anxiety or depression experienced in coping with a particular event can linger on and will affect responses in other related situations. If the individual predisposed toward anxiety or depression is not treated effectively, his condition will generalize and become chronic. Anxiety or a depression that has become chronic can pose special problems for the therapist. When, for instance, a patient's anxiety is powerful enough to interfere with the treatment of his phobic, compulsive, or somatic condition, the therapist must resort to an initial relaxation approach designed to facilitate the therapeutic process.

However, in cases of generalized or chronic anxiety or depression, the relaxation approach rarely succeeds. Then, mild tranquilizers or antidepressants may be needed to control the emotional state of the patient. Otherwise he will remain resistant to the necessity for a new pattern of thinking. The clinical reasons for this are simple: the anxiety or depression, though induced by a defective thinking style and a faulty way of coping with events, causes, at its most basic level, a neurophysiological reaction of the brain expressed by a change in neurochemistry. Any emotional state is the expression of a chemical change in the activity of the brain neurotransmitters (specific chemical substances responsible for the transmission of neuroelectrical impulses in the brain, such as norepinephrine, dopamine, serotonin, cortisol, and others). The more persistent the emotional state, the more unchangeable it becomes because the chemical imbalance of the neurotransmitters is sustained. Although the mechanism by which the brain neurotransmitters produce these emotional states is not fully understood, the fact remains that the presence or absence of certain neurochemicals can be linked to certain emotional states: norepinephrine, for instance, is found to increase in periods of anxiety and depression, while cortisol appears to increase only with depression. Similarly, tranquilizers, by affecting neurosynaptic activity, are able to control anxiety, while antidepressants, with the same effect, alleviate depression.

The lessening of the patient's anxiety or depression reduces the power of his reflexive neurotic responses to events. When these reflexive responses are freed of their emotional context, the patient can begin to look at events in a new, more objective way. He is then able to assess his past experiences more realistically and to appreciate his present capabilities more fully. With an outlook free of magical beliefs he is able to explore fresh solutions to his problems. Gradually the need for tranquilizers or antidepressants is also eliminated.

THE TREATMENT OF PARANOID THINKING

The paranoid individual reacts with a variety of emotional responses, from anxiety and depression to frustration and anger, in circumstances that he considers hostile to him. His reactions are determined by his slanted interpretation of events. He is anxious and belligerent when his suspicious nature leads him to believe that something is being plotted against him by others; he is depressed when he is convinced that "they" have destroyed his chances of succeeding in the pursuit of his goals; he is angry when he is frustrated by others whom he feels are against him. The primary trait of the paranoid is this unjustified, inappropriate suspicion, anger, and hostility toward others whom he considers his enemies.

While mobilizing anger can be helpful in treating the depressed patient, in the treatment of the paranoid patient, anger is the first emotional response that must be controlled. Any attempt to modify by psychoanalytic interpretation or by desensitization the anger produced by an event proves counterproductive in the case of the paranoid. His thinking is too strongly oriented toward self-protection against a hostile world for him to be able to change it by, for instance, simple mental representation of the anger-producing event, as is required in desensitization. Such a representation would be likely to rekindle his anger. It can be controlled only when he ceases to see the world as aligned against him, when his set of beliefs and false assumptions about human interaction is corrected.

The paranoid's pseudological thinking patterns are built on perceptions of pseudocausal relationships between events that are in fact unrelated, or related only coincidentally or inferentially. They must be carefully reexamined by the therapist and patient together, and tested against the evidence of the patient's present life. This will help the patient gradually change his thinking from an evaluation of reality based on meaningful or assumed connections to one based on the tenets of logical causality. The tactful questioning of the patient's distortion in interpreting events, the logical reconstruction of an objective view of those events, will permit him to face errors in his thinking and seek alternatives for handling events that appear threatening to him. When the paranoid person becomes convinced that his personal expectations and assumptions, his preconceived view of reality, are responsible for his conflict with others, he will be able to seek alternative approaches to handling his relationship with others.

To reach this level of objectivity in the appraisal of events, he also has to change his perception of himself in his interaction with others. He must realize that his certainty that other people will try to take advantage of him or infringe his rights causes him to be argumentative and difficult toward them, and that his behavior contributes to the tension he interprets as proof of others' antagonism toward him. Furthermore, as long as he maintains an opinion about himself that is in discord with his real abilities and achievements, or with the opinion of him held by the world at large, he will have difficulty seeing himself and events objectively. The reevaluation of his view of himself requires careful analysis of the discrepancies between the reasons he gives for his failures and the real nature of the events that frustrate his efforts. Achieving an objective view of his frustrated need for self-realization will enable him to correct his view of himself and to eliminate his hostility toward others.

The therapist must expose and debate the hidden motives and special meanings that the paranoid assumes to be present in his interactions with others. In the final analysis, the gap in the evaluation of reality between the therapist and the paranoid person lies not in the factual presentation of events but in the significance attributed to them.

The therapist must provide the paranoid individual with alternative models for dealing with the events he considers hostile. In this way he will be able to learn to negotiate situations evenhandedly, free of distorted assumptions. Proof of the validity of his new type of thinking will be provided by the fact that the new approach will be beneficial to him in his dealings with others. This should represent the ultimate incentive for the paranoid person to change his mode of interpreting his interactions with others.

THE TREATMENT OF HYSTERICAL THINKING

One of the greatest challenges to the concept of maturational thought-process therapy is posed by the magical thinking of hysteria. In hysteria, the anxiety of the patient is dispelled and instead he develops either bizarre physical symptoms or an altered state of consciousness for which he denies any responsibility. The magical thinking of the hysteric is dependent on the satisfaction of the egocentric needs of his personality and his inability to cope with the adversities of adult life.

The "illness" of a conversion reaction, or the amnesia associated with hysterical dissociation, represents a magical solution that precludes confrontation with the situations that arouse anxiety; it is a childlike way of "making the problem go away." For instance, a woman in her late thirties, faced with a confrontation with her lover, whom she wanted to leave, unable to offer a satisfactory explanation for her behavior, threw herself down on the floor claiming that she was fainting. When pulled up by her lover she became uncontrollably excited and hostile. Rather than coping with the situation she "played dead."

Because the mechanism responsible for this type of reaction is autosuggestion, the therapy should also use the power of suggestion to free the patient. To facilitate this process, the patient's anxiety must be relieved as well. For instance, in the case of Gail (chap. 7), the threat of being confronted with a relationship with a new man had to be played down in order to alleviate the anxiety that had brought about the hysterical response.

Regardless of how successful this method may be, it represents only a temporary solution to the hysteric's problems. In order to achieve more permanent results, the therapy must analyze his incompetent coping style in order to demonstrate its inefficacy in adult situations. The hysteric's perception of certain situations as threatening, because of his lack of tolerance to frustration and to his egocentric thinking patterns, requires reorganization on a logical level. His projection of his helplessness in certain situations should be scrutinized as a manifestation of his poor self-image. His thinking will mature only when he learns to appraise his environment more objectively, when he changes his view of himself and of his unrealistic expectations of others. As part of this maturational process the hysteric must become less susceptible to the influences of others' opinions, more critical of human interaction, so that he becomes able to project more reasonable expectations. The impressionistic evaluation of an experience must be replaced by an analytic, systematic one in order to eliminate the subjective, immediate response that reduces his ability to cope successfully with the event.

THE TREATMENT OF SEXUAL DEVIANCE

Because of the failure of the psychoanalytic approach in treating sexual problems, deviant sexual behavior has been treated with various degrees of success by means of desensitization, aversion therapy, and other types of deconditioning. The idea behind this approach is simple: to provoke in the patient a feeling of gradual or total aversion toward the behavior that before the deconditioning had been exciting to him. The association of unpleasant experiences with the deviant behavior is supposed to reduce the desire for it to the point of extinction. This type of therapy, while it may temporarily modify the specific behavioral expression, does not basically alter the individual's concept of sexuality or of his relationship to the opposite sex. In order to develop a satisfactory sexual relationship with a member of the opposite sex, he must first acquire an altogether more mature concept of sexuality. In other cases simple desensitization by positive reinforcement will free the individual from the inhibiting anxiety (impotence, frigidity, premature ejaculation).

The sexual deviant is an individual who has remained sexually immature, controlled by childish fantasies about sex and about his sexual role. At some point during the development of his thinking and of his sexual behavior he came to identify sexuality with some specific form of sexual activity that aroused him, and this activity became for him the normal mode of sexual expression and gratification. Therapy must help him separate the meaning given to sexuality at this immature stage of development from its significance in the world of the mature adult. The magical or symbolic meaning that he attaches to sexuality must be replaced by a desire for a real member of the opposite sex.

The therapist must examine with the patient the specific nature of his misdirected sexual drive—whether this involves festishism, with its substitution of a symbolic object for a real partner, or homosexuality, with its illusion of the incorporation of the masculinity or femininity of the partner through sexual contact—and analyze it in the light of its relation to normal male-female sexual interaction and to the patient's other personality problems, such as shyness, awkwardness with the opposite sex, or poor identification with the male or female sexual role. The solution of these personality difficulties will permit the patient to redirect his sexual activity toward more normal patterns.

In the case of Ken, discussed in chapter 8, the therapeutic process must strengthen his male identity role before helping him to give up the symbolic meaning attached to female clothing. His fetishistic activity is part of his confused sexual identity; thus when he accepts his maleness in his relationships with women, then the magic of possessing a woman's qualities through wearing her clothes will lose its meaning. During therapy, the wearing of female clothes must be associated mentally with a grotesque travesty of his masculinity. This will act negatively on his sexual arousal, ultimately allowing him to relinquish this orientation. Concomitantly, the positive reinforcement of his male image, freed from the distorted sexual concepts of childhood, will help him recapture his male sexual identity. The emotional investment he had had in female clothes will be replaced by the positive experience of interacting with a woman.

The therapy must also analyze the patient's concept of his own body, with its sexual connotations for himself and others (as presented in chapter 8 in the case of Ron), and the therapist must seek to explore and elucidate the psychology of the patient's emotional interaction with the opposite sex, in order to free him of any sense of inadequacy and fear of rejection.

In the case of the male homosexual who is unhappy with his orientation and wishes to establish a meaningful relationship with a woman, the therapist must help him readjust his concept of women and his sexual drives toward a new set of stimuli, toward a new sexual physiognomy. He must replace his feelings toward the male erogenous zones with new feelings toward those of the female, within the context of his own arousal. This means that, at the beginning, the patient must associate the same methods of stimulation with the opposite sex as he used with the same sex, in order to be satisfactorily aroused and have a positive experience in his new sexual orientation.

This gradual orientation toward heterosexuality can be helped by a discussion of the patient's fears of women in general and sexual activity in particular, and the gradual elimination of them through positive imagery oriented toward his new form of sexual interaction. The main problem encountered in changing sexual orientation is that of anxiety. Ultimately, the anxiety in men is related to the fear of inadequate performance, whereas in women it is related to the fear of rejection. The solution to the problem is the patient's understanding of his needs in the sexual interaction with the opposite sex and gradual acceptance of his sexual capability, which gradually makes him more comfortable with his partner, provided he relates to a suitable one.

The same theoretical concepts apply to sadomasochistic behavior. Sadomasochists associated pain with sex in their childhood fantasies, and these fantasies are relived in the act of receiving or inflicting pain, which become as such a modality of sexual interaction. Later in life they remain accustomed to it and compensate for a lack of sexual passion in their lives by using pain to intensify their erotic pleasure. These concepts of sexuality must be replaced with normal, healthy attitudes about sex through the therapeutic process. The secondary benefit of intensifying erotic pleasure through pain will lose its appeal as the patient learns to appreciate the intensification of sexual passion that can occur in an atmosphere of love and trust.

A few conclusions can be drawn from these discussions of the general principles of maturational thought-process therapy. The most important point about this therapeutic strategy is that the emotional response is only a result of the individual's inability to appraise, cope with, and control a situation that he perceives as unfavorable. The fact that the patient comes to the therapist to allay his emotional suffering does not change the reality that the underlying causes of that suffering are distorted perceptions and magical judgments. Just because the patient is seeking help and recognizes his behavior as irrational, he does not necessarily have any insight into the thought processes that are at the root of his suffering.

In this context, the debate in psychotherapy about whether the psychologist should offer solutions to the patient's problem or should only interpret its emotional significance is pointless. The therapist's role is neither to be an adviser to the patient nor to be a theoretical instructor who will help him solve his conflict by merely offering explanations. Either of these approaches, applied rigidly, would be of little value in helping the individual develop new modes of coping on his own with events perceived by him as threatening. It is important that the patient not only realize his distorted appraisal of events and apprehend his possibilities for coping with them but be able to find, with the help of his therapist, new choices within the framework of a new outlook and a new, objective evaluation of his environment. The therapist, by evaluating, together with the patient, various courses of action or available choices in keeping with the patient's true opportunities and abilities, will help him indirectly to make the appropriate decisions.

It is important also to emphasize that all therapeutic methods, directly or indirectly, regardless of what they theoretically claim, try to deal with the elements of magical belief in the patient's conception of reality that interfere with his functioning. The problem is that the methods they use are sometimes counterproductive. For instance, the therapeutic method used by psychoanalysts more often than not reinforces the childish patterns of thinking by justifying the patient's behavior as the result of the alleged irrepressible power of the unconscious sexual conflict developed in childhood. The individual is somehow not responsible for his actions, as long as the conflict is unconscious and the patient is resistant to freeing himself from it. Ironically, the resistance itself is unconscious, which absolves the patient of any responsibility to change.

The behaviorists, on the other hand, although somewhat successful at eradicating certain neurotic symptoms, are unable to correct the infantile patterns of thinking that are and will continue to be responsible for a patient's maladjustment. The behaviorists do not focus on helping the individual develop a new style of coping with stressful life events, to demythologize his thinking about reality. They merely modify behavior through the removal of symptoms.

Only a therapeutic approach that changes the organization of the thought processes of the individual from magical to rational, and changes the patient's view of himself and of his interaction with others, can help him adjust properly to life. Because the aim of therapy is to improve the individual's ability to function in his areas of high vulnerability and to adjust to situations perceived as stressful, its ultimate focus should be on factors involved in the decision-making process, starting with his ability to appraise events that are anxiety-arousing or depressive and ending with his real skills for coping with such events. The following steps must be taken if this goal is to be achieved:

1. Identification of the patient's unique perception of reality and concept of the world.
2. Assessment of the areas of the individual's conflict with his environment and himself resulting from his particular view of reality.
3. Identification of the pattern of magical thinking, based on beliefs about himself, situations, and other people, that is responsible for his distortions.
4. Tracing of these patterns of magical thinking from their emergence at the prelogical level of evaluation of reality to the present time.
5. Dissociation of these pseudological patterns of thinking from their reflexive emotional component.
6. Gradual replacement of the pseudological thoughts, beliefs, and magical expectations with the realistic evaluation of conflictual events; reassessment of the patient's expectations of himself and others according to his new coping skills.

7. Step-by-step testing of reality as each pseudological judgment is eliminated (this process reinforces further removal of the old behaviors).
8. Actualization of the individual's potential by freeing him from his past ambiguous approach to life, which has stifled his freedom of choice in any decision-making process.

In summary, the effect of childhood patterns of thinking on the evaluation and analysis of new events must be examined and made clear to the patient. Also, his inner world must be explored and reconstructed in order to find the particular meaning and importance given by him to things and events that have shaped his concept of reality. Then the pseudological components must gradually be eliminated from his thinking. The emotional element of the pseudologic will lose its impact when the infantile beliefs, symbols, and distortions are eliminated from his thinking. The expression of feeling should not be suppressed by changing the therapeutic process to an intellectual exercise, as is done by the cognitive therapist. On the contrary, the emotional component of his thinking should be fully expressed and discussed at the same time as it is evaluated within the context of his judgment If his judgment is proven to the patient to be incorrect, it is obvious that the emotional state will change.

The whole therapeutic process is based on the sincere attempt to verbalize the most intimate thoughts, intentions, and convictions in order to reveal the meanings that the individual attaches to his actions and life.

The relationship between patient and therapist is a continuous, dynamic dialogue, a process of sharing, questioning, and probing the experiences of the patient in the light of the insight and knowledge offered by the therapist In this interpersonal communication and expression of feelings the therapist should not be a cold, dispassionate, authoritarian figure but a warm human being who understands and tries to help the patient free himself from the style of thinking that has long controlled him.

After therapy is completed the individual may still experience anxiety or depression, or hostility from others—as who does not?—but these feelings will be transitory, and he will be able to assess them within the context of a realistic view of the world. When they arise he will deal with such situations according to his objectively defined options.

Let us remember that only 30 percent of normal adult individuals function on a fully mature logical level, and that 55 percent operate only partially on this level. The remaining 15 percent use only rudiments of mature logic. It is not within the scope of maturational thought-process therapy to make the patient think completely logically in all of his social interactions. However, changing the patterns of pseudological thinking in areas of his emotional-cognitive conflict will give him alternatives in approaching reality that will lead to new possibilities for the organization of his behavior and activity. As long as the patient's beliefs do not conflict with his social intercourse with others, however, they should not be the subject of therapeutic thought modification. On the contrary, they may play an important adaptive role in his life.

Finally, therapy should help the individual to exercise his free choice in evaluating and coping with significant events in his life. This freedom of choice will permit him to give new meaning to his actions and to live free from the hindrances of past beliefs and unrealistic expectations. Only then will he be able to grow, affirm himself, and realize his true potential.

AFTERWORD

If an individual frees himself from the constraints of magical thinking and is able to reason logically about situations which frightened or upset him before, we should be able to assume that his therapy is terminated. Yet it rarely happens that people's problems are clearly circumscribed and do not permeate into other areas of life, either directly or indirectly.

In addition, an individual's beliefs and expectations for life might actually interfere with the full expression of his potential, and as a result he could experience a further sense of anguish at his lack of self-fulfillment. Even the individual who chooses to deny his opportunities for self-realization and attempts to rationalize self-imposed constraints may still feel discontented, frustrated, and cheated by life. When this happens, either of these people can feel that life has lost its meaning, that it is controlled by others, and that they must conform to a set of values imposed on them for the benefit of others. Simply, they feel alienated and self-estranged; that they live inauthentic lives.

In these cases the therapist can only help the individual try to redefine the meaning of his life toward a new social and personal perspective, and to try to point out to the individual when he is imposing self-restrictions based on distorted concepts, unjustified assumptions, and beliefs. Basically, the individual has to understand that his life takes place in the midst of shifting societal forces that can either advance or interfere with his self-actualization. Most likely in the course of his life he will be faced with dynamic situations, toward which he has to take positions according to his convictions and knowledge. While he should attempt to weigh his options objectively in any situation and press for a favorable solution, he also has to recognize that he might fail to succeed and that this does not mean that he is a failure or even that he would not be able to achieve his goals under a different set of circumstances.

The ability to develop a flexible outlook toward life unfortunately escapes most people. The result is either a tendency to feel overwhelmed and to give up or to feel that one must obstinately keep trying in the same manner despite nonexistent opportunities for success. Either way, individuals come to feel defeated. They have difficulty accepting this basic predicament of the human condition: that we are subject to unpredictability and uncertainty while committed to an elusive future. When confronted with disappointment or failure they look for explanations that border more on the irrational and magic than on reality and facts.

Furthermore, when projected plans collapse, most people take these situations as an act of personal injustice instead of seeing them as a simple sign of miscalculation or the result of unfortunate chance. It is hard for many people to admit that sometimes events in their lives are determined by random factors to which they can only react according to their best abilities and possibilities, if not passively. Yet, only the ability to maintain a sense of objectivity in a stressful event will permit an individual to evaluate the situation coolly and to handle it properly. In general, a person has to develop a dynamic view of life, which will help him understand that although his choices might appear to be limited in a particular situation, the situation will probably change with time and this will permit him to explore new choices not available to him before.

In this context life stops being an implacable and oppressive Greek tragedy or an ambiguous and frustrating Shakespearean drama, and becomes a meaningful and goal-directed continuum in which diverse forces temporarily counterbalance each other in order to change their equilibrium and develop a new position. The key to this is the perspective of the individual, who has to see himself as the master of himself *within his range of meaningful choices.* In the quest to satisfy his urges and drives, he has to learn to manipulate the complex external forces that confront him and accept an outcome that is sometimes favorable, at other times unfavorable, and always seen as temporal—subject to change.

His view of life has to embrace contentment and discontentment, success and failure, joy and suffering, and finally inescapable termination by death. His view of human nature should go beyond a static and fragmented concept that reduces its complex aspects to some categorical definitions of good or bad, noble or vulgar, egotistic or altruistic, cruel or self-sacrificing. Man is all these and more. He will always delight, surprise, or shock us by his creative actions or outrageous behavior, because he is sometimes rational and at other times irrational. Various sides of his nature will alternate according to his perception of events. We should never ignore these facts in our interaction with others.

Within this framework it is part of a responsible therapy to broaden a patient's view of life in order to help him to accept the responsibility he has toward himself to reach his full potential according to the choices available to him against the inevitable background of societal and environmental adversities. Certainly every individual will still experience anxiety and depression, but they will, we hope, be transient responses to temporary obstructions of plans or aspirations. These feelings, however, will dissipate if the individual approaches events with a flexible philosophy of life. A workable philosophy not only will help him overcome his negative feelings toward himself but will help him transcend crises by looking forward to better circumstances and a different strategy for self-expression, one that will continue to help him in his lifelong exploration of his own potential.

REFERENCES

Introduction

Brentano, F. *Psychology from an Empirical Standpoint.* New York: Humanities Press, 1973.
Breuer, J., and Freud, S. *Studies in Hysteria.* Boston: Beacon Press, 1950.
Cassirèr, E. *An Essay on Man.* New Haven: Yale University Press, 1965.
Darwin, C. *Darwin.* Edited by P. Appleman. New York: W. W. Norton, 1970.
Descartes, R. *Discourse on Method and Meditations.* Indianapolis: Bobbs-Merrill, 1979.
Eysenck, H. J. "Learning Theory and Behavior Therapy." In *Behavior Therapy and the Neuroses.* New York and Oxford: Pergamon Press, 1960.
Freud, S. *Autobiography.* New York: W. W. Norton & Company, 1937, pp. 82–110.
———. "A Neurosis of Demoniacal Possession in the Seventeenth Century." In *Collected Papers.* vol. 4, p. 637. London: The Hogarth Press, 1950.
Heidegger, M. *Being and Time.* New York: Harper & Row, 1962.
Hook, S., ed. "Psychoanalysis: Scientific Method and Philosophy." In *Methodological Issues,* ed. E. Nagel. London: Grove Press, 1960, pp. 38–47.
Husserl, E. *Ideas.* New York: Collier Books, 1967.
Jaspers, K. *Man in the Modern Age.* New York: Doubleday & Co., 1967.
Kierkegaard, S. *Fear and Trembling: Sickness unto Death.* New York: Doubleday Anchor Books, 1954.
Kohlberg, L. "Moral Stages and Moralization: The Cognitive Developmental Approach." In *Moral Development and Behavior,* ed. T. Lickona. New York: Holt, Rinehart & Winston, 1976.
Lévi-Strauss, C. *Structural Anthropology.* New York: Doubleday Anchor Books, 1967.
Merleau-Ponty, M. *Phénoménologie de la Perception.* Paris: Gallimard, 1966.
Nietzsche, F. *The Philosophy of Nietzsche.* New York: Modern Library, 1954.
Pascal, B. *Penseés and the Provincial Letters.* New York: Modern Library, 1941.
Pavlov, P. I. *Conditioned Reflexes and Psychiatry.* Edited by H. Gantt. New York: International Publishers, 1941.
Piaget, J. *The Child's Conception of the World.* Totowa, N.J.: Littlefield, Adams, 1967.
———. *The Child and Reality.* New York: Viking Compass Books, 1974.
———. *Judgment and Reasoning in the Child.* Totowa, N.J.: Littlefield, Adams, 1966.
———. *Psychology of Intelligence.* Totowa, N.J.: Littlefield, Adams, 1968.
Radin, P. *The World of Primitive Man.* New York: Grove Press, 1953.
Sartre, J. P. *Being and Nothingness.* New York: Philosophical Library, 1956.
Schopenhauer, A. *The Philosophy of Schopenhauer.* 2d ed. Edited by Irwin Edman. New York: Modern Library, 1956.

Serban, G. "The Cognitive Origin of Neurotic Thinking." In *Development of the Cognitive Defect in Mental Illness*. New York: Brunner/Mazel, 1978.

———. "Freudian Man Versus Existential Man." *Archives of General Psychiatry* 17 (1967), pp. 598–607.

———. "Piaget's Significance for Psychiatry." *Journal of Adolescence and Youth* (July 1974).

———. "The Process of Neurotic Thinking." *American Journal of Psychotherapy* 28, no. 3 (1974), pp. 418–429.

Skinner, B. F. *The Behavior of Organisms*. New York: Appleton-Century, 1938.

Tillich, P. *The Protestant Era*. Chicago: The University of Chicago Press, 1948.

Tolman, E. C. "Cognitive Maps in Rats and Men." *Psychological Review* 55 (1948), pp. 189–208.

Volpe, J. *The Practice of Behavior Therapy*. Oxford & New York: Pergamon Press, 1973.

Whyte, L. L. *The Unconscious Before Freud*. New York: Doubleday Anchor Books, 1962.

CHAPTER 1

Adler, A. *The Neurotic Constitution*. New York: Dodd, Mead, 1930.

Appley, H. M., and Trumbull, R., eds. *Psychological Stress*. New York: Appleton-Century Crofts, 1967.

Allport, G. W. *Personality and Social Encounters*. Boston: Beacon Press, 1960.

Bolles, R. *Theory of Motivation*. New York: Harper & Row, 1976.

Cassirer, E. *The Logic of the Humanities*. New Haven: Yale University Press, 1966.

Dubos, R. *Man Adapting*. New Haven: Yale University Press, 1965.

Festinger, L. *A Theory of Cognitive Dissonance*. Stanford, Calif.: Stanford University Press, 1957.

Freud, S. *Civilization and Its Discontents*. New York: W. W. Norton, 1962.

Hall, C. S., and Lindsey, G. *Theories of Personality*. New York: John Wiley & Sons, 1978.

Hamilton, V., and Vernon, M. D. *The Development of Cognitive Processes*. London and New York: Academic Press, 1976.

Horney, K. *The Neurotic Personality of Our Time*. New York: W. W. Norton, 1937.

———. *Our Inner Conflicts*. New York: W. W. Norton, 1945.

Lazarus, R. S. *Adjustment and Personality*. New York: McGraw-Hill, 1961.

Levi, L., ed. *Stress and Disease*. vol. 1. London: Oxford University Press, 1971.

Maslow, A. H. *Motivation and Personality*. New York: Harper & Row, 1959.

McClelland, J. C., Atkinson, J. W., and Clark, R. A. *Achievement Motive*. New York: Appleton, 1953.

Ryan, A. T. *Intentional Behavior*. New York: The Ronald Press, 1970.

CHAPTER 2

Bakwin, H. "Emotional Deprivation in Infants." *Journal of Pediatrics* 35 (1949), p. 512.

Bowlby, J. *Maternal Care and Mental Health and Deprivation of Maternal Care*. New York: Schocken Books, 1966.

———. *Attachment and Loss*. vols. 1 and 2. New York: Basic Books, 1973.

————. "Human Personality Development in an Ethological Light." In *Animal Models in Human Psychobiology*, ed. G. Serban and A. Kling. New York: Plenum Press, 1976.

Brentano, F. *Psychology from an Empirical Standpoint.* New York: Humanities Press, 1973.

Bruner, S. J., Olner, R. R., and Greenfield, M. P. *Studies in Cognitive Growth.* New York: John Wiley & Sons, 1966.

Erikson, E. H. *Discussions on Child Development.* In *Comments at a Round Table Discussion*, ed. J. M. Tanner and B. Inhelder. New York: International Universities Press, vol. 3, pp. 91–215, 1958; vol. 4, pp. 136–154, 1960.

————. *Childhood and Society.* New York: W. W. Norton, 1963.

Fenichel, O. *The Psychoanalytic Theory of Neurosis.* New York: W. W. Norton, 1945.

Freud, S. "Fragment of an Analysis of a Case of Hysteria." In *Collected Papers*, vol. 3, pp. 13–134. London: The Hogarth Press, 1950.

————. "Analysis of a Phobia in a Five-Year-Old Boy." In *Collected Papers*, vol. 3, pp. 149–259. London: The Hogarth Press, 1950.

————. "From the History of an Infantile Neurosis (1918)." In *Collected Papers*, vol. 3, pp. 473–585. London: The Hogarth Press, 1950.

————. "Paper on Metapsychology." In *Collected Papers*, vol. 4, pp. 13–137. London: The Hogarth Press, 1950.

————. *Three Essays on the Theory of Sexuality.* New York: Avon Books, 1965.

Goldfarb, W. "The Effects of Early Institutional Care on Adolescent Personality." *Journal of Experimental Education* 12 (1943), p. 106.

Harlow, H. F. "The Nature of Love." *American Psychologist* 13 (1958), pp. 673–685.

————, Gluck, J. P., and Suomi, S. J. "Generalization of Behavioral Data Between Nonhuman and Human Animals. *American Psychologist* 27 (1972), pp. 709–716.

————, and Novack, M. A. "Psychopathological Perspectives." *Perspectives in Biology and Medicine* 16, (1973), pp. 461–478.

Jones, M. C. "A Laboratory Study of Fear. The Case of Peter." In *Behavior Therapy and the Neuroses*, ed. H. J. Eysenck, pp. 45–51. New York: Pergamon Press, 1960.

Kohlberg, L. "Moral Stages and Moralization: The Cognitive Developmental Approach." In *Moral Development and Behavior*, ed. T. Lickona. New York: Holt, Rinehart & Winston, 1976.

Money, J., and Ehrhardt, A. A. *Man and Woman, Boy and Girl. The Differentiation and Dimorphism of Gender Identity from Conception to Maturity.* Baltimore: Johns Hopkins University Press, 1972.

Piaget, J. *Play, Dreams and Imitation in Childhood.* New York: W. W. Norton, 1951.

————. *The Child's Construction of Reality.* London: Routledge & Kegan Paul, 1955.

————. *The Moral Judgment of the Child.* New York: Collier Books, 1962.

————. *Judgment and Reasoning in the Child.* Totowa, N.J.: Littlefield, Adams, 1966.

————. *The Child's Conception of the World.* Totowa, N.J.: Littlefield, Adams, 1967.

————. *Psychology of Intelligence.* Totowa, N.J.: Littlefield, Adams, 1968.

————, and Inhelder, B. *The Psychology of the Child.* New York: Basic Books, 1969.

————. *The Child and Reality.* New York: Penguin Books, 1976.

Rapaport, D. *Emotions and Memory.* New York: Science Editions, 1961.

Rie, H. E. "Depression in Childhood." *Journal of the American Academy of Child Psychiatry* 5 (1966), pp. 653–685.

Serban, G. "The Significance of Ethology for Psychiatry." In *Animal Models in Human Psychobiology*, ed. G. Serban and A. Kling. New York: Plenum Press, 1976.

Spitz, R. A. "Hospitalism." In *Psychoanalytic Study of the Child*. vol. 1, p. 53. New York: International Universities Press, 1945.

———. "Hospitalism: A Follow-Up Report." In *Psychoanalytic Study of the Child*. vol. 2, p. 113. New York: International Universities Press, 1946.

———, and Wolf, K. M. "Anaclitic Depression." In *Psychoanalytic Study of the Child*. vol. 2, pp. 313–315. New York: International Universities Press, 1946.

Watson, B. J., and Rayner, R. "Conditioned Emotional Reactions." In *Behavior Therapy and the Neuroses*, ed. H. J. Eysenck, pp. 28–37. New York: Pergamon Press, 1960.

CHAPTER 3

Cannon, W. B. " 'Voodoo' Death." *American Anthropologist* 44 (1942).

Cassirer, E. *An Essay on Man*. New Haven and London: Yale University Press, 1944.

Comte, A. *Positive Philosophy*. Translated by Harriet Martineau. London: Trubner, 1831.

Crawley, E. *The Mystic Rose*. New York: Meridian Books, 1960.

Dement, W. C., and Kleitman, N. "The Relation of Eye Movements During Sleep to Dream Activity, an Objective Method for the Study of Dreaming." *Journal of Experimental Psychology* 53 (1957), p. 339.

Witkins, H. A., and Lewis, H. B., eds. *Experimental Studies of Dreaming*. New York: Random House, 1967.

Fisher, C., Gross, J., and Zuch, J. "Cycle of Penile Erection Synchronous with Dreaming (REM) Sleep." *Archives of General Psychiatry* 12 (1965), p. 29.

Foulkes, W. D. "Dream Reports from Different Stages of Sleep." *Journal of Abnormal Social Psychology* 65 (1962), p. 14.

———, and Vogel, G. "Mental Activity at Sleep Onset." *Journal of Abnormal Social Psychology* 70 (1965), p. 231.

Freud, S. *The Interpretation of Dreams*. New York: Modern Library, 1950.

Gorer, G. *Exploring the English Character*. London: Cresset Press, 1955.

Jung, C. G., and Kerényi, C. *Essays on a Science of Mythology*. London: Pantheon Books, 1949.

———. *Psychological Reflections*. New York: Harper Torchbooks, 1953.

———. *Memories, Dreams, Reflections*. London: Routledge & Kegan, 1963.

———. *Man and His Symbols*. London: Aldus Books, 1964.

Kiev, A., ed. *Magic, Faith and Healing*. London: Free Press/Collier-Macmillan, 1964.

Kleitman, N. *Sleep and Wakefulness*. Chicago: University of Chicago Press, 1963.

Lévi-Strauss, C. *Structural Anthropology*. New York: Doubleday Anchor Books, 1967.

Levy-Bruhl, L. *How Natives Think*. London: Allen, 1926.

Oesterreich, K. T. *Possessions and Exorcism*. New York: Causeway Books, 1974.

Opler, M. K. "Dream Analysis in Ute Indian Therapy." In *Culture and Mental Health*, ed. M. K. Opler, pp. 97–118. New York: The Macmillan Co., 1959.

Oswald, I. *Sleeping and Waking*. New York: Elsevier Press, 1962.

Piaget, J. *The Language and Thought of the Child*. New York: Meridian Books, 1959.

———. *Play, Dreams and Imitation in Childhood*. New York: W. W. Norton, 1962.

——, and Inhelder, B. *The Origins of the Idea of Chance in Children*. New York: W. W. Norton, 1975.

Radin, P. *The World of Primitive Man*. New York: Grove Press, 1960.

Sartre, J. P. *Being and Nothingness*. New York: Philosophical Library, 1956.

——. *Psychology of Imagination*. New York: Washington Square Press, 1966.

Skinner, B. F. *Science and Human Behavior*. New York: The Macmillan Co., 1953.

Whitman, R. M., Kramer, M., and Baldridge, B. "Which Dream Does the Patient Tell?" *Archives of General Psychiatry* 2 (1961), p. 219.

CHAPTER 4

Adams, L. P. *Obsessive Children*. New York: Penquin Books, 1973.

Appley, M. H., and Trumbull, R., eds. *Psychological Stress*. New York: Appleton-Century-Crofts, 1967.

Bandura, A. *Principles of Behavior Modification*. New York: Holt, Rinehart & Winston, 1969.

Eysenck, H. J. "Anxiety and the Natural History of Neurosis." In *Stress and Anxiety*, chapter edited by C. D. Spielberger and Irwin G. Sarason, pp. 51–88. New York: John Wiley & Sons, 1975.

Fenichel, O. *The Psychoanalytic Theory of Neurosis*. New York: W. W. Norton, 1945.

Freud, S. *The Problem of Anxiety*. New York: W. W. Norton, 1936.

——. *An Outline of Psychoanalysis*. New York: W. W. Norton, 1949.

——. "Obsessions and Phobias: Their Psychical Mechanism and Their Etiology." In *Collected Papers*, vol. 1, ed. James Strachey, pp. 128–137. London: The Hogarth Press, 1953.

Heidegger, M. *Being and Time*. New York: Harper & Row, 1962, pp. 179–182.

Janet, P. *Les Obsessions et la Psychasthénie*. vol. 1. Paris: Felen Alcan, 1903.

——. *De l'Angoisse à l'Extase*. Paris: Alcan, 1928.

Jaspers, K. *Man in the Modern Age*. Garden City, N.Y.: Doubleday Anchor Books, 1957.

Kierkegaard, S. *Fear and Trembling. The Sickness unto Death*. Garden City, N.Y.: Doubleday Anchor Books, 1954, pp. 155–207.

Kimmell, D. H. "Conditioned Fear and Anxiety." In *Stress and Anxiety*, vol. 1, ed. D. Spielberger and I. G. Sarason, pp. 189–200. New York: John Wiley & Sons, 1975.

Lader, M., and Marks, I. M. *Clinical Anxiety*. London: Heinemann, 1971.

——. "The Nature of Clinical Anxiety in Modern Society." In *Stress and Anxiety*, vol. 1, ed. C. D. Spielberger and I. G. Sarason, pp. 3–24. New York: John Wiley & Sons, 1975.

Lazarus, A. A. "Behavior Therapy." *International Journal of Psychiatry* 9 (1970), pp. 113–139.

Marks, I. M. *Fears and Phobias*. London: Heinemann, 1969.

May, R. *The Meaning of Anxiety*. New York: The Ronald Press, 1950.

Mowrer, O. H. "A Stimulus-Response Analysis of Anxiety and Its Role as a Reinforcing Agent." *Psychological Review* 46 (1939), pp. 553–565.

Odier, C. *Anxiety and Magic Thinking*. New York: International Universities Press, 1956.

Pascal, B. *Pensées*. New York: Modern Library, 1941.

Rachman, S., Hodgson, R., and Marks, I. M. "The Treatment of Obsessive Compulsive Neurosis." *Behavior Research and Therapy* 9 (1971), pp. 237–247.

Rappaport, H., and Katkin, E. S. "Relationship Among Manifest Anxiety, Response to Stress, and the Perception of Autonomic Activity." *Journal of Consulting and Clinical Psychology* 38 (1972), pp. 219–224.

Rioch, M. D. "Psychological and Pharmacological Manipulation." In *Emotions—Their Parameters and Measurement*, ed. L. Levi. New York: Raven Press, 1975.

Sartre, J. P. *Essays in Existentialism*. New York: Citadel Press, 1956.

Serban, G. "The Theory and Practice of Existential Analysis." *Behavioral Neuropsychiatry* 1 (1969), p. 7.

———. "Neurotic Thinking." *American Journal of Psychotherapy* 48 (July 1974), pp. 418–429.

———. "The Cognitive Origin of Neurotic Thinking." In *Development of the Cognitive Defect in Mental Illness*, ed. G. Serban. New York: Brunner/Mazel, 1978.

Tyrer, P. "Anxiety States." In *Recent Advances in Clinical Psychiatry*. ed. Kenneth Granville Grossman, pp. 161–182. Edinburgh: Churchill Livingstone, 1979.

Volpe, J. *The Practice of Behavior Therapy*. Oxford: Pergamon General Psychology Series, 1973.

CHAPTER 5

Beck, A. T.. *Cognitive Therapy and the Emotional Disorders*. New York: International Universities Press, 1976.

Bibring, E. "The Mechanism of Depression," In *Affective Disorders*, ed. P. Greenacre, pp. 13–48. New York: International Universities Press, 1953.

Bowlby, J. *Attachment and Loss*. vols. 1 and 2. London and New York: The Hogarth Press, 1969, 1973.

———. "Human Personality Development in an Ethological Light." In *Animal Models in Human Psychobiology*, ed. G. Serban and A. Kling. New York: Plenum Press, 1976.

Brown, G. W. "A Three-Factor Causal Model of Depression." In *Stress and Mental Disorder*, ed. J. Barrett, pp. 111–120. New York: Raven Press, 1979.

Bunney, W. E., Jr., Gershon, E., Murphy, D. et al. "Psychobiological and Pharmacological Studies of Manic Depressive Illness." *Journal of Psychiatric Research* 9 (1972), p. 207.

Clayton, J. P., and Darvish, S. H. "Course of Depressive Symptoms Following the Stress of Bereavement." In *Stress and Mental Disorder*, ed. J. E. Barrett et al., pp. 121–136. New York: Raven Press, 1979.

Davies, B. "Depression and Anxiety Contrasted." *Australian-New Zealand Journal of Psychiatry* 3 (1969), pp. 223–226.

Durkheim, E. *Suicide*. Illinois: The Free Press, 1951.

Fawcett, J. A., and Bunney, W. E. "Pituitary Adrenal Function and Depression." *Archives of General Psychiatry* 16 (1969), pp. 517–535.

———,Leff, H., and Bunney, W. E. "Suicide." *Archives of General Psychiatry* 21 (1969), pp. 129–151.

Freud, S. "Mourning and Melancholia." In *Collected Papers*, pp. 27–36, 152–172. London: The Hogarth Press, 1950.

Gershon, E. S., Cromer, M., and Klerman, G. L. "Hostility and Depression."
    Psychiatry 31 (1968), pp. 224–235.
Goodwin, F. K., and Bunney, W. E. "A Psychological Approach to Affective Ill-
    ness." *Psychiatric Annals* 3 (1973), pp. 19–55.
Hamburg, A. D., Hamburg, B. A., and Barchos, J. D. "Anger and Depression in
    Perspective of Behavioral Biology." In *Emotions—Their Parameters and Mea-
    surement*, ed. L. Levi. New York: Raven Press, 1975.
Harlow, H. F. "The Nature of Love." *American Psychologist* 13 (1958), pp. 673–685.
———, and Zimmerman, R. R. "Affectional Responses in the Infant Monkey."
    Science 130 (1959), p. 421.
Paykel, S. E. "Causal Relationship Between Clinical Depression and Life Events." In
    Stress and Mental Disorder, ed. James E. Barrett et al., pp. 71–85. New York:
    Raven Press, 1979.
Pilowsky, I., and Spence, N. D. "Hostility and Depressive Illness." *Archives of
    General Psychiatry* 32 (1975), pp. 1154–1159.
Sachar, E. J. "Corticosteroid Responses to Psychotherapy of Depression." *Archives of
    General Psychiatry* 16 (1967), pp. 461–470.
Seligman, M., and Groves, D. "Non-transient Learned Helplessness." *Psychosomatic
    Science* 19 (1970), p. 191.
Serban, G. "The Phenomenology of Depression." *American Journal of Psychotherapy* 29
    (July 1975), pp. 355–362.
Spitz, R. "Anaclitic Depression: An Inquiry into the Genesis of Psychiatric Condi-
    tions in Early Childhood." *Psychoanalytic Study of the Child* 2 (1946), p. 213.

CHAPTER 6

Freud, S. "Psychoanalytic Notes on an Autobiographic Account of a Case of Paranoia
    (Dementia Paranoides)." In *Collected Papers*. vol. 3, pp. 390–467. London: The
    Hogarth Press, 1950.
——— "Some Neurotic Mechanisms in Jealousy, Paranoia and Homosexuality." In
    Standard Edition, vol. 18, pp. 221–232. London: The Hogarth Press, 1955.
McCawley, A. "Paranoia and Homosexuality: Schreber Reconsidered." *New York
    State Journal of Medicine* 71 (1971), pp. 1505–1513.
Merleau-Ponty, M. *Phenomenology of Perception*. New York: Humanities Press, 1970.
Ovesey, L. "Pseudohomosexuality: The Paranoid Mechanism and Paranoia."
    Psychiatry 18 (1969), pp. 163–173.
Rickles, N. K. "The Angry Woman Syndrome." *Archives of General Psychiatry* 24
    (1971), pp. 91–96.
Sarvis, M. H. "Paranoid Reactions: Perceptual Distortions as an Etiological Agent."
    Archives of General Psychiatry 6 (1962), pp. 157–162.
Schoeck, H. *Envy*. New York: Harcourt, Brace & World, 1969.
Schwartz, D. A. "A Review of the Paranoid Concept." *Archives of General Psychiatry* 8
    (1963), pp. 349–361.

CHAPTER 7

Boss, M. *Psychoanalysis and Daseinanalysis*. New York: Basic Books, 1963, pp. 133–186.
Breuer, J., and Freud, S. *Studies in Hysteria*. New York: Basic Books, 1957.

Chodoff, P. "The Diagnosis of Hysteria: An Overview." *American Journal of Psychiatry* 137, no. 10 (1974), pp. 1073–1078.

Eysenck, H. J. ed. *Behavior Therapy and the Neuroses.* New York & Oxford: Pergamon Press, 1960, pp. 337–432.

———. "Anxiety and the Natural History of Neurosis." In *Stress and Anxiety*, ed. C. D. Spielberger and I. G. Sarason. New York: John Wiley & Sons, 1975.

Fenichel, O. *The Psychoanalytic Theory of Neurosis.* New York: W. W. Norton, 1945, pp. 216–219.

Freud, S. "The Etiology of Hysteria." In *Collected Papers*, vol. 1, pp. 183–219. London: The Hogarth Press, 1946.

Hollender, M. H. "Conversion Hysteria." *Archives of General Psychiatry* 26, no. 4 (1972), pp. 311–314.

Janet, P. *The Major Symptoms of Hysteria.* New York: Hafner Press, 1965.

Kretschmer, E. *Hysteria.* New York: Nervous and Mental Disease Publishing Co., 1926.

Ladee, G. A. *Hypochondriacal Syndromes.* Amsterdam: Elsevier, 1966.

Lerner, H. E. "The Hysterical Personality: A 'Woman's Disease.'" *Comprehensive Psychiatry* 15 (1974), pp. 157–164.

Nemiah, J. C. "Conversion: Fact or Chimera." *International Journal of Psychiatry in Medicine* 5, no. 4 (1974), pp. 443–448.

Pope, K. S., and Singer, J. L. eds. *The Stream of Consciousness.* New York: Plenum Press, 1978.

Wittkower, E. D. "Trance and Possession States." *International Journal of Social Psychiatry.* 16 (1970), pp. 153–169.

Woodruff, R. A., Jr., Clayton, P. J., and Guze, S. B. "Hysteria Studies of Diagnosis, Outcome and Deviance." *Journal of the American Medical Association* 215 (1971), pp. 425–428.

CHAPTER 8

Bieber, I., Dain, H. et al. *Homosexuality.* New York: Basic Books, 1962.

Boss, M. *Meaning and Content of Sexual Perversions.* New York: Grune & Stratton, 1949.

de Beauvoir, Simone. "The Lesbian." In *The Problem of Homosexuality in Modern Society*, ed. H. M. Ruitenbeek. New York: Dutton Paperbacks, 1963.

Fenichel, O. *The Psychoanalytic Theory of Neurosis.* New York: W. W. Norton, 1945.

Freud, S. "My View on the Past Role Played by Sexuality in the Aetiology of the Neuroses." In *Collected Papers*, vol. 1, pp. 272–283. London: The Hogarth Press, 1950.

———. "Certain Neurotic Mechanisms in Jealousy, Paranoia and Homosexuality." In *Collected Papers*, vol. 2, pp. 232–243. London: The Hogarth Press, 1950.

———. "The Infantile Genital Organization of the Libido." In *Collected Papers*, vol. 2, pp. 244–249. London: The Hogarth Press, 1950.

———. "From the History of an Infantile Neurosis." In *Collected Papers*, vol. 3, pp. 480–568. London: The Hogarth Press, 1950.

———. "Fetishes: Female Sexuality Screen Memories." In *Collected Papers*, vol. 5, pp. 47–70, 198–205, 252–273. London: The Hogarth Press, 1950.

———. *Three Essays on the Theory of Sexuality.* New York: Avon Books, 1965.

Freund, K. "Some Problems in the Treatment of Homosexuality." In *Behavior Therapy and the Neuroses*, ed. H. J. Eysenck, pp. 312–326. Oxford: Pergamon Press, 1960.

Gebhard, P. H., Gagnon, J. H., Pomeroy, W. B. et al. *Sex Offenders*. New York: Harper & Row, 1965.

Hatterer, L. I. *Changing Homosexuality in the Male*. New York: McGraw-Hill, 1970.

Lorenz, K. *On Aggression*. New York: Bantam Books, 1969.

Money, J., and Pollit, E. "Psychogenetic and Psychosexual Ambiguities." *Archives of General Psychiatry* 11 (1964), pp. 589–595.

Ovesey, L. *Homosexuality and Pseudohomosexuality*. New York: Science House, 1969.

Serban G. "The Existential Therapeutic Approach to Homosexuality." *American Journal of Psychotherapy* 22, no. 3 (1968), pp. 491–501.

———. "The Phenomenological Concept of Homosexuality." *Journal of Existential Psychiatry* 28 (Winter 1970), unpaged.

———. "The Significance of Ethology for Psychiatry." In *Animal Models in Human Psychopathology*, ed. G. Serban. New York: Plenum Press, 1976.

———. "The Cognitive Origin of Neurotic Thinking." In *The Development of the Cognitive Defect in Mental Illness*, ed. G. Serban. New York: Brenner/Mazel Inc., 1979.

Steckel, W. *Sadism and Masochism*. vols. 1 and 2. New York: Liveright, 1939.

Stoller, R. J. "The Transsexual Boy: Mother's Feminized Phallus." *British Journal of Medical Psychology* 43 (1970), pp. 117–128.

———. "Transsexualism and Transvestism." *Psychiatric Annals* 1 (1972), pp. 6–72.

———. *Sex and Gender*. vol. 2. New York: Jason-Aronson, 1975.

Storr, H. *Human Aggression*. New York: Bantam Books, 1970.

Volpe, J. *The Practice of Behavior Therapy*. Oxford: Pergamon Press, 1973, pp. 238–264.

CHAPTER 9

Eysenck, H. J. *Experiments in Behavior Therapy*. Oxford: Pergamon Press, 1964.

Foreyt, J. P., and Rathjen, D. P. *Cognitive Behavior Therapy*. New York: Plenum Press, 1978.

Frank, J. A. *Persuasion and Healing*. New York: Schocken Books, 1967.

Kelly, G. A. *The Psychology of Personality*. New York: W. W. Norton, 1963.

Lazarus, A. A. *Multimodal Behavior Therapy*. New York: Springer, 1976.

Malan, D. H. *The Frontier of Brief Psychotherapy*. New York: Plenum Press, 1976.

Sartre, J. P. *Being and Nothingness*. Translated by H. Barnes. New York: Philosophical Library, 1956.

Serban, G. "The Theory and Practice of Existential Analysis." *Behavioral Neuropsychiatry* 117 (1969), pp. 8–14.

———. "Neurotic Thinking." *American Journal of Psychotherapy* 28 (July 1974), pp. 418–429.

———. "The Development of Neurotic Thinking." *Journal of Youth and Adolescence* (1974), p. 2.

————. "The Phenomenology of Depression." *American Journal of Psychotherapy* 29 (1975), pp. 355–362.

Strupp, H. H., and Hadley, S. W. "Specific vs. Nonspecific Factors in Psychotherapy." *Archives of General Psychiatry* 36 (September 1979), pp. 1125–1136.

Volpe, J. *The Practice of Behavior Therapy.* Oxford: Pergamon Press, 1973.

SELECTED
READING

Ayer, A. J., ed. *Logical Positivism*. Glencoe, Ill.: The Free Press, 1960.
Bakan, D. *Sigmund Freud and the Jewish Mystical Traditions*. New York: Schocken Books. 1969.
Bandura, H. *Principles of Behavior Modification*. New York: Holt, Rinehart & Winston, 1969.
Beck, T. A. *Cognitive Therapy and the Emotional Disorders*. New York: International Universities Press, 1976.
Binswanger, L. *Being in the World*. New York: Basic Books, 1963.
Breuer, J., and Freud, S. *Studies in Hysteria*. Boston: Beacon Press, 1937.
Bruner, J. S., Goodnow, J. J., and Austin, G. A. *A Study of Thinking*. New York: John Wiley & Sons, 1956.
——, Olner, R. R., and Greenfield, M. P. *Studies in Cognitive Growth*. New York: John Wiley & Sons, 1966.
Cassirer, E. *The Philosophy of Symbolic Forms*. New Haven: Yale University Press, vol. 2, 1955; vol. 3, 1957.
Eliade, M. *Myths, Dreams and Mysteries*. New York: Harper Torchbooks, 1960.
Eysenck, H. J., ed. *Behavior Therapy and the Neuroses*. New York & Oxford: Pergamon Press, 1960.
Frank, J. B. *Persuasion and Healing*. New York: Schocken Books, 1967.
Freud, S. *Civilization and Its Discontents*. New York: W. W. Norton, 1962.
Hartman, E. von. *Philosophy of the Unconscious*. New York: P. Kegan, Trench, Trubner, 1931.
Heidegger, M. *Existence and Being*. Chicago: Henry Regnery, 1949.
Horney, K. *The Neurotic Personality of Our Time*. New York: W. W. Norton, 1937.
Husserl, E. *Méditations Cartésiennes*. Paris: Vrin Press, 1967.
Jaspers, K. *Man in the Modern Age*. New York: Doubleday Anchor Books, 1957.
Kierkegaard, S. *Fear and Trembling: Sickness unto Death*. New York: Doubleday Anchor Books, 1954.
Kohlberg, L. "Moral Stages and Moralization: The Cognitive Developmental Approach." In *Moral Development and Behavior*, ed. T. Lickona. New York: Holt, Rinehart & Winston, 1976.
Levi, L., ed. *Emotions*. New York: Raven Press, 1975.
Lorenz, K. *Behind the Mirror*, New York: Harcourt, Brace, Jovanovich, 1978.
MacIntosh, and Coval, S. C. *The Business of Reason*. New York: Humanitites Press, 1969.

Mackay, C. H. *Extraordinary Popular Delusions and the Madness of Crowds.* L. C. Page, 1932.

Maier, W. H. *Three Theories of Child Development.* New York: Harper & Row, 1969.

Malinowski, B. *Magic, Science and Religion.* New York: Doubleday Anchor Books, 1948.

Merleau-Ponty, M. *Phénoménologie de la Perception.* Paris: Gallimard, 1966.

————. *The Structure of Behavior.* Boston: Beacon Press, 1967.

Nye, Robert D. *Conflict Among Humans.* New York: Springer, 1973.

Ortega y Gasset, J. *Man and People.* New York: W. W. Norton, 1957.

Piaget, J. *Play, Dreams and Imitation in Childhood.* New York: W. W. Norton, 1951.

————. *Judgment and Reasoning in the Child.* Totowa, N.J.: Littlefield, Adams, 1966.

————. *The Child's Conception of the World.* Totowa, N.J.: Littlefield, Adams, 1967.

————. *Psychology of Intelligence.* Totowa, N.J.: Littlefield, Adams, 1968.

————. *Six Psychological Studies.* New York: Vintage Books, 1968.

————. *Understanding Causality.* New York: W. W. Norton, 1974.

————, and Inhelder, B. *The Origins of the Idea of Chance in Children.* New York: W. W. Norton, 1975.

————. *Behavior and Evolution.* New York: Pantheon Books, 1978.

Sartre, J. P. *Being and Nothingness.* New York: Philosophical Library, 1956.

————. *Essays in Existentialism.* New York: Citadel Press, 1967.

Serban, G., ed. *Psychopathology of Human Adaptation.* New York: Plenum Press, 1976.

————. *Cognitive Defects in the Development of Mental Illness.* New York: Brunner/-Mazel, 1978.

Spielberger, C., and Sarason, I. eds. *Stress and Anxieties.* vols. 1, 2, 3. Washington, D.C.: Hemisphere, 1975.

Tart, C. T. ed. *Altered States of Consciousness.* New York: John Wiley & Sons, 1969.

Thomas, A., Chess, S., and Birch, H. *Temperament and Behavior Disorders.* New York: New York University Press, 1968.

Tinbergen, N. *The Study of Instinct.* London: Oxford University Press, 1951.

Unamuno, M. de. *Tragic Sense of Life.* New York: Dover, 1954.

Volpe, J. *The Practice of Behavior Therapy.* New York & Oxford: Pergamon Books, 1973.

Zimbardo, P. G. *The Cognitive Control of Motivation.* Glenview, Ill.: Scott, Foresman, 1969.

Zinberg, N., ed. *Alternate States of Consciousness.* New York & London: The Free Press, 1977.

INDEX